The
Purification
Prescription

The Purification Prescription

Sheldon Saul Hendler, M.D., Ph.D.

WILLIAM MORROW AND COMPANY, INC.
New York

NOTE TO THE READER: Discuss all items and programs mentioned in this book with your physician before embarking on their use. Some require continuous medical supervision.

To maintain confidentiality, patient identities and histories have been altered.

Library of Congress Cataloging-in-Publication Data

Hendler, Sheldon Saul.
    The purification prescription / Sheldon Saul Hendler.
        p.   cm.
    Includes bibliographical references.
    ISBN 0-688-08770-1
    1. Orthomolecular therapy.   2. Nutrition.   3. Substance abuse—
Diet therapy.   I. Title.   II. Title: Purification prescription.
    [DNLM: 1. Diet—popular works.   2. Health Promotion—popular
works.   3. Substance Dependence—diet therapy—popular works.   WM
270 H497z]
RM235.5   1990
613.2'6—dc20

Printed in the United States of America   89-14520

First Edition   CIP

1 2 3 4 5 6 7 8 9 10

BOOK DESIGN BY BERNARD SCHLEIFER

This book is dedicated to my aunt Fay,
in whom hope springs eternal

Acknowledgments

I would like to express my sincere thanks to the following for their aid and/or encouragement: Joseph D. Beasley, Murray Jarvik, Robert Nagourney, Red Rodney, Richard Wachsman, Debbie Waters, and Saul White.

Special thanks: To my agent, friend, and snorkel-pal, David M. Rorvik of Proteus, Inc., for invaluable assistance in creating and producing this book. And to my editor, Margaret M. Talcott, for excellent insight and assistance throughout this project.

Contents

PART I

THE PURIFICATION PRINCIPLES

1 *The Purification Promise: What This Book Can Do for You*

WHOM THIS BOOK IS FOR

Before I tell you *what* this book can do, I'd like to tell you *who* this book can benefit:

- Anyone still breathing. We *all* live in an increasingly polluted world. We're *all* beset by ever more hazardous air and water pollutants, natural and man-generated radiation, pesticides, herbicides, food contaminants, and additives.
- Anyone who eats the "standard" American diet, with its excesses of cholesterol, saturated fat, refined carbohydrates, sugar, salt, and calories.
- Anyone who is overweight.
- Anyone who has an eating disorder.
- Anyone who has allergies or sensitivities.
- Anyone who has been exposed to radiation or is undergoing chemo- or radiotherapy.
- Anyone who regularly:
    —drinks alcohol;
    —smokes or is exposed to the cigarette smoke of others;

—uses cocaine and/or other stimulants or uppers;
—uses opiates (such as codeine and various opiate prescription painkillers, morphine, heroin, methadone);
—uses benzodiazapines and other sedatives or downers.

WHAT THIS BOOK CAN DO FOR YOU

The toxins that foul our brains and bodies include the harmful residues of legal—as well as illegal—drugs, heavy metals, pesticides, herbicides, innumerable chemical food additives, water and air pollutants, radioactive materials, fats, and cholesterol. The Purification Prescription is capable of *dramatically* reducing the burden of all of these toxins. In as little as *five weeks*, by following programs that utilize pragmatic regimens of purifying elements, the drug or alcohol or nicotine addict can essentially detoxify his or her system, greatly reduce the pain and stress of withdrawal, and significantly increase the chance of long-term abstinence.

The food addict can, similarly, reduce cravings, and the fat addict can purge himself or herself of dangerous accumulations of cholesterol, saturated fats, and toxic sugars in blood, vessels, organs, and cells, with 20 percent *or greater* reductions in cholesterol, for example, within just five weeks.

Others, in the same five-week period, can substantially rid their bodies and brains of a broad spectrum of harmful chemicals present in our increasingly airtight, energy-efficient homes and workplaces and in our water, air, and food. The Purification Prescription can even remove radioactive material from our cells and help protect against future contamination.

The benefits of the Purification Prescription are multiple:

- increased physical energy

- enhanced feeling of well-being

- heightened mental acuity and mood

- weight control

- improved memory

- greater ability to resist obsessive-compulsive and addictive behaviors

- enhanced immunity

- reduced risk of cancer, heart attack, stroke

- greater longevity

In sum, the Purification Prescription restores biochemical *balance*, short-circuiting addictive or compulsive behavior while purging the body and brain of impurities. This balance imparts a feeling of *wholeness*. It is when we are out of balance and do *not* feel whole that we are most vulnerable to addictive or compulsive behavior. (See further discussion of this concept under Purification Principles, below.)

ELEMENTS OF THE PRESCRIPTION

In Part II of this book, you'll learn about the individual elements that make up the Purification Prescriptions detailed in Part III. The elements include selected vitamins and minerals, amino acids, lipids, seaweeds and seaweed derivatives, herbs, pharmaceuticals, diet, light, exercise, and relaxation and stress-management techniques.

Here's a sampling of some of these elements and what they can do, when used in proper amounts and combinations. Remember, this is just a *sampling*. Refer to Parts II and III to learn how to use these elements in the proper way.

L-tyrosine is an amino acid (the kind you can buy in a health-food store) that has remarkable detoxifying capabilities. Through its influences on key brain neurotransmitters, it can be a very useful stress detoxifier. It is also proving quite effective in cocaine withdrawal and detoxification.

The Chinese herbs astragalus and ligustrum have been shown to reduce and protect against the toxic effects of chemo- and radiotherapies. The herb milk thistle has been proven capable of detoxifying a number of dangerous chemicals. Extracts of young oat plants have exhibited, in intriguing pilot studies and in clinical practice, an ability to reduce nicotine craving.

Lipids (more commonly known as fats) are a complex family of substances, some of which can be used to help improve memory, cleanse the cells, and make them more responsive; they can also alleviate the pain of withdrawal from opiate drugs. Some can be effective in protecting and restoring liver cells, of crucial importance in purification since the liver is the body's principal organ of detoxification. Certain of the lipids may be among the most important detoxifiers of the aging process itself.

Substances derived from several types of seaweed have very potent purifying effects. Ongoing studies are revealing more of these capabilities all the time. They are particularly useful for cleansing the body of a number of highly detrimental environmental pollutants, such as lead and some of the other heavy metals. They can even protect against some forms of radioactive waste and may be able to clear certain viruses from the body.

Several pharmaceuticals are showing great promise in treating and curbing addictive behavior. Piracetam, to cite one example, may greatly ease withdrawal from alcohol without any adverse side effects. Prozac is another new drug that has the potential to actually reduce both food and alcohol craving. It may also be able to diminish other cravings related to obsessive-compulsive behavior. Again, all of these substances work by helping to restore biochemical *balance*.

Light is another of the purifying elements you'll soon be learning more about. Adequate exposure to the right kind of light can be useful in a number of purifying programs. One recent pilot study demonstrated the power of light in alcohol withdrawal. It can also help suppress appetite.

THE PURIFICATION PRESCRIPTIONS

In Part III, you'll learn about the five-week Purification Prescriptions themselves. These include prescriptions for withdrawal from and detoxification of alcohol, nicotine, caffeine, cocaine, opiates, and some other drugs. They also include regimens for the detoxification of environmental pollutants, chemo- and radiotoxins, cholesterol, fat, and "stagnant" blood (characterized by sticky platelets that predispose to potentially lethal clots). Still other prescriptions address food addictions and eating disorders.

THE PURIFICATION PRINCIPLES

When it comes to cleansing the body and brain of impurities that accumulate *without* the active cooperation and complicity of the individual, the purification process is straightforward. No one *know-*

ingly contaminates one's body with lead or radioactive strontium 90, for example. Discovery of such contamination or even possible contamination results in an immediate desire to avoid further and future contamination and immediate efforts to purge the body of the contamination that has already taken place. This book powerfully facilitates that process.

Another set of principles comes into play, however, when the contamination of the body, brain, and mind is the result of apparent *conscious* behavior, as in the case of addictions. Then the purification process is somewhat more complex. But *not* as complex as some would have you believe.

Most addicts *know* that they are harming themselves, and they want to stop. Furthermore, the reasons why they became addicted to various substances are, in the majority of cases, perfectly comprehensible and can thus be addressed without resort to labyrinthine psychological analysis. There has been far too much "psychologizing" of the addictive process and far too little "biologizing." This book begins to correct that error, highlighting the biochemical bases of addiction.

I feel that I must interject, at this point, that it is not the purpose of this book to attempt to supplant supportive psychological therapies related to drug and other addictions. I endorse many such therapies, and I support such groups as Alcoholics Anonymous. The information in this book can be used in conjunction with such therapies. More attention, however, needs to be paid to the biochemical components of addictive behavior. This book is an effort toward that end. The advice in this book related to drug addiction is for the addict who is making the effort to withdraw from drugs, detoxify the body and brain, and reduce drug craving so that the chances of continued abstinence are enhanced. The book is also for the physician who counsels and manages those with addictions.

The reality is that most addicts are in hot pursuit of *normalcy*, not mindless ecstasy or escape. They want to feel *well*. They want to feel *whole*. I have no desire to excuse (or to judge) addictive behavior—only to understand it. And what I understand from my own study of addictive processes and from my own clinical experience, as well as that of many of my colleagues, is that most people who end up abusing drugs do so in an effort to alleviate pain, in one form or another. The pain, depending upon how you define your terms, may be purely physical or it may be psychological or even spiritual. The individual feels something vital is wrong or something vital is missing. Drugs alter those perceptions—not magically or mystically, but *predictably*, in ways that can be scientifically elucidated. The drugs work—at least for a while—because they *fill in* what's missing or impaired in the biochemistry of the body and the brain.

It is important to note that most of the drugs that are typically abused have *short-term* effects that are actually health-giving and energy- and life-enhancing. They are often, initially, membrane fluidizers. They make the membranes of cells in all parts of the body and brain less rigid, more alive and responsive, better able to cope with pain, stress, depression, illness. They also help normalize, however briefly, disordered brain neurotransmitters, the chemical transporters of thought, emotion, behavior. They make the individual feel young and whole again.

The problem is this: All of these "gains" are short-term. In the long run, these drugs are membrane *rigidifiers*. Ever larger doses are required, over time, to achieve the fluid boost that rapidly becomes the objective. Meanwhile, the drugs actually accelerate aging and further deplete the very neurotransmitters they all too fleetingly fill in for.

Until we begin to recognize addictive behavior for what it really is, we will make little, if any, progress against the drug problem. And when it comes to making judgments about drug addiction, we need to achieve a clearer perspective. We attach great opprobrium to heroin addiction, for example, while at the same time approving and even admiring some other addictions that may actually be more destructive to individuals and to society.

Many workaholics I've treated, for example, are engaging in behavior more self-destructive than that of heroin addicts. And the typical workaholic—I'm talking about people truly addicted to work—is often highly neglectful or directly abusive of spouse, children, and others.

The person addicted to compulsive cleanliness or to sex or to food or to exacting ritual or to obsessive exercise—all of these people are frequently just as likely to destroy themselves and those around them as are the alcoholic or the heroin or cocaine addict.

The bottom line—and the good news—for all of these people is that *there's a better way*. There's a way to achieve health and wholeness that will *last*, a way that will actually strengthen and not weaken, a way that will not only eradicate the present addiction but inoculate against addictive tendencies in the future.

This book is all about that way. That way is an orderly, constructive rebuilding of the biochemical bases of health, normalcy, well-being. Some people seek themselves in drugs—or in things outside themselves—because they've forgotten, or never had the chance to experience, how good their *own* chemistry, when properly ordered, can make them feel.

True, the Purification Prescription uses a number of substances, including even drugs, but all of these substances, most of which are nutrients, have been carefully selected to rebuild, reorder, and restore the body's and brain's own natural biochemical balances. Once their missions are accomplished, some can be discontinued. Others are prudent additions to everyday life in this increasingly polluted world, a world we will explore in the following chapter.

2 Polluted Body/Impure Mind: Scope of the Epidemic

"WHAT'S HAPPENING TO US?"

I couldn't forget Alicia's first visit if I wanted to. This well-educated professional woman filled my office with her woes—and as it turns out, the world's woes. She also filled my small office with herself. Nearly eighty pounds overweight, Alicia groaned and the chair under her groaned with her. So did I, for as Alicia spoke, her mantle of miseries settled down around us so oppressively that even I could not escape its relentless weight. Alicia, thirty-eight going on sixty-eight, was addicted to food (especially dicey in her case since she was also beset by a number of nasty food sensitivities), nicotine, and, most recently, opiates (in the form of a painkilling drug that had been prescribed for injuries sustained in an alcohol-caused auto accident). Alicia admitted to liking "a few drinks in the evening."

Now Alicia was "wondering" if she needed tranquilizers as well, since "so many bad things" were happening in her life. Her husband had been an alcoholic for some time and was abusive. He had, in addition, a number of "maddening compulsive-obsessive hang-ups" that Alicia said had driven her to start drinking. Their fifteen-year-old daughter, following in her older sister's footsteps, had run away twice already and was "strung out on one thing or another half the time." Alicia feared her daughter might even be "prostituting herself to get money for cocaine." Alicia's father, a lifelong chain smoker, had died some years earlier of lung cancer and now Alicia's favorite brother, also a heavy smoker, had been diagnosed with the same disease. Another brother, also overweight, had recently had a heart attack. Both Alicia and her sister were finding it difficult to remain employed because of sensitivities and allergies not only to many foods and food additives, but also to many chemicals and synthetic substances typically encountered in the workplace. Alicia said she'd tried to quit smoking many times, hoping that would help, but had never succeeded. Each time she stopped, her weight problem became even worse.

At the end of this recitation, Alicia (about whom I'll have more to say at the end of this chapter) laughed ruefully and said, "The only wonder is I'm not crazy—yet. I probably would be if practically everybody I know wasn't in the same boat. What's *happening* to us?"

THE TERRIBLE NUMBERS

The terrible truth is that we live in an increasingly polluted, toxic, and intoxicated world. Our brains and bodies are being tainted not only by alcohol, nicotine, amphetamines, opiates, and misused prescription and over-the-counter drugs, but also by an ever-expanding spectrum of air and water pollutants, food additives, radiation, noxious chemicals in both the home and the workplace, and the cholesterol and saturated fats in the food we eat.

Here are some sad statistics and terrible numbers:

- Thirty percent of all adults in the U.S. are smokers (nicotine addicts). Most say they want to quit. Nicotine is now recognized to be as addictive as cocaine and heroin.

- Smoking kills 320,000 Americans each year, accounting for 16 percent of *all* deaths in the U.S.

- "Involuntary smoking"—nonsmokers inhaling the cigarette smoke of others—kills more people each year than do all the other man-made air pollutants combined.

- Nearly 11 million American adults are chronic alcoholics and another 7–8 million are problem drinkers. An additional 4–5 million teenagers aged fourteen to seventeen are also problem drinkers.

- Alcohol kills 125,000 Americans annually. Thousands more die due to alcohol-induced accidents and violence.

- There are 5–6 million regular users of cocaine in the U.S., and five thousand more people try cocaine for the first time *each day*. Cocaine is highly addictive, and one form of it—crack—may be the most addictive substance known.

- Half a million Americans are addicted to heroin, and use of this drug is again on the rise due to lower street prices and purer product.

- Eighty percent of the U.S. population uses caffeine, consuming an average 200 mg of it daily—mostly from coffee, tea, some over-the-counter drugs, soft drinks, and chocolate.

- Those who drink five or more cups of caffeinated coffee daily are at two to three times higher risk of developing coronary heart disease than are non-coffee users, according to the most authoritative long-term study ever conducted on this issue. Fibrocystic breast disease in women and elevated cholesterol levels in men have also been linked to caffeine intake.

- Pharmacists are filling more than *1.5 billion* drug prescriptions for Americans each year. Prescription-drug misuse and abuse is on the rise. Some 350 people in the U.S. die *each day* due to prescription-drug misuse and abuse.

- The elderly have been found to be at particularly high risk of chemical dependency due to their higher incidence of pain, depression, loneliness, and physical disability.

- Just *five* pollutants account for 98 percent of *all* air pollution—but all can be deadly and all are becoming more prevalent in many parts of the country.

- Indoor pollution—caused by a variety of substances being used in increasingly "energy efficient" (air-sealed) homes, office buildings, factories, and other workplaces—is increasing sharply, resulting in the sick-building syndrome and in pollution levels that, in some homes and offices, have been found to exceed maximum safe levels that have been set for toxic-waste sites!

- At least 40 million Americans, according to the Environmental Protection Agency (EPA), are now regularly consuming water with unsafe levels of lead. Millions of others are exposed to numerous other toxins in their water. The EPA has identified more than seven hundred known hazardous substances in various samples of U.S. water supplies.

- Numerous potentially carcinogenic substances (including some of the thirty thousand pesticides currently in use in the U.S.) continue to taint some produce and other food supplies. And various food additives continue to trigger sometimes severe sensitivities and allergies in susceptible individuals.

- Radon gas, a radium decay product that arises out of natural radioactive deposits in the soil, may be causing twenty thousand or more lung cancer deaths annually, according to the National Cancer Institute. Some 8 million or more homes are believed to be contaminated by significant amounts of this radioactive gas. Some experts believe that up to 20 percent of all homes in the U.S. may be affected.

- X rays, radiopharmaceuticals, and radioisotopes used in diagnosis and treatment of several diseases and disorders have proliferated with highly toxic results in some individuals. Faulty equipment and poorly trained technicians further boost the risks. Even dental X rays, when overused or when equipment is faulty, can significantly elevate cancer risks.

- At least 34 million adult Americans are obese (20 percent over ideal weight); 13 million of these are *severely* obese (40 percent over ideal weight). Food addiction is now a recognized disease, and obesity is linked to heart disease, hormonal disturbances, high blood pressure, elevated cholesterol, diabetes, stroke, some cancers, and gallbladder difficulties.

- Up to 100 million Americans have cardiovascular systems polluted by dangerously elevated levels of blood cholesterol and blood fats.

- Disordered brain chemistry, sometimes similar to that seen in toxic and addictive states, contributes to an increasing number of mental problems, including eating disorders such as anorexia and bulimia, various obsessive-compulsive disorders (characterized by repetitive, ritualistic behavior), addictive sexual behavior, memory and cognitive difficulties, depression, and mania. The prevalence of obsessive-compulsive disorders, according to the best recent studies, is twenty-five to sixty times greater than previously estimated.

• There are now 750,000 members of Alcoholics Anonymous in the United States, up from 550,000 five years ago. There are 28,000 Al-Anon groups and 1,100 adult-children-of-alcoholics groups nationwide, up from only 14 such groups in 1981.

• The typical community now has not only Alcoholics Anonymous but also chapters of such groups as Narcotics Anonymous, Overeaters Anonymous, Gamblers Anonymous, Debtors Anonymous, Sex and Love Addicts Anonymous, Cocaine Anonymous, Smokers Anonymous, Shoplifters Anonymous, Spenders Anonymous, Adult Children of Alcoholics, Adult Children of Sex Addicts, Coc-Anon, Al-Anon, Eating Disorders, Men for Sobriety, Women for Sobriety, Pills Anonymous, Sex-oholics Anonymous, and so on.

COSTS OF THE EPIDEMIC

Let's look now at some of the additional costs this epidemic is producing. First, consider alcohol abuse. The country's annual bar bill, what the nation pays for the harm done by this drug each year, comes to a staggering (pun intended) *$120 billion*. More than 50 percent of all highway deaths are alcohol-related. Such deaths are the number one killer of fifteen- to twenty-four-year-olds. Other alcohol-related accidents claim another 25,000 lives each year. As many as 40 percent of all accidental deaths in industry involve alcohol abuse; 50 percent of all fatal fires are due to alcohol-induced negligence or misbehavior; almost 70 percent of all drownings and 70 percent of all injurious and fatal falls are due, in significant part, to alcohol abuse. Some 33 to 50 percent of *all* injuries and deaths caused by accident, crime, and suicide are alcohol-related.

The damage doesn't stop there, unfortunately. Women who drink regularly during pregnancy annually deliver more than three thousand severely defective babies. Nobody knows how many additional thousands are robbed in the womb of their full physical and mental endowment.

Alcoholism contributes to malnutrition, depression, gastrointestinal disorders, memory impairment, liver disease, heart problems, central-nervous-system disorders and hormonal disturbances, among other problems. Even moderate drinking (15 to 39 ounces of alcohol *per month*) doubles a person's risk of bursting a blood vessel in the brain (hemorrhagic stroke). Heavy drinkers (those who consume 40 or more ounces of alcohol per month) have a three times greater risk of stroke than do nondrinkers. (A 12-ounce beer delivers about half an ounce of alcohol; a 4-ounce glass of wine also contains about half an ounce of alcohol, as does a shot [1¼ ounces] of hard liquor.) These risks are independent of all other risk factors for stroke (such as age, weight, and cigarette smoking).

Heavy drinking has now also been linked to substantially increased risks of cancer of the tongue, mouth, pharynx, larynx, esophagus, and liver. These account for about 10 percent of *all* cancers in the U.S.

Alcohol abuse also leads to impaired immunity and increased risk of infection. In some areas, 50 percent of all those admitted to hospitals for treatment of pneumonia are alcoholics. In fact, 40 to 50 percent of *all* hospital admissions in some centers are alcohol-related.

Then there is the enormous cost to individuals, families, and society as a whole that results from alcohol-influenced cases of rape, assault, and abuse. Alcohol intoxication can significantly increase the chances of being both victim and victimizer in such crimes. From 25 to 50 percent of all cases of spouse abuse involve alcohol.

Given the monstrous tax this drug imposes on society, it is amazing that we continue to regard it with ambivalence. The noted author and researcher Alex Comfort, writing in *The Lancet* (February 25, 1984), summed it up this way:

> Our attitude towards alcohol is basically not evidential but sentimental, rather as we are slow to admit that a family member is delinquent or insane. If cocaine is an Edwardian roué, marijuana a grubby counterculturist, and LSD a crazy with a knife, alcohol is a beloved if disreputable old uncle whose peccadilloes are excused because he is friendly and keeps a good cellar. So much so

that even substance abuse experts bridle at the idea that he is a
child molester who should be incarcerated. We obviously need to
moderate his excesses, but suggesting that he be banished is like
attacking Santa Claus.

We've grown considerably more intolerant of another "relative,"
however, that once racy cousin from the sophisticated city—nicotine. Perhaps we've finally recognized you can only bury so many
bodies in the basement. Cousin Nic, as even many of those who keep
sucking up to him agree, has to go. It's not just the death toll,
appalling as that is. People have exhibited a remarkable willingness
to risk distant (even if distinctly premature) death for instant and
immediate gratification. But there are also more immediate costs
(than death) associated with smoking—and people have begun to pay
heed.

For one thing, the damage smoking does is costing the economy
(and the taxpayers) about $65 billion a year. Nonsmokers are footing
a large part of that bill. They are also suffering—physically—from the
cigarette smoke of others: spouses, friends, coworkers, strangers. Involuntary smoking (inhaling the smoke from other people's cigarettes)
is killing thousands of Americans annually; it is also impairing the
health of thousands of children, predisposing them to asthma and
other respiratory problems that may persist into adult life. When the
involuntary smoker is a pregnant woman, her baby is likely to be born
with low birth weight, a factor associated with risk of significant health
problems both in infancy and later in life. Women regularly exposed
to cigarette smoke (that of their spouses, typically) are more likely to
experience earlier-than-normal menopause.

Smokers themselves, even when they are not daunted by the
data showing that they are at enormously increased risk of dying
of heart attack, lung cancer, or other malignancy or respiratory
ailment, are sometimes moved by other adverse findings. Younger
people, in particular, appear more responsive to studies showing that
smoking can significantly impair fertility, cause premature aging and
wrinkling of the skin, and substantially reduce athletic endurance and
energy.

The new understanding of nicotine's powerful addictive capacity
also appears to be having some positive influence on younger, prospective, and beginning smokers. Surveys have previously shown
that the young mistakenly believe it is relatively easy to quit smoking.

We now know this is not the case—and that knowledge is beginning to have some impact among younger people.

After fifty years of research and thousands of studies, science, through the office of the surgeon general, officially declared nicotine addictive in 1988. The tobacco companies, of course, deny it. But researchers have known for some time that nicotine is highly addictive, and so, for that matter, have many smokers. When the really terrifying health hazards of smoking first began to be made known in the 1950s, many people assumed everyone would quickly quit smoking. Some immediately sold their shares in tobacco companies, thinking they would soon be worthless.

Those who held on to their shares are richer today. Despite an onslaught of negative reports related to smoking over the past several decades, the percentage of Americans who smoke remains high— around 50 percent. It isn't ignorance that keeps people puffing. More than 70 percent of those polled know that smoking causes cancer. Almost 80 percent of Americans who smoke, according to an even more recent poll, say they want to quit.

Why don't they? For this "simple" reason: They have a monkey on their back with a grip every bit as ferocious and tenacious as the one heroin, alcohol, and cocaine addicts have to contend with. In fact, once hooked, it is actually a little easier, studies show, to abstain from heroin and alcohol than it is to say no to nicotine. Only one smoker in ten can hold consumption down to under five cigarettes per day for any length of time without some form of treatment.

Because abstinence from smoking does not produce the dramatic symptoms that withdrawal from heroin, for example, does, some insisted that nicotine is not truly addictive. But studies have now proved beyond any doubt that nicotine withdrawal is real and intense. The scientific evidence is all in place now, but we needn't belabor that. Just ask anyone who has tried to quit.

Or consider the case of the three-year-old child in rural India who was admitted to a hospital with anemia, bronchitis, and malnutrition. The child was in a state of irritation and agitation that persisted even after being given tranquilizers in an effort to sedate him during blood transfusion. The child could not sleep, wouldn't eat, and was up, "crying and fretting through much of the night, begging for bidis," as his doctors recalled it.

The child, it developed, had been smoking bidis—crude cigars— for the past six months. His grandmother had supplied him with the bidis, usually eight to ten per day. The doctors wrote the case up for *Clinical Pediatrics*, calling their paper, "Probable Tobacco Addiction in a Three-Year-Old Child."

Then there's cocaine. It was always costly, in more ways than one; we just didn't know it. In fact, for a long time—and as recently as a few years ago—many people, including a fair number of researchers, regarded cocaine as a relatively harmless, nonaddicting euphoriant. By contrast, amphetamines, another class of stimulants, were regarded as major evils. The prevailing misperception of cocaine resulted in literally millions of people suddenly trying cocaine. And today we have more than 5 million cocaine abusers in this country. Already by 1986, approximately 40 percent of those in the twenty-five-to-thirty-year-old range had tried cocaine. By the same date, cocaine-caused emergency room visits were up *fifteenfold* over where they had been a decade earlier.

What we're seeing now actually occurred on two other occasions. In the late 1800s, word went out that you could use cocaine and not get hooked. People believed, responded—and ultimately paid the price. Word got around on the often extreme dangers of cocaine, and its use gradually declined. The cycle repeated itself in the 1920s. The same thing occurred in the early 1950s and again in the late 1960s, but this time with other stimulants—amphetamines and methamphetamine. As Drs. Frank Gawin and Everett H. Ellinwood Jr. have noted in a recent paper in the *New England Journal of Medicine*, history has repeated itself with regularity in this context, partly because these stimulant drugs, with the exception noted below, have a long lag time in terms of producing addiction—often two to five years. That doesn't necessarily mean, however, that it's going to be easy to quit cocaine if you stop before taking it for two years. Cocaine delivers a sense of well-being and wholeness that, for many, is difficult to abandon. Instead, it is actively pursued—with higher doses of cocaine taken with increasing frequency.

As for the exploding number of people smoking crack (a chemically altered form of cocaine), the addictive lag time drops from years to *weeks*. The advent of crack has resulted in virtual epidemics of addiction in many major cities. Crack is cheaper than regular cocaine and is readily available in most areas. The compulsion to smoke crack develops very rapidly; it is almost impossible to make a distinction between crack use and crack abuse. Here is one case where merely using a drug—for even a very short time—almost guarantees abuse. Crack, as noted earlier, may well be the most addictive drug there is.

Many use alcohol and crack cyclically, crack to go up, alcohol to come down.

It is estimated that it will take up to $30 billion per year just to treat those presently addicted to cocaine and crack. And the fear is well founded that the number of addicted will continue to soar.

IS THERE HOPE?

We could also examine the extended costs of heroin and prescription-drug abuse; the social and psychological costs of all manner of compulsive and addictive behavior; the toll air and water pollution is taking; the awful price we're paying for our love affair with rich and fatty foods—but the point, I believe, has been made. We're in a mess of our own making. We've not only fouled our own nest—our environment—we've polluted our very cells, poisoned our neurons, and short-circuited our synapses.

Can we ever "get clean?" *Yes.* I said at the beginning of this chapter that I would return to the case of Alicia. I am happy to report that Alicia, who used many of the elements of the Purification Prescription you will learn about in Part Two of this book, *is* clean today and has been for over a year. She has shed those eighty excess pounds and shows every sign of being capable of maintaining an ideal body weight indefinitely. She has not had a drink or smoked a cigarette in nearly a year. Her opiate (painkiller) addiction is a thing of the past. She did *not* start on tranquilizers. Her cholesterol and triglyceride levels are ideal, and her once-high risk for heart disease has evaporated. Her food sensitivities are entirely under control, and her allergic symptoms have been substantially reduced. She is relaxed, she exercises regularly, and she looks as she should, instead of like a much older woman.

Alicia's mind and her resolve are clearer and stronger than they have been in years. The cleansing of her mind and body has given her power, the strength to deal in new and more prudent ways with her wayward daughter and abusive husband. Her codependency with them has been severed. This has meant a separation from her husband, but she sees hopeful signs and believes that the separation has benefited him as much as it has her. She believes her marriage may ultimately be restored, but even if it isn't, she says, "It's better for even one of us to be alone and whole than for both of us to be together and broken."

I don't claim credit for this miracle—nor do I attribute it to those elements we'll be discussing shortly. I attribute it to the strength and creativity that were always present in Alicia—to a presence that the purifying elements of my Prescription merely helped clarify through a restoration of vital, *innate* biochemical balances.

PART

II

THE ELEMENTS OF THE PRESCRIPTIONS

NOTE ON THE ELEMENTS

Descriptions of the major elements of the Purification Prescriptions follow. They include vitamins and minerals, amino acids, lipids, seaweeds, herbs, pharmaceuticals, diet, light, exercise, and meditation. The purpose of this part of the book is to familiarize you with the individual elements and alert you to some of their remarkable purifying properties. *Do not attempt to use any of these substances, however, until after you have read and studied the actual Prescriptions themselves in Part III*. It is important that these substances be used in the *proper doses, proper combinations,* and under the *proper circumstances. Discuss all items and programs mentioned in this book with your physician before embarking on their use*. Some require continuous medical supervision.

1 Vitamins and Minerals: The Essential Purifiers

FROM ADDICTIONS TO ALZHEIMER'S

Vitamins and minerals are the essential elements of detoxification and purification in the body, blood, and brain. They are the vital precursors of the antioxidants that protect us against those highly reactive molecules called free radicals. Free radicals are the real culprits in all of the pollutants that beset us. They are the very agents of aging and the degenerative processes that characterize aging.

Let's look at alcohol for a moment to see how vitamins can help protect us against the ravages of free-radical attack. Alcohol is liquid aging—or the fountain of aging, as I sometimes call it. It's an elixir of free radicals waiting to be liberated in your blood, tissues, and brain. Free radicals start smoldering biological fires and spew toxic sparks and exhaust, impairing cell membranes and ultimately destroying whole cells. These free-radical fires use up oxygen the cells need and thus interrupt the proper flow of energy throughout body and brain. In the process, everything from immunity to psychological equilibrium gets thrown out of whack. The consequences can be cancer, heart disease, arthritis, liver failure, chronic fatigue, memory loss, depression, mania, psychosis, and more.

The more alcohol (or other toxin) that is consumed, the more antioxidant vitamins and minerals are needed to help put out the biological fires that accelerate aging and cause disease. For years, animal experiments have demonstrated the enormous power vitamins can have over addictive behavior. If rats are given the choice between drinking plain water and water spiked with alcohol, they will almost always choose the latter. Researchers have found that when animals are deficient in the B vitamins, they are even more eager to drink alcohol. Alcohol provides an initial rush, a quick energy fix—a means of replacing, in effect, whatever is missing or deficient in the body. Unfortunately, the fix is short-lived and contributes very quickly to even greater nutrient deficiencies.

But what happens when you supplement the diet of animals with the B vitamins? The supplementation *delays* the voluntary consumption of alcohol. And when vitamins C and E are given along with the B vitamins, consumption is delayed ever further. Finally, the further addition of a liver extract stopped alcohol consumption altogether in these experiments.

Early studies related to vitamin supplementation in human alcoholics have also shown positive results, but such studies have been few in number. One of the earliest, using vitamins A, C, and E, in addition to the B vitamins, was suggestive of an effect that decreased desire for alcohol. A better-designed follow-up study involving far more alcoholics and better scientific controls found that the same vitamins benefited a number of patients, promoting abstinence in some and better control over alcohol intake in some others.

Vitamin and mineral therapies are now being used in *most* detoxification and withdrawal programs—but often with little understanding of their proper use. When the prescription is right, the effects can be quite dramatic (see Part III). Oddly, though, vitamins and minerals are almost never prescribed for long-term substance-abuse rehabilitation and prevention. This is unfortunate, because these micronutrients may be even more effective in that context, as the late (and, yes, great) nutritional pioneer Roger Williams suggested years ago.

Williams, who helped discover the vitamins pantothenic acid and folic acid, believed that inadequate intake of dietary vitamins, minerals, and other nutrients increases vulnerability to addiction, whether of drugs or of foods. He was the first to question seriously the adequacy of the standard American diet. He believed that while we are born free in this country, we are *not* biochemically equal. Our biochemical individuality requires not one standard diet but, in many cases, additional supplementation based upon many environmental and hereditary variables.

In the pages that follow, you will learn about some of the most important vitamin and mineral supplements that can be used in the effort to deal with those variables. These supplements may help prevent and treat addictive behavior and toxic conditions ranging from alcoholism to Alzheimer's disease.

Vitamin A and Beta Carotene

There are several substances that have vitamin A activity. The best known and most important of these are preformed vitamin A and beta carotene. Beta carotene is the best extinguisher of one of the most toxic free radicals—the singlet oxygen free radicals. Beta carotene is far superior to vitamin A in putting out oxygen free-radical fires in cell membranes. Vitamin A deficiency and low beta carotene intake increase the risk of several cancers.

Alcohol consumption often leads to vitamin A deficiencies. People who drink a lot usually have bad nutrition in general. Alcohol specifically depletes vitamin A stores in the liver, leaving that crucial organ undefended against free-radical destruction. High doses of vitamin A itself can be toxic, but beta carotene has extremely low toxicity even in high doses and so provides an ideal supplement for heavy drinkers and some others with toxic liver damage.

Beta carotene may also help detoxify barbiturates and nicotine. It has been shown, in animal experiments, to help protect against cancer caused by certain chemicals found in cigarettes. And human studies show that smokers with low intakes of beta carotene are much more likely to get lung cancer than are those with adequate or higher intakes of this nutrient. Smoking itself depletes beta carotene, so it is wise for smokers and those withdrawing from nicotine to make sure they are getting even more beta carotene than is considered adequate. (See Part III for specific recommendations.)

A 1988 study has found that supplemental beta carotene and/or vitamin A can actually *prevent* precancerous lesions (the result of using chewing tobacco and snuff) and can cause existing lesions to *regress*. Other studies indicate that vitamin A and beta carotene can provide some protection against radiation damage—of the sort inflicted in some cancer treatments, for example.

Vitamin B₁ (Thiamine)

One of the most devastating effects of chronic alcoholism is known as the Wernicke-Korsakoff syndrome. The syndrome is characterized by severe confusion and abnormal eye movements. The disease has approximately the same incidence as muscular dystrophy, and most who develop it require long-term care. The disease is caused by vitamin B₁ or thiamine deficiency and *can* be prevented.

Thiamine is a B vitamin that is crucial to the smooth working of the cellular machinery involved in the production of energy. The processing of blood sugar or glucose to produce energy depends on an adequate amount of thiamine. Under conditions of thiamine deficiency, biological energy production is decreased, lactic acid builds up in the blood, and if the deficiency is severe enough, death can occur. Alcohol is known to interfere with thiamine absorption and metabolism, and alcoholics are at high risk for deficiency of the vitamin.

Heavy drinkers who suddenly stop drinking often start to eat ravenously and are thus at particularly high risk for developing the Wernicke-Korsakoff syndrome, lactic acidosis, paralysis of some eye muscles, heart failure, and even death. The reason for this is when these people eat—and they typically eat foods high in refined sugar—the sugar that enters their cells ends up mainly as lactic acid due to their thiamine deficiencies. Thiamine supplementation can prevent all of this from happening. In fact, whenever an alcoholic enters the hospital for treatment of alcohol withdrawal or acute alcoholism, thiamine should *always* be administered before the patient is given any food either by mouth or intravenously. The administration of an injection of thiamine is often life-saving in these cases.

For many years it has been suggested that alcoholic beverages be fortified with thiamine to prevent the development of deficiency of the vitamin and, in particular, the Wernicke-Korsakoff syndrome. Two researchers at the University of California, San Diego, school of medicine published a paper in the *New England Journal of Medicine* dealing with this issue. They showed that by investing $17 million annually to fortify all domestic alcoholic beverages with thiamine, $70 million could be saved each year in medical payments for the long-term care of patients with the Wernicke-Korsakoff syndrome. Has anything been done toward this end? In a word, *no*. Why not?

Some believe that more research is needed before thiamine fortification is implemented. Others ask, Who will pay for the vitamin? Some argue that if Americans know that their alcohol contains thiamine, they will drink *more* of it. Some are concerned about the *taste* of fortified alcohol, though in a test no difference could be detected between fortified and unfortified beer. It is highly likely that thiamine fortification will diminish the incidence of some of the most devastating aspects of alcoholism, and it is highly *unlikely* that alcoholism would increase if this were done. Fortification should be started as soon as possible. It will save society money and reduce human suffering enormously. In the meantime, those who do consume alcoholic beverages are advised to take thiamine supplements.

I mentioned above that severe confusion is the major manifestation of the Wernicke-Korsakoff syndrome. Severe confusion is also the major symptom of an equally devastating and even more common disorder, Alzheimer's disease. Some enzymes (biological catalysts) that require thiamine for their activity have been found to have reduced activity in this disease. It is of great interest that a recent placebo-controlled study (reported on in a 1988 edition of *Archives of Neurology*) demonstrated significant improvement in cognitive function in patients with Alzheimer's disease who got *massive* doses of thiamine for a period of three months.

Vitamin B_2 (Riboflavin)

Vitamin B_2 (riboflavin) is another vitamin essential in energy production. Deficiency of the vitamin is manifested mainly as skin and mucous-membrane disorders, particularly those of the mouth. There is some evidence that severe riboflavin deficiency may be an important causative factor in cancer of the esophagus. Megadoses of the vitamin, given to those living in an area where incidence of esophageal cancer is very high, resulted in fewer esophageal lesions thought to be precancerous. These studies are ongoing.

Chronic consumers of alcohol are at risk for riboflavin deficiency. Significant deficiency of the vitamin is found in alcoholics with marginally adequate diets. The combination of alcohol consumption and cigarette smoking significantly increases one's chances of getting esophageal cancer, among other things. Increased vitamin B_2 intake is extremely important in those who drink, particularly if they smoke as well.

Vitamin B₃ (Niacin)

The term *niacin* commonly refers to the two forms of vitamin B_3: nicotinic acid and nicotinamide. Neither nicotinic acid nor nicotinamide are related to nicotine, the addictive element of cigarettes. Niacin plays a crucial role in energy production and nicotinic acid has recently received wide attention for its dramatic cholesterol-lowering effect when used at high doses.

An active form of niacin (nicotinamide adenine dinucleotide) that is produced in the body is required for the metabolism of alcohol. Chronic consumers of alcohol thus have *greater* need of niacin and are often at risk for niacin deficiency. Such deficiencies are frequently found in alcoholics with even marginally deficient diets. Increased intake of niacin is obviously a good idea for those who drink.

There are some anecdotal reports and speculation that niacin may be helpful in alcoholic detoxification. Niacin, along with saunas and exercise, are used by some in an effort to detoxify the body of all pollutants, including alcohol, recreational drugs, Agent Orange, pesticides, herbicides, formaldehyde, nicotine, and so on. But no scientific studies have been done to prove that this regimen really works.

On the other hand, there is no doubt that niacin can help purify the body of one of its most potent endogenous toxins, cholesterol. We all need a certain amount of cholesterol for normal body function, but most of us have too much cholesterol in our blood and also in our cells. Abnormally elevated blood cholesterol is a major factor in the formation of deposits that restrict the flow of blood through the arteries that feed the heart, brain, and other tissues of the body. Accumulation of cholesterol in cellular membranes creates a type of atherosclerosis at the cellular level, restricting the flow of oxygen and other nutrients into the cell and diminishing the responsiveness of cells in general. Increased amounts of cholesterol in cell membranes make the cells, and ultimately the whole body, more rigid, a process most of us are familiar with as we age. This is a process that can be slowed and even, to some extent, reversed. High-dose nicotinic-acid therapy is very useful in lowering elevated cholesterol, especially in combination with other elements you will learn about in this book. In addition to lowering cholesterol, nicotinic acid also raises serum HDL cholesterol (high density lipoprotein—"good" cholesterol)—and lowers serum triglyceride levels.

Vitamin B$_6$

Vitamin B$_6$ consists of three substances, all of which have equivalent activity: pyridoxine, pyridoxal, and pyridoxamine. Pyridoxine is the form most commonly used for supplementation. The vitamin is converted in the body to compounds that are of utmost importance in the metabolism of amino acids. Some amino acids are precursors of the neurotransmitters. Neurotransmitters are the molecules that make connections between the basic elements of our nervous system and that facilitate thoughts, feelings, and actions. B$_6$ deficiency can diminish neurotransmitter synthesis and cause problems in all these spheres. In addition, vitamin B$_6$ is, among the B vitamins, most important for maintenance of the immune system. Vitamin B$_6$ deficiency can cause depression, confusion, convulsions, increased susceptibility to infection, and abnormalities of the skin and mucous membranes.

Insufficient intake of B$_6$ is common in the U.S. A number of widely used drugs, including oral contraceptives, diminish the body's ability to utilize this vitamin, and contribute to deficiencies. Chronic alcohol users are at particular risk for B$_6$ deficiency since alcohol affects B$_6$ metabolism and may stimulate urinary excretion of B$_6$. Deficiency of B$_6$ is quite common among alcoholics, and its incidence may be as high as 80 to 100 percent in those with alcoholic liver disease. Alcoholics have abnormal serum amino acid levels, and it's probable that B$_6$ deficiency is one of the causes. These abnormalities contribute to the sort of neurological and mental problems commonly seen in alcoholics, problems that are often traceable to B$_6$ deficiency.

Vitamin B$_6$ has been found to ease symptoms of asthma. Scientists at Columbia University and the USDA Agricultural Research Service have reported that asthmatics who were given B$_6$ supplements had a significant reduction in the occurrence, duration, and frequency of asthmatic attacks and wheezing episodes. Others are confirming these results. Many who drink alcohol or use other commonly abused drugs often suffer from asthma. Alcoholic beverages and many other drugs often contain additives that can precipitate asthmatic attack. Many champagnes and wines contain sulfites (usually stated somewhere on the label), and wines may also contain urethanes. Both of these additives can cause serious reactions in those susceptible to them. (See also B$_{12}$, another vitamin that can detoxify some of these additives.)

Folic Acid

Folic acid, a member of the B vitamin family, is essential for the synthesis of the molecule that contains our genetic endowment, DNA. Deficiency of the vitamin results in impaired cell division, particularly in rapidly growing tissues. Folic-acid deficiency is typically first manifested in the decreased production of red blood cells leading to a kind of anemia known as megaloblastic anemia. Deficiency of the vitamin can contribute to carcinogenesis and teratogenesis (birth defects) because of impaired ability of nucleic acids to be repaired if damaged. Recent research indicates that high doses of folic acid can reverse premalignant lung lesions of the sort often seen in smokers.

Chronic consumers of alcohol with inadequate nutrition or even marginally adequate diet can very quickly become deficient in folic acid. Alcohol causes a marked increase in urinary excretion of folic acid and adversely affects its metabolism. Low serum folic acid has been seen in 40 to 87 percent of alcoholic persons admitted to municipal hospitals, and 40 to 61 percent of these individuals had megaloblastic anemia. One report showed that 38 percent of a random group of alcoholics had low serum folic acid. Alcoholics with deficiency of this vitamin have an increased incidence of esophageal cancer.

Certain drugs, such as oral contraceptive agents and the anticonvulsants phenytoin (Dilantin), phenobarbital, and primidone, all increase the risk of folic acid deficiency. *All* barbiturates increase this risk. Women on the pill are more likely to get precancerous cervical lesions, especially if they have folic-acid deficiencies. And folic-acid supplements have been shown to produce beneficial effects on the course of cervical dysplasia in women using oral contraceptives.

An important study on the effect of folic acid and vitamin B_{12} in heavy smokers came out of the University of Alabama and was reported in a 1988 edition of the *Journal of the American Medical Association*. Components of cigarette smoke can partially inactivate folic acid, leading to a deficiency of the vitamin in the bronchial tissues. This deficiency makes those tissues more vulnerable to the effects of cancer-causing agents. Other components, such as nitrous oxide, can break down vitamin B_{12}, leading to deficiencies in it as well. Cigarette smoke places tremendous oxidant stress on the lungs while robbing the tissues of their defenses (e.g., folic acid and vitamin

B_{12}). The researchers wanted to see whether supplemental folic acid and B_{12} could help heavy smokers who had already developed precancerous bronchial lesions.

The subjects were randomly assigned to treatment with 10 milligrams of oral folic acid, plus 500 micrograms of oral B_{12} in the form of hydroxycobalamin or a placebo. The study lasted for four months. In those who got the vitamins, there was a significant reduction in the number of patients with precancerous cells. This very important study is being continued. No adverse side effects from the vitamin megadoses were observed.

Vitamin B_{12}

Vitamin B_{12} refers to a group of substances called cobalamins (thus named because they all contain the mineral cobalt). The vitamin is essential for synthesis of DNA, cell replication, and the normal function of the nervous system. B_{12} deficiency can produce an anemia similar in nature to that caused by folic-acid deficiency (megaloblastic anemia) and neurologic symptoms such as difficulty in walking, weakness in arms and legs, confusion, and fatigue. Chronic alcohol ingestion decreases B_{12} absorption, and alcoholic patients often have decreased amounts of B_{12} in their liver and red blood cells.

B_{12}, in the form of cyanocobalamin, can block adverse responses to sulfites, additives used in foods, drugs, and alcoholic beverages as preservatives. Those sensitive to sulfites can develop symptoms that include bronchospasm, wheezing, and asthmatic attack (which could be fatal), sinus congestion, nasal blockage, runny nose, headache, itchy throat, and skin rash. Sulfites are present in some wines, beers, mixed drinks, and champagnes. Some manufacturers of these products list the presence of sulfites on the label; others do not. Sulfite sensitivity is common; there are at least 500,000 people in the U.S. susceptible to asthmatic attack triggered by sulfites. See Part III for more details and the Resources section for information on a home sulfite-testing kit.

Vitamin B_{12} supplementation has a beneficial effect in the treatment of precancerous bronchial lesions found in heavy smokers. Refer to folic acid discussion for details.

Pantethine

Pantethine is a metabolic derivative of the B vitamin pantothenic acid. Pantethine has recently become available as a nutritional supplement. Clinical research indicates that supplementary pantethine can lower blood levels of cholesterol and triglycerides, as well as decrease the stickiness of blood platelets.

A recent study by Japanese scientists suggests that supplementary pantethine can have favorable effects on the metabolism of alcohol. Alcohol is metabolized to acetaldehyde (similar to formaldehyde) in the liver. Acetaldehyde has many toxic effects, especially in the liver. The Japanese investigators reported that pantethine supplements significantly decrease acetaldehyde blood levels in some alcoholics. The substance appears to accelerate the metabolism of acetaldehyde.

Vitamin C (Ascorbic Acid)

Vitamin C (ascorbic acid) is the most popular of all the micronutrients. This popularity, to a large degree, is due to the suggestions of Linus Pauling; he believes that megadoses of vitamin C can prevent and cure the common cold and that it can be beneficial in the treatment of cancer. Although vitamin C therapy has fallen short of these claims, there is scientific evidence that it *can* reduce the severity and duration of colds and that it offers some measure of protection against certain types of cancer and ischemic heart disease.

Vitamin C is necessary for the formation of collagen, which holds connective tissue and bone together. It is also a major antioxidant. Deficiency of the vitamin can lead to scurvy, a disease characterized by bleeding guns, wounds that don't heal, skin that is rough, muscles that waste away and, sometimes, difficulty in breathing. Scurvy is not a disease of the past, as many believe. There are plenty of cases in the U.S. even today. Alcohol abusers are at particularly high risk.

The incidence of ascorbic acid deficiency in chronic alcoholics is reported to be as high as 91 percent. Chronic alcohol intake is associated with decreased absorption, increased urinary excretion, and altered metabolism of the vitamin—even in those with "adequate" RDA dietary intake of vitamin C. It is apparent that chronic consumers of alcohol require higher amounts of vitamin C for their health.

Cigarette smoking also depletes vitamin C. Many studies have documented the lower serum and white-blood-cell levels of ascorbic acid in smokers. These levels are diminished by 25 percent in those who smoke fewer than twenty cigarettes per day. They are diminished by up to *40 percent* in those who smoke more than twenty cigarettes daily. There is evidence that vitamin C supplementation can restore ascorbic-acid levels to normal in smokers. Most of the toxic effects of smoking, such as emphysema, heart disease, and lung cancer, are due, in great part, to runaway free-radical activity of the sort vitamin C can blunt.

Vitamin C can prevent the formation of nitrosamines, which are known to cause a wide variety of cancers in experimental animals and are thought to do the same in humans. Cigarette smoke, some food and alcoholic beverages, as well as some air and water pollutants, can give rise to nitrosamines. Much has been done to remove or inactivate these substances in food, but cigarette smoke and air and water pollutants remain major sources of exposure. Diet contributes about 1 microgram of these toxins daily while a pack of filtered cigarettes contributes at least 17 micrograms.

Asthmatics are particularly vulnerable to air pollutants and the noxious elements in cigarette smoke. Vitamin C can decrease bronchial irritability in asthmatics. One study showed that supplementation of 1 gram daily of vitamin C could significantly reduce airway reactivity to toxins in asthmatics. Another study indicated that a 500 milligram dose of the vitamin taken an hour and a half prior to vigorous exercise lessened bronchial spasms in some asthmatic patients.

Chloramine is being used, increasingly, in the purification of public water. Many object to the taste it confers and worry about its long-term effects. Chloramine can be neutralized by adding 30 milligrams of ascorbic acid to each quart of water.

Vitamin D

Vitamin D is derived from the diet but is also made in the skin by the action of ultraviolet light from the sun's rays. The active form of vitamin D is a hormone. Vitamin D is essential for the health of our bones. Deficiency of the vitamin leads to the bone disorder rickets in children and to bones that are soft and deficient in calcium in adults. The active form of vitamin D works, among other ways, by assisting the uptake of calcium into the body to be processed into bone. We are finding now that vitamin D is also involved in the production of white blood cells and the immune system. It appears to protect against some forms of cancer, especially cancer of the colon and rectum.

Those at risk for vitamin D deficiency include people who don't get much sun and whose diets are low in the vitamin. The elderly absorb less vitamin D from their diet and are not as efficient in producing vitamin D in their skin, even if exposed to sunlight. Regular users of certain drugs, including alcohol; anticonvulsants (such as phenytoin [Dilantin], phenobarbital, and primidone); barbiturates;

and laxatives, such as mineral oil and stool softeners (including Colace and Surfac) are all also risking vitamin D deficiency. Alcoholics have decreased bone density and bone mass, increased incidence of osteoporosis, and increased susceptibility to fractures. These problems are in part due to decreased absorption of vitamin D, as well as to interference with metabolism of the vitamin to its active hormonal form. Alcohol has adverse effects on calcium and magnesium nutrition, which are also involved in these problems.

Vitamin E

Vitamin E is the generic term for several molecules, the most active of which is called d-alpha-tocopherol. The vitamin is found in cell membranes and directly scavenges any free radical that threatens the membrane, provided it is present in adequate quantities. Vitamin E is essential for the healthy operation of the nervous system and immune system and for the maintenance of the fluidity of the blood as well as the cellular membranes. Studies at the Tufts University Human Nutrition Research Center on Aging show that high levels of supplementary vitamin E in experimental animals *reverse* the decline in immunological responsiveness that occurs with aging. More recently, investigators at this institution reported that supplementary vitamin E in humans enhanced immune responsiveness. Epidemiological studies reveal that low blood levels of vitamin E correlate with higher risk of lung cancer in humans.

Low vitamin E levels have been found in some alcoholics—but not in as many as one would expect. This may be because vitamin E is such an important antioxidant that all the other antioxidants work overtime when necessary to help conserve it. Vitamin E is the last antioxidant to go—and when it does go, the situation may well be terminal. Smokers are also at risk for vitamin E deficiency. Cigarette smoke contains many oxidants that increase free-radical production in the lungs and consequently increase membrane peroxidation (rancidification). A 1988 report from Toronto General Hospital demonstrated that cigarette smokers given supplementary vitamin E had a significantly lower amount of lipid peroxidation, which again increased after the vitamin E supplementation was discontinued. Vitamin E, like vitamin C, blocks the formation of cancer-causing nitrosamines and this may further contribute to a cancer-protective role.

Doxorubicin, or Adriamycin, is a drug widely used in cancer chemotherapy. Its usefulness is limited, however, by its potentially serious toxicity to heart muscle. This toxicity is probably due to free-radical activity generated by this drug. Supplementary vitamin E protects against this toxicity to some degree.

One of the more interesting studies related to the antioxidant effects of vitamin E was reported by German researchers in 1987. A group of six high-altitude mountain climbers was given 400 IUs of the vitamin daily, while another group of six was given a placebo. It was shown that the group receiving vitamin E performed significantly better, with less membrane lipid peroxidation, than the placebo group. Decreased lipid peroxidation translates into maintenance of membrane fluidity, which further translates into increased tissue oxygenation and, at the bottom line, increased production of biological energy.

Calcium

Calcium has received a lot of attention for its importance in the structure and metabolism of bone and its beneficial role in the prevention of osteoporosis. Adequate calcium nutrition also appears to be beneficial in the control of hypertension, and in the protection against cancer of the colon and rectum. Chronic consumers of alcohol are especially likely to have calcium deficiency.

Many chronic alcoholics have bone disease of one sort or another. They often have too little bone mass and are at increased risk of fracture. The cause of alcoholic bone disease appears to be related to defective calcium nutrition, as well as vitamin D and magnesium deficiencies. Alcohol inhibits the absorption of calcium and affects its metabolism. Vitamin D deficiency associated with chronic alcohol intake leads to inhibition of calcium absorption, as well. Low magnesium, common in alcoholics, can itself cause low blood levels of calcium.

Adequate calcium nutrition can also protect against the toxicity of such environmental toxins as lead and cadmium. This may in part explain why calcium is beneficial in the control of hypertension, a condition that may sometimes result from heavy-metal toxicity.

Magnesium

It is increasingly evident that magnesium deficiency is widespread. In 1988, the average American reportedly consumed approximately 40 percent of the recommended daily allowance of magnesium. Some experts believe that 80 to 90 percent of the U.S. population may be magnesium deficient. Magnesium is absolutely essential for life. It is necessary for every major biological process, including the metabolism of glucose, production of cellular energy, and the synthesis of nucleic acids and proteins. It is also important for the maintenance of cellular-membrane integrity, the electrical stability of cells, muscle contraction, nerve conduction, and the regulation of the muscle tone of blood vessels.

Magnesium deficiency has global adverse effects on the body. Manifestations of its deficiency include loss of appetite, nausea, vomiting, diarrhea, muscle weakness, muscle twitching and tremor, loss of coordination, heart arrhythmias, aggravation of angina, delirium, convulsions, coma, and sudden death—to name just a few! There are links between magnesium deficiency and high blood pressure, coronary heart disease, pregnancy problems, diabetes, and asthmatic attacks. The major reason magnesium deficiency has not been widely recognized until recently is that blood levels of the mineral are frequently normal even though *cellular* levels of the mineral are abnormally low. These abnormalities can be detected with special tests not yet widely available.

Magnesium deficiency, which is common among alcoholics, is sometimes severe enough to cause death. Supplementation with magnesium is crucial for the treatment of alcohol withdrawal, detoxification, and rehabilitation. It may also play a role in *prevention* of alcoholism. There is a striking similarity between the neuromuscular excitability seen in situations of low blood magnesium and that seen during acute alcohol withdrawal. One can postulate that alcoholics try, in effect, to self-treat their magnesium deficiency with alcohol.

Magnesium deficiency is also common in those with eating disorders, which often involve another type of addictive behavior. A report delivered at the 1988 meeting of the American Psychiatric Association revealed that about 25 percent of patients with eating disorders, especially those with bulimia (binging-and-purging disorder), have low serum magnesium levels. Magnesium deficiency appears to be associated with many of the emotional symptoms that characterize eating disorders. Clinical symptoms improve when patients are given supplementary magnesium.

Those who take diuretics are another group at risk for magnesium deficiency. More and more physicians are becoming aware of this problem and are giving these patients magnesium supplements, accordingly. Many people, particularly those with eating disorders, abuse diuretics. This abuse can be life-threatening in some circumstances.

Other drugs that cause magnesium deficiency include Cisplatin, widely used in cancer chemotherapy, cyclosporin, used to prevent rejection of organ transplants, antibiotics (such as gentamicin, carbenicillin, and ticarcillin), and digitalis.

Selenium

It has recently been shown that selenium—an essential trace mineral required by the body in minute quantities—can have enormous beneficial effects for human health. A large body of epidemiological evidence now exists that suggests that the incidence of many types of cancer is lower in regions where dietary selenium intake is higher. A few studies have shown that low levels of serum selenium is a risk factor for gastrointestinal and prostatic cancer. Low selenium intake also appears to be a risk factor for atherosclerosis and its consequences, heart attacks and strokes. Two very important enzymes involved in antioxidant activity require selenium for their synthesis and function. And there is probably no other micronutrient that is as important as selenium in helping conserve vitamin E.

Selenium deficiency increases the risk of various cancers. The effects of long-term selenium supplementation on cancer incidence are currently being studied. The animal studies have already demonstrated significant protective effects, with respect to chemically and virally induced cancers. Selenium appears to benefit virtually every component of the immune system. Selenium deficiency, on the other hand, leads to immune suppression.

Alcoholics are at particular risk for selenium deficiency. As we already know, alcohol places an increased oxidant stress on the body at the same time that it robs it of ways to deal with this stress. A 1988 study at the University of Helsinki demonstrated that alcohol intake significantly decreased serum selenium levels. The subjects apparently had "adequate" dietary intake of selenium, so it can be postulated that alcohol interferes with the absorption and metabolism of selenium.

Selenium protects against the toxic effects of such heavy metals as cadmium, mercury, lead and arsenic. It can also protect against toxins in cigarette smoke.

Zinc

Zinc is another mineral superpower when it comes to promoting good health. More than two hundred enzymes (biologic catalysts) require the trace element for their activity; among these are the enzymes involved in the production of nucleic acids (DNA and RNA), as well as the enzyme that metabolizes alcohol (alcohol dehydrogenase). Zinc is a biological antioxidant that, like selenium, spares vitamin E and is essential for normal immune function, the maintenance of taste, smell, and vision, and accelerates wound healing, among other things.

Heavy drinkers are at risk for zinc deficiency. Unfortunately, ordinary tests inadequately assess zinc status. Better tests are currently being developed. Zinc deficiencies are almost certainly extremely common in alcoholics. Alcohol is known to interfere with the absorption and metabolism of zinc. In those with alcoholic cirrhosis (advanced alcoholic liver disease), problems of immunity are common. Zinc supplementation may help with these problems.

Diuretic users and abusers (such as those with some eating disorders) are at risk for zinc deficiency. It has even been speculated that zinc deficiency itself may be a cause of some eating disorders, such as anorexia nervosa.

Other Trace Minerals

CHROMIUM

Chromium is an essential trace element that appears to protect against atherosclerosis and diabetes. Inadequate chromium intake is probably common in the U.S. There are some studies showing that chromium supplementation increases HDL cholesterol (the good form of cholesterol), and recently a new form of chromium, chromium picolinate, has been found to have a small but significant effect in the lowering of serum cholesterol and the raising of serum HDL cholesterol. Chromium supplementation has been found, in some cases, both to lower elevated blood sugar values and to normalize blood sugar in those with hypoglycemia. Heavy drinkers, heavy exercisers, diuretic users and abusers, and those with eating disorders are at risk for chromium deficiency.

COPPER

Copper is a trace element that participates in many free-radical defense strategies. Copper, however, also has its dark side. Those with advanced liver disease may accumulate copper in the liver, further accelerating the disease process. For these people, *decreased* (rather than increased) copper intake is important. For others, increased copper intake is prudent, as you'll see in Part III.

IODINE

Iodine is crucial for the normal working of the thyroid gland, the body's master regulator of energy metabolism. High doses of iodine are protective against the toxic effects of radioactive iodine, or Iodine 131, which is released following a nuclear-power-plant catastrophe.

IRON

Iron is an enormously important trace mineral, essential for, among other things, the production of red blood cells. Iron, like copper, also has its dark side. Those with advanced liver disease may have too much iron in their bodies. This can easily be determined by appropriate blood tests. Too much iron itself increases oxidant stress. For people who suffer from this problem, the prudent thing is to stay clear of iron. For others, adequate iron nutrition is mandatory.

MANGANESE

Manganese is an essential trace element that is, among other things, an important antioxidant. It is an integral component of one of the major free-radical defense substances, the enzyme manganese superoxide dismutase. Adequate manganese nutrition is essential, particularly for those subject to increased oxidant stress—smokers, heavy drinkers, and those exposed to air and water pollutants.

MOLYBDENUM

Molybdenum is an essential trace mineral. It is an essential component of the enzyme sulfite oxidase, which is involved in the detoxification of sulfites.

2 Amino Acids: The Mind Menders

CHEMICALS OF COMMUNICATION

There is nothing as magnificent as the human brain—the culmination of 18 billion years of cosmic evolution. We've only recently begun to understand how the brain works. One of the most fascinating things we have learned is that the brain's neurotransmitters are *all* derived from what we eat. Neurotransmitters are the chemicals that communicate feelings, thoughts, emotions, actions, behavior. Nearly all neurotransmitters are derived from amino acids in the foods we eat or are amino acids themselves. Amino acids are small chemical units that make up larger molecules called proteins. They also participate in energy formation and, as noted, neurotransmitter production.

There is now evidence indicating that all addictive behavior produces imbalances and deficiencies in the neurotransmitter systems of the brain. The amino-acid precursors of neurotransmitters are, increasingly, being used in the treatment of drug addiction. The amino acids most commonly used are L-tyrosine and, until recently, L-tryptophan. Other amino acids in use include L-glutamine, L-phenylalanine, L-aspartic acid, and the nonprotein amino acid D-phenylalanine.

Only recently has the idea been taken seriously that addiction to drugs is coupled to imbalances and deficiencies in the brain's neurotransmitters. But the late Roger Williams, as early as the 1940s, postulated that addiction to drugs, particularly alcohol, had to do with disorders in metabolism. He believed that every individual had a different metabolism (the chemical reactions of the body) and called this concept biochemical individuality. Because of different metabolisms, individuals, he argued, require different amounts of the various nutrients, a concept he later called differential nutrition. Williams and his colleagues found that *some* alcoholics, given supplementary L-glutamine, showed dramatic improvement. Because of individual metabolic differences among alcoholics, Williams did not expect L-glutamine to work for all alcoholics.

It turns out that Williams was really onto something. His postulates came before anyone knew very much about the metabolism of the brain or neurotransmitters. But recent research proves that nutrients can dramatically influence behavior and can be very useful in the treatment of drug addiction. There is now evidence that genetic factors, as well as chronic physical and psychological stress (including poor nutrition and exposure to pollutants), can lead to neurotransmitter malfunction, making many individuals more vulnerable to drug addiction of all types. Let's look now at some of the "mind menders" that are proving most useful in the detoxification, withdrawal, and purification processes.

L-Tyrosine

L-tyrosine has remarkable properties. It has been used as an antidepressant and is often effective in the treatment of addiction to cocaine and other drugs. Likewise, it is useful for those who must endure very harsh physical stresses (soldiers, for example) and is also helpful to many with premenstrual syndrome (PMS). L-tyrosine is the amino-acid precursor to the brain neurotransmitters dopamine and norepinephrine. These neurotransmitters help regulate alertness and mood and appear to buffer the effects of stress. There is evidence that cocaine and many other addictive drugs produce their initial pleasurable effects by stimulating the production of dopamine in the reward centers of the brain. Continued use of these drugs, however, results in burnout of dopamine (and other) neurotransmitters.

L-tyrosine has been used with success in the treatment of cocaine addiction, usually as part of a detoxification program that typically included L-tryptophan and antidepressants. In open clinical trials of such a program, Columbia University investigators reported that 75 to 80 percent of those thus treated were able to stop cocaine use completely or decrease usage by at least 50 percent. For most of the patients, the treatment blocked the cocaine high, diminished the craving for the drug, and prevented the rebound depression that follows when it is discontinued. Other researchers, at UCLA and elsewhere, have also reported favorably on this regimen for the treatment of cocaine abuse. It is highly likely that such a regimen would be useful in treating amphetamine abuse, as well as abuse of some other addictive substances.

L-tyrosine is an effective stress detoxifier. In experimental animals, acute stress increases norepinephrine activity in certain regions in the brain; this results in the depletion of the neurotransmitter in those regions. The consequences of this depletion include reduction in physical activity and exploratory behavior and increase in blood levels of an immunosuppressive cortisone-type steroid. When these animals were pretreated with supplemental L-tyrosine, not only were norepinephrine depletion and consequent behavioral depression prevented, but elevation of the cortisone-type steroid in the blood was also suppressed.

L-tyrosine supplementation also appears to be a useful antidote to sudden, extreme stress in humans. Researchers at the United States Army Research Institute of Environmental Medicine recently reported on soldiers who were subjected to stress and received either supplementary L-tyrosine or a matching placebo. The most extreme simulated stress situation was the equivalent of being taken suddenly to a height of about 15,500 feet and exposed to the cool temperatures of that altitude while wearing light clothing. The sudden drop in oxygen pressure produces a condition that can result in acute altitude sickness. Most people require at least several hours to adjust to the change in oxygen before they can even think clearly. The soldiers who were given L-tyrosine, however, adjusted rapidly, compared with those who got placebos. They were significantly more mentally alert and better able to make complex decisions and they had more energy and endurance. Their moods were better and they were less tense. They also suffered less from the physical rigors of the test, such as muscle discomfort, coldness, and headaches.

The beneficial effects of L-tyrosine appear to be directly related to the degree of stress. The greater the stress, the greater the benefit. Acute stress, especially of the sort imposed by sustained cocaine and amphetamine abuse, rob key areas of the brain of the neurotransmitters dopamine and norepinephrine. L-tyrosine is remarkably able to replace these crucial brain chemicals.

L-Tryptophan

L-tryptophan is another amino acid with notable beneficial properties. This amino acid was found to be useful in the treatment of cocaine, amphetamine, alcohol, and other drug abuse; it was helpful in treating insomnia and helping people adjust to jet lag. It was also effective in treating both depression and manic illness in some and was often a beneficial adjunct for the treatment of anxiety, pain disorders, and the hyperventilation syndrome in others. It was found to be helpful in the treatment of tardive dyskinesia, a serious neurological disorder. L-tryptophan is the amino-acid precursor for the neurotransmitter serotonin, and it appears that all of the above effects are mediated through serotonin in one way or another.

The bad news is that in November 1989, the FDA recalled suplementary L-tryptophan because of several reports associating the amino acid with some severe side effects, mainly affecting the blood and muscles (the eosinophilia-myalgia syndrome). It appears that these side effects are due to a contaminant(s) in the L-tryptophan products and *not* the L-tryptophan itself. *However, to be completely on the safe side, supplementary L-tryptophan should not be used until it has been determined that the available products are completely safe to take.* The following discussion and comments reflect research that had been performed before L-tryptophan was recalled.

Chronic use of alcohol, cocaine, and amphetamines, as well as many other drugs, burns up serotonin. L-tryptophan appears to exert several actions that can be helpful in the treatment of cocaine addiction. It may decrease anxiety and drug craving, help control both depressive and manic symptoms, and promote restorative sleep. Animal research supports the idea that L-tryptophan can be useful in treating both cocaine and amphetamine abuse. Amphetamine-dependent rats increased the rate of self-administered amphetamine twofold when their brain serotonin was depleted. Pretreatment with L-tryptophan markedly reduced their amphetamine intake. The greater the L-tryptophan dose, the less the rats craved amphetamines.

Chronic alcohol consumers frequently have decreased serum levels of L-tryptophan. Consequently, they would be expected to have lower brain serotonin levels. Brain serotonin deficiency could contribute to increased cravings for alcohol, to memory problems, sleep problems, depression, and to agitated behavior and hallucinations, all of which are often seen in alcoholics. Animal research supports these conclusions. Administration of alcohol to rats and baboons produces a decrease in the ratio of L-tryptophan to branched-chain amino acids in their serum. Branched-chain amino acids (L-valine, L-isoleucine, and L-leucine) are competitive with L-tryptophan for entry into the brain. Decrease in brain serotonin was found in the rats. L-tryptophan supplementation could thus be helpful in the treatment of alcoholism. (See section on branched-chain amino acids.)

The sedative and sleep-inducing effects of L-tryptophan have been known for some time. L-tryptophan has been shown to reduce sleep latency (time needed to fall asleep) in rats without disturbing sleep patterns (as so many sedative drugs do). Subsequent studies in humans showed that large doses of L-tryptophan increased sleepiness. L-tryptophan may be especially helpful in promoting restorative sleep among those with manic tendencies and cocaine- (and other drug-) induced brain serotonin depletion.

The hypnotic effect of L-tryptophan may also be useful in combating the toxic effects of jet lag. A study from the department of psychiatry at the University of California, San Diego, reported in 1987, found that L-tryptophan benefited U.S. marines who crossed eight time zones during a flight from California to Okinawa. Some fifty-one marines were involved in this study; half of them received L-tryptophan during the flight and for the first three nights after arriving in Okinawa, while the other half were given only placebos. Those who received L-tryptophan enjoyed significantly longer total sleep time on the plane flight and during the first night after arrival. They also scored higher on several measures of performance the day after arrival.

L-tryptophan had been shown to alleviate anxiety, panic attacks, and depression in some people. It was found to be more consistently beneficial in those with hypomania, manic illness, and in manic-depressives who were in their manic cycles.

Supplementary L-tryptophan has been found to increase pain tolerance—useful in some drug withdrawal situations. Animals fed L-tryptophan-poor diets were found to have diminished brain serotonin and decreased pain thresholds. The administering of L-tryptophan reverses the increased pain sensitivity by restoring brain serotonin levels to normal. There exist some clinical reports suggesting L-tryptophan may be beneficial for humans as well, in the treatment of chronic pain disorder, migraine headaches, and dental pain. Studies at Temple University School of Dentistry showed that subjects receiving L-tryptophan had significantly higher dental pain-tolerance levels when compared with subjects who received placebos. It appears that adequate brain serotonin levels are necessary for the control of pain symptoms.

Tardive dyskinesia is about the worst side effect from taking antipsychotic medications. It is characterized by bizarre facial tics, grimaces, and involuntary body movements. A report from the University of Arizona suggests that high doses of L-tryptophan helped detoxify these medications and provided relief from some of these symptoms. Further, L-tryptophan appears to *prevent* the onset of this disorder in experimental animals.

Phenylalanine

Astonishing as it may seem, our bodies have the capability of making opiatelike substances. These opiatelike substances are polypeptides that belong to a family of compounds known as neuropeptides, which are produced in the brain. Polypeptides are, like proteins, made up of amino acids, but they are much smaller in size than proteins. There are at least three types of these substances: endorphins, enkephalins, and dynorphins. They are involved in the regulation of pain and mood, among other things. There is evidence that chronic alcohol and opiate use produces or worsens deficiencies of these neuropeptides, increasing drug craving in the process. Restoring normal levels of these opiatelike substances appears to diminish the hunger for drugs.

D-phenylalanine is a nonprotein amino acid that inhibits the breakdown of enkephalins in the brain. Researchers at the University of Texas Health Science Center, San Antonio, recently reported that D-phenylalanine given to alcoholic mice significantly decreased their alcohol intake. These mice had a genetic predisposition to alcohol preference and were known to have brain enkephalin deficiencies. D-phenylalanine, by preventing the breakdown of enkephalins, produced higher levels of brain enkephalins. There is evidence that D-phenylalanine can also reduce human drug craving.

D-phenylalanine is available (in health-food stores and some supermarkets and drugstores) in the form of DL-phenylalanine. This consists of an equal mixture of D-phenylalanine and the protein amino acid L-phenylalanine. L-phenylalanine itself has shown benefits in the treatment of some depressives. This is not surprising, since the amino acid is converted in the body to L-tyrosine, which, as we have seen, is helpful for treating some with depression.

D-phenylalanine can help alleviate chronic pain. It also has anti-inflammatory action. Chronic-pain patients who benefit most from D-phenylalanine are those who have some inflammatory condition, such as arthritis.

It appears that the combination of D-phenylalanine and D-leucine (a nonprotein branched-chain amino acid) may be especially useful in helping control drug hunger. These amino acids have a synergistic action, since they work by different means to help prevent enkephalin breakdown. Hopefully, pure D-phenylalanine and D-leucine will soon be made available for use in these problems as well as others (chronic pain, arthritis, fibrositis, etc.). These nonprotein amino acids appear to be relatively free of side effects.

L-Glutamine and L-Glutamic Acid

L-glutamine was the first amino acid ever used for the treatment of addictive behavior, in this case alcoholism. At the time, very little was known about neurotransmitters. The initial studies were performed by Roger Williams and his colleague, William Shive. You will recall that Williams proposed that alcoholism, as well as other addictive behaviors, is related to nutritional deficiencies.

Alcohol inhibits the growth of the bacterium *Streptococcus faecalis,* among other bacteria. Shive discovered that an extract of liver could reverse this bacterial inhibition. The active substance in the liver extract is L-glutamine. Williams and colleagues subsequently showed that L-glutamine can substantially decrease voluntary consumption of alcohol by rats. Other amino acids, including the related L-glutamic acid, did not have this effect. Shive and Williams also found that rats fed nutritionally poor diets consumed relatively large quantities of alcohol. When these same rats were given L-glutamine supplements, however, their alcohol consumption went down 40 percent. Human studies by Shive and colleagues at the University of Texas at Austin, Fincle at the Veterans Administration Hospital in Bedford, Massachusetts, and French researchers all found glutamine to be helpful in the treatment of *some* cases of chronic alcoholism; they also found it could help some alcoholics *stay off* alcohol. L-glutamic acid was not similarly beneficial. This is not surprising, since L-glutamine passes much more readily into the brain than L-glutamic acid.

L-glutamine is a precursor of the neurotransmitters gamma amino-butyric acid (GABA) and L-glutamic acid. It also contributes to the production of energy in the brain and to the formation of glutathione, a very important antioxidant. Though some of the initial relaxing effects of alcohol appear to be mediated through increased GABA transmission, long-term alcohol production *depletes* GABA. It is only logical to include L-glutamine in alcohol- (and some other drug-) rehabilitation programs. And, in fact, it is now being used in an increasing number of such programs.

L-glutamic acid, which is similar but *not* identical to L-glutamine, has been found to limit the neurotoxicity of vincristine, a drug used extensively in cancer chemotherapy. Researchers at the Bowman Gray School of Medicine reported in 1988 on a double-blind, placebo-controlled, randomized study designed to determine if giving L-glutamic acid along with vincristine would limit the incidence of vincristine neurotoxicity in eighty-four women with breast cancer. Those who got the L-glutamic acid did, in fact, suffer significantly less toxicity, and no adverse effects were reported from the L-glutamic acid.

Other Amino Acids

L-ASPARTIC ACID
L-aspartic acid itself is a neurotransmitter. Chronic opiate use appears to deplete brain L-aspartic acid, and administration of L-aspartic acid has been shown to decrease intake of opiates. In a recent report, thirty-one opiate addicts were given L-aspartic acid during drug withdrawal. Another twelve opiate addicts were given high doses of diazepam (Valium) and chlorpromazine (Thorazine), a major tranquilizer. The intensity and duration of withdrawal symptoms were significantly less in those given aspartic acid than in those given the tranquilizing drugs.

BRANCHED-CHAIN AMINO ACIDS
Depletion of the branched-chain amino acids L-valine, L-isoleucine, and L-leucine characterizes some advanced liver diseases, such as severe alcoholic cirrhosis. This depletion contributes to

the marked clouding of consciousness known as hepatic encephalopathy—a condition that can lead to coma. Branched-chain amino acids are beneficial in the treatment of hepatic encephalopathy and may even *reverse* this terrible condition. These amino acids work, in part, by stimulating the conversion of L-glutamic acid into energy in the brain. They also have *anabolic* effects (promoting muscle growth) in those with severe liver disease. The anabolic process helps detoxify ammonia, which plays a large adverse role in hepatic encephalopathy.

L-Cysteine and L-Methionine

The metabolism of alcohol to acetaldehyde creates increased oxidant stress in cells, particularly in liver cells; acetaldehyde thus accounts for most of the adverse effects of alcohol, including liver disease. A major protective antioxidant, glutathione, is typically depleted in the liver cells of chronic alcohol users. Glutathione depletion promotes the rancidification and rigidification of cell membranes, leading to destruction of liver cells and brain cells, among others. Glutathione is produced from the amino acids L-cysteine, L-glutamic acid, and glycine. L-cysteine, in turn, is produced from L-methionine. Large doses of L-methionine have been found to protect against liver injury caused by lipid peroxidation in animals. Chronic alcohol use necessarily increases requirements for the precursors of glutathionine—L-cysteine and L-methionine. It is prudent to consider including L-methionine or L-cysteine in an alcohol-treatment program. In addition to this, L-methionine is involved in the synthesis of phosphatidylcholine, a crucial component in the maintenance of optimal cell-membrane fluidity (see discussion of Lipids).

Taurine

Japanese researchers have recently demonstrated that daily use of the nonprotein amino acid taurine lowers dangerous blood acetaldehyde levels in alcoholics. Taurine levels are usually low in chronic alcoholics.

Taurine has been found to significantly protect the lung against damage produced by the chemotherapeutic agent bleomycin in experimental animals.

3 Lipids: The Fabulous Fats

THE PURIFYING PROPERTIES OF "PURE FAT"

Lipids, commonly known as fats, comprise a group of biological substances that include triglycerides (the true fats), cholesterol, fatty acids, phospholipids, and prostaglandins. Most of us think of fats as universally bad, but in reality, the body and brain depend, crucially, upon a variety of lipids for proper functioning, and it is now becoming clear that several of the lipids can have extraordinary therapeutic and disease-preventive effects. Some of these remarkable substances are showing particular promise in regulating mood and memory; in purifying the cells, tissues, organs (especially the liver); and in alleviating the pain of withdrawal from those most addictive of drugs, the opiates. Studies indicate these lipids may assist in withdrawal from other types of drug dependency, as well.

Lecithin and Addictive Drugs

About sixty years ago, a most extraordinary report appeared in the *Chinese Journal of Physiology*, noting that, in animal experiments, soy lecithin could both *prevent* morphine dependence and make withdrawal from even severe chronic morphine addiction much easier. This research, conducted at one of the major Chinese medical schools of that period, went unnoticed in the Western world until the early 1980s, when a group of Israeli researchers unearthed it and began their own investigation.

Scientists at the Weizmann Institute of Science in Rehovot, Israel, found that a "special lipid mixture . . . which is a highly potent membrane fluidizer" could reduce or even completely abolish opiate withdrawal symptoms in experimental animals. They call their lipid mixture AL-721. Its most active ingredient is lecithin.

A number of different medical investigators have found evidence that our ability to tolerate and become dependent upon a variety of drugs is mediated by the lipid component of nerve cell membranes. The opiates, alcohol, barbiturates and some other drugs initially increase the fluidity of these membranes but, with continued use, have the opposite effect, making them more rigid and less functional. They do this by increasing the cholesterol content of the membranes, among other things. A vicious cycle ensues in which the membranes require more and more of the drugs in order to maintain short-term fluidity; the cost of this, however, is ever greater long-term rigidity. In a sense, you can see a reflection of this in the heavy user of alcohol or other drugs, who, while high, appears loose and fluid (frequently *too* loose and fluid) but who, during periods of abstinence, is increasingly stiff, rigid, and in pain. It is evident that those with chronic drug dependencies are aging at a significantly accelerated rate and that one of the clearest markers of aging is rigidification of cell membranes throughout the body and brain.

Pure lecithin is phosphatidylcholine, which includes fatty acids that may be of the saturated, polyunsaturated, and/or mono-unsaturated varieties. Those lecithins that contain the *polyunsaturated* fatty acids have the greatest membrane-fluidizing potential, although the Israeli product, AL-721, uses lipids extracted from egg yolks. Its special structure, however, is said to give it marked membrane-fluidizing properties. It is a structure specially designed to "capture" cholesterol. The Israelis have reported that fully saturated lecithins (against which they have compared AL-721) have actually made drug withdrawal symptoms *worse*—as would be expected, since the more saturated the fat, the more rigidifying the effect. In the original Chinese work, as previously noted, a soy lecithin was used. Soy contains mainly polyunsaturated fatty acids.

There are many mechanisms by which disturbances in cell-membrane fluidity may contribute to drug dependence and the rigors of detoxification and withdrawal. The lipid content of these membranes embraces a complex biochemistry with direct links to important neurotransmitters. Disturbances in membrane equilibrium echo throughout the brain and body. Almost all drugs deplete dopamine, a crucial chemical of the brain and central nervous system. And dopamine, in turn, is a stimulator of phosphatidylcholine in the brain.

Lecithin and the Mind

As a "purifier" of brain or central-nervous-system functions, pure lecithin—phosphatidylcholine—certainly has few, if any, equals. Phosphatidylcholine gives rise to acetylcholine, one of the most important of the body's neurotransmitters (chemicals that regulate and determine behavior). Acetylcholine disturbances and deficiencies contribute to a broad spectrum of ills, including memory disorders, Alzheimer's disease, mania, some psychoses, and tardive dyskinesia. Various environmental and genetic factors can foul our systems and, with continued exposure and aging, can pollute, impair, and deplete our acetylcholine biochemistry. Fortunately, there is a growing body of good evidence that increasing phosphatidylcholine intake can help prevent and reverse some of this damage—sometimes dramatically.

Lecithin has not proven to be the magic bullet we hoped it would be in the treatment of Alzheimer's disease (that severe presenile dementia that robs an increasing number of people of their memory, judgment, and orientation), but it *has* proved useful even in that extreme disorder *in some cases*. It remains quite possible that *combinations* of phosphatidylcholine with other substances (including some of the other elements discussed in this book) *will* eventually yield the answer to this frightening disease. In addition, it is possible that we may *prevent* Alzheimer's by ensuring that we get adequate amounts of phosphatidylcholine in our diets. There is evidence that many of us are deficient in this vital nutrient.

A deficiency of acetylcholine in certain areas of the brain is the most striking abnormality thus far discovered in victims of Alzheimer's. Phosphatidylcholine, the precursor of acetylcholine, has been given to these patients in an effort to make up for this deficit. Short-term memory was improved in some of these individuals, but lasting results have so far not been achieved. In one study, no improvement was noted in Alzheimer's patients until after they had been given daily doses of phosphatidylcholine for four months, after which a slowing in disease progression was noted. In another study, positive results were seen at certain doses but not at others.

Of perhaps greater significance to the general population are findings that when acetylcholine synthesis is artificially suppressed in humans, short-term memory impairment quickly develops. Giving supplemental choline, on the other hand, *enhanced* short-term memory. From these human and a variety of animal experiments, it appears that our memory skills are quite sensitive to our phosphatidylcholine status. This suggests that we should be vigilant about getting adequate amounts of this substance, either through diet or supplementation.

Lecithin has proved very useful in detoxifying even some of the most severe side effects of the neuroleptic drugs, major tranquilizers used in the management of various psychological disorders, including psychosis. One of the worst of these side effects is a condition called tardive dyskinesia. It is a serious neurological disorder characterized by involuntary movements of the neck, head, tongue and, sometimes, the entire body. The neuroleptic drugs, especially when used for six months or longer, cause serious deficiencies in brain choline and acetylcholine, and these deficiencies often persist long after the neuroleptic drugs are withdrawn. Many considered tardive dyskinesia to be irreversible, but supplemental phosphatidylcholine can be quite effective in quieting the involuntary movements caused by this disorder and is now the preferred treatment. Choline and lecithin have similarly been used, with some success, in treating other neurological disorders, such as Gilles de la Tourette's syndrome, Friedreich's ataxia, and another form of dyskinesia (this one caused by use of Levodopa, the anti-Parkinson's disease drug).

Some excellent results have been obtained, as well, with the use of choline and phosphatidylcholine in the management of some forms of mania (and, specifically, the manic phases of manic-depressive illness). In some studies, these substances have been shown to work even in cases where lithium failed to control the mania. In one study, lecithin, given along with lithium, significantly lessened the severity of manic episodes, but when the lecithin was withdrawn (and the patients were getting only lithium), 75 percent worsened markedly.

Researchers have compared the phosphatidylcholine content of cell membranes from psychotic and/or manic patients with those of healthy controls. They have found that the cell membranes of these mentally disturbed individuals contain significantly less phosphatidylcholine than do the membranes of cells from healthy individuals.

Once again, then, in addition to all else, the ability of the lecithins to keep cell membranes fluid and youthful is one of the keys to their mind-purifying properties.

Lecithin, Liver Detoxification, Hepatitis, AIDS, and Other Viruses

Hepatitis B is a viral disorder that can be very serious. In numerous recent animal and human studies, polyunsaturated phosphatidylcholine has demonstrated protective and restorative effects in liver cells damaged by hepatitis B virus. In a British study of patients with chronic active hepatitis, phosphatidylcholine, taken orally, resulted in substantial improvement. In some of these patients, the disease was completely inactivated. In several other studies of acute viral hepatitis B, equally good results were obtained using oral phosphatidylcholine. Recovery was speedier and there were fewer relapses than among those receiving only standard treatments. Laboratory values returned to normal much more quickly.

The liver, of course, is the body's primary organ of detoxification. By now it will come as no surprise to you to learn that the membranes of these liver cells have as their main component phosphatidylcholine. The stability, health, and resistance to infection and other assaults on these membranes are directly dependent upon their lecithin content. The lecithin may produce its positive effects in a number of ways. First of all, its incorporation into the damaged liver cells restores the proper amount of fluidity to their membranes, enabling them to function more normally again. The lecithin may also alter the membrane of the virus itself, making it less infective.

Numerous viruses that cause serious diseases in humans have lipid envelopes, or outer coatings. Recently, a number of researchers have demonstrated that if the fluidity of these viral membranes are increased, they can be destabilized and even inactivated. The lipid-envelope viruses vulnerable to this mode of attack include some of the most troublesome and dangerous viruses known, including hepatitis, the whole family of herpes viruses, and HIV (the AIDS-associated virus). AL-721 is, in fact, being tested experimentally in AIDS and other HIV-infected individuals. It appears that the lecithins may have a bright future in immunology and virology as well as in the other domains already discussed.

Lecithin Versus Aging

Substances that are truly purifying are also, ultimately, "anti-aging" elements. This is certainly true of the lecithins. In fact, Israeli researchers were primarily interested in discovering anti-aging elements when they developed AL-721, and they still believe that AL-721 and similar substances will have their greatest impact in slowing the progression of degenerative processes. The ability of polyunsaturated phosphatidylcholine to purge the cells of rigidifying cholesterol is, in itself, a profound anti-aging effect. Two different research groups have shown that phosphatidylcholine can have what appear to be genuine rejuvenating effects on vital biochemical activities in the brains of aging laboratory animals, with the activities under study returning to levels normally found only in much younger animals. In still other animal work, it was demonstrated that the liver cells of old animals could still be fluidized by giving supplemental oral phosphatidylcholine, also returning those cells to a condition closer to what is normally seen only among far younger animals.

Fish Oils/Marine Lipids and Cholesterol

There is another class of lipids that can have significant purifying effects in the human body and brain. These are the fish oils and marine lipids, especially eicosapentaenoic acid (EPA), one of the omega-3 fatty acids. EPA is involved in the synthesis of prostaglandins, substances that have broad hormonelike effects in the body. EPA has been marketed as a substance that can lower cholesterol.

Even though Eskimos typically consume a diet very high in fat and cholesterol, they have an unusually low incidence of heart attacks, strokes, blood clots, and atherosclerosis (narrowing of the arteries). They consume large amounts of whale blubber, seal meat, and fish. Scientists, puzzled by this situation, finally isolated the EPA in the Eskimo diet and determined that it is the factor that protects them from all those other fats and the cholesterol. It has now been demonstrated that EPA, through its effects on the prostaglandins, inhibits dangerous blood-clot formation, of the sort that can lead to heart attacks and stroke. In general, EPA, like the polyunsaturated lecithins, has a fluidizing effect.

One recent study found that EPA could significantly lower both total cholesterol and the particularly dangerous LDL form of cholesterol. This study also showed that the blood platelets of those with atherosclerosis have less phosphatidylcholine, relative to cholesterol, than do platelets in people who are healthy. With EPA treatment, phosphatidylcholine content of platelets rose in atherosclerotic patients.

Again, EPA, like polyunsaturated phosphatidylcholine, lives up to the "anti-aging" purification principle. By lowering cholesterol and fluidizing the blood platelets, it certainly slows and, to some extent, even reverses some of the aging processes. (It is also showing promise in alleviating some of the symptoms of arthritis.) But in a more direct test of its anti-aging properties, EPA was recently given to mice that otherwise ate a normal (mouse) diet. These EPA-supplemented mice were then compared with a group of mice on a calorie-restricted diet, of the sort that has promoted unusually great longevity. To the surprise of many, the EPA-fed mice lived just as long as the other group. Both groups lived *much* longer than is normal for laboratory mice.

4 Seaweed: Cleansers from the Sea

PURGING VIRUSES, HEAVY METALS, RADIOACTIVE POISONS, CHOLESTEROL

The sea plants that washup on ocean beaches are regarded by many as nothing more than debris. The very name—seaweed—suggests a nuisance plant with no real value. Nothing could be further from the truth. Seaweed has been used as a food by the Orientals for many years and is now becoming more popular in the American diet. Seaweed is used in folk medicine to treat a wide range of illnesses, and there is emerging scientific evidence that constituents of seaweed lower serum cholesterol, protect against cancer, boost immune function, and have antiviral activity against a number of viruses including the one associated with AIDS. Seaweed can also help cleanse the body of some nasty environmental pollutants such as cadmium, lead, and radioactive strontium.

In reality, seaweed is *not* a true plant—since it has no leaves, stems, or roots and develops differently from plants. Most seaweeds belong to the Protoctista Kingdom, but some, such as the blue-green algae, belong to the Monera Kingdom and are actually bacteria. Seaweeds (or algae, as they are often called) are also classified according to their color. There are the brown algae, the red algae, the green algae, and the blue-green algae. Kelp refers to brown seaweed. Hijiki, kombu, wakame, and arame are types of brown seaweed. Nori and dulse are types of red seaweed. The microalgae chlorella is a green seaweed, and spirulina is a type of blue-green algae.

Some of the most interesting substances derived from seaweeds are the polysaccharide gums. These are alginic acid or algin, which comes from the brown seaweeds; carrageenan, which comes from the red seaweeds; agar or agar-agar, also from the red seaweeds; and fucoidan, from brown seaweeds.

The Astonishing Alginates

Alginic acid and its salts are widely used in the food and medical industries. Among other things, these seaweed derivatives maintain the "heads" of beer, provide creamy bodies to milk shakes, are used to make dental impressions, and are beneficial for the treatment of heartburn caused by acid reflux from the stomach.

Alginates have been found to strongly bind strontium. Radioactive strontium-90 is one of the more common radioactive pollutants. Strontium-90 gets deposited in the bones and has been associated with increased incidence of bone cancer and other forms of cancer. Sodium and calcium alginate both bind to radioactive strontium in the gastrointestinal tract, preventing its absorption into the body. In addition, the alginates have been shown to reduce the amount of radioactive strontium that has *already* accumulated in the bones. The alginates can thus be used as both preventives and as treatments.

Alginates also bind to cadmium, barium, radium and, to a lesser extent, to lead. Ouch-ouch disease, found in Japan, is due to poisoning by cadmium-contaminated water used in the irrigation of rice fields. The disease is called ouch-ouch because the major symptom is painful joints. Ingestion of alginates has been reported to be beneficial in its treatment.

The Even More Astonishing Carrageenans

Carrageenans are sulfated polysaccharides that are derived from red algae. Carrageenans, like the alginates, are also widely used in the food industry as stabilizers and emulsifiers. The carrageenans used in the food industry come from the red algae known as *Chondrus crispus* (better known as Irish moss). Irish moss is found along the coasts of eastern Canada, Maine, Scandinavia, France, and the British Isles. Carrageenans are used as emulsifiers in ice cream, sherbets, frozen custard, chocolate products, cheese spreads, artificially sweetened jellies and jams, chocolate milk, and evaporated milk. They are also used to stabilize the foam in beer.

Carrageenans are more potent detoxifiers of lead than are the alginates. Carrageenans, in addition, have recently been found to inhibit a wide spectrum of disease-causing viruses in test-tube studies. These viruses include HIV (associated with AIDS) and some of the herpes viruses. The inhibitory effects appear to be quite powerful. Clinical studies are planned.

Agar is a polysaccharide gum that, like carrageenan, comes from red algae. It has many uses in the food industry; it can serve as a substitute for gelatin and as a thickening agent for milk and cream. Agar (also known as agar-agar) is sold in flakes, in powder form, and as sticks or bars called kanten. It is excellent for aspics, soups, pâtés, desserts, jellies, fillings, ice cream, etc.

Alginates, carrageenans, and agar all have potential cholesterol-lowering activity. This alone should be sufficient reason to increase consumption of seaweed, especially of the brown and red varieties.

The plant kingdom has been responsible for many drugs commonly used in the practice of medicine. The surface has only been scratched regarding the health benefits of seaweeds. Some recent research indicates that substances in brown seaweed are protective against various cancers in experimental animals. The polysaccharide fucoidan, found in these seaweeds, is believed to play a principal anticancer role, probably through an immune-enhancing effect.

5 Herbs: The Purifying Plants

HERBS THAT CLEANSE AND HEAL

If you've ever tried to read an herbal "guide," you've probably felt your head begin to spin and your yin begin to yang. Until recently, Western medicine paid scant attention to the Chinese and other "traditional" medicinal herbs. Part of the reason for this no doubt has to do with Western medicine's crisis-directed orientation (not to mention its sometimes smug insularity) and its attendant perplexity over and impatience with medical disciplines that seem to revolve around long-term difficult-to-quantify gains and seemingly oblique preventive strategies (not to mention vague "energies"). In fairness to the West, it must be said that the herbal literature *is* frequently ambiguous, poorly documented, and sometimes maddeningly self-contradictory and downright inscrutable. Lack of standardization and often unpredictable reliability of different herbal preparations contribute to further frustration. It must also be said, however, that there *are* herbs that have remarkable purifying and healing properties— and Western medicine is not only finally acknowledging this but, faced with stubborn cancers, AIDS, drug dependence, and a widening spectrum of environmental illness, is actively searching among the herbs for additional remedies.

Fortunately for all of us, it is finding some. In this chapter you'll learn about the purifying properties of Siberian and Chinese ginseng, astragalus, ligustrum, licorice, valerian, milk thistle, and wild oats. These plants are showing promise in a number of circumstances, including detoxification of chemo- and radiotherapies and nicotine, alcohol, and other drug withdrawal. A report in a U.S. medical publication not long ago noted, with a hint of envy, that doctors in the department of oncology at the Beijing Hospital of Traditional Medicine in China are enjoying significantly extended survival rates among many of their cancer patients, owing to the use of Chinese herbs that appear to counteract the toxicity of standard chemotherapies and radiation.

Astragalus and Ligustrum

Astragalus membranaceus and *Ligustrum lucidum* are two herbs long used in traditional Chinese medicine. Recently, they have begun to stir excitement in Western medicine as well, owing to research here showing that they are potent biological response modifiers. Substances found in the astragalus root include a polysaccharide called astragalan B, as well as choline and a bioflavonoid. That is a very interesting combination, to say the least. (See discussions of lecithin and choline, bioflavonoids, and polysaccharides elsewhere in this book.) Astragalan B has demonstrated detoxifying and immune-stimulating effects in animal studies. It appears, among other things, to have membrane-fluidizing properties. Ligustrum, often used in conjunction with astragalus, contains syringin and a terpene compound, both of which are also potential membrane fluidizers. Ligustrum has also demonstrated immune-stimulating properties.

Extracts of these herbs have restored immune response in human cells damaged by cancer chemotherapies and radiation treatments. Researchers in the U.S. have been very favorably impressed by the apparent potency of these immunorestorative test-tube effects. In China, doctors are using these herbs as adjuncts in the treatment of cancer, both to boost immunity and to detoxify some of the adverse effects of chemo- and radiotherapies, with reported good results. There is now also interest in these herbs among AIDS patients and some AIDS researchers.

Dr. Giora Mavligit, of the University of Texas M. D. Anderson Hospital and Tumor Institute, directed some of the cancer research. He and his colleagues reported that important immune responses were restored in 90 percent of those cells treated with astragalus and in 70 percent of those treated with ligustrum. "We have not seen anything close to this in terms of immune augmentation or restoration," he told *Medical Tribune.*

Ginseng

There are many types of ginseng, but the two that are most interesting medicinally are Siberian ginseng (*Eleutherococcus senticosus*) and *Panax ginseng, (Panax schinseng)* found in China, Japan, and Korea. These herbs contain a complexity of active substances, including polysaccharides, sterols, and germanium. They can have highly variable effects, depending upon their potency. Their complexity and variability have made them difficult to study, but there is no doubt that they are very significant medicinal herbs. With further study, and with development of ginseng products in reliable, standardized doses, they are apt to yield some truly startling results in a number of conditions.

Even though few well-controlled studies have been done on the effects of ginseng, the hundreds, perhaps thousands, of favorable anecdotal and uncontrolled reports that continue to accumulate are cause enough for us to sit up and pay some notice. An increasing number of studies are being launched now in Russia, Japan, and other countries. Most studies completed, to date, show positive results of one sort or another.

Work with Siberian ginseng has been encouraging. This herb is from a family different from that of all the other ginsengs. Extracts of this herb, according to overseas researchers, may help protect the body against a broad range of environmental pollutants as well as various drugs and radiation. It is also said to boost energy and immunity and fight stress. It is widely used by Soviet athletes and soldiers and even by the Soviet cosmonauts.

Panax ginseng is attracting more serious scientific attention these days, as well. A number of researchers, in Japan and elsewhere, have recently reported that *Panax ginseng* can protect animals against X rays, even against radiation doses that are normally fatal. In other experiments, *Panax ginseng* has exhibited significant restorative effects even when it is not given until *after* serious radiation damage has already taken place. It seems to work, at least in part, by stimulating the synthesis of substances crucial for bone-marrow repair and function. Bone marrow, in which the red blood cells form, is particularly vulnerable to X rays and other forms of radiation. In some experiments, a single injection of *Panax ginseng* following exposure to normally damaging levels of X radiation largely prevented adverse effects.

Soviet research, some of it reportedly conducted with good scientific controls, suggested some time ago that ginseng is an antagonist of alcohol and barbiturates and might thus be helpful in those seeking to disengage from those drugs. More recently, Korean researchers have conducted a human study showing that *Panax ginseng* extract can speed up the clearance of alcohol in the blood. Others have shown that *Panax ginseng* enhances enzymatic activity that oxidizes—burns up—alcohol. When ginseng is given to those consuming alcohol, the alcohol is eliminated more quickly. In another recent, placebo-controlled study done in Italy, researchers found that ginseng extract could significantly improve the liver's ability to detoxify alcohol and some other drugs. This was true even though the patients studied were elderly and had already been suffering for some time from chronic liver disease caused by substance abuse.

Licorice

Licorice is sometimes called the great detoxifier. Chinese licorice (*Glycyrrhiza uralensis*) is preferred over Western licorice (*Glycyrrhiza glabra*). Chinese herbalists claim that extracts of licorice can detoxify hundreds of noxious substances. They often use licorice in combination with other herbs in the belief that it helps blend them, potentiate them, and dampen any side effects. It is used not only as a detoxifier but also as a tonic and energizer.

Active substances found in licorice include glycyrrhizin, licoricidin, liquiritin, iso-liquiritin, and dihydroxyglycyrrhetic acid. Glycyrrhizin has attracted a lot of attention recently since it has been shown to inactivate HIV, the AIDS-related virus, in test-tube experiments. Like some of the other active ingredients in licorice, glycyrrhizin is a potential membrane fluidizer.

Licorice must be used with caution by those with high blood pressure. One of the herb's active ingredients appears to cause salt retention, which, in turn, can aggravate hypertension.

Milk Thistle

Ingredients of milk thistle (*Silybum marianum*) are powerful detoxifiers of a number of liver toxins, including carbon tetrachloride, the hydrazines, phallotoxins, alpha-amanitin, and radiation. It may also be protective against some of the toxic effects of alcohol. Milk thistle is best known for its ability to detoxify the liver-destroying poisons of the so-called deathcap mushrooms (*Amanita phalloides*).

Milk thistle contains a bioflavonoid called silymarin, which has been shown, in animal experiments, to prevent alcohol-caused lipid rancidification and other oxidant damage due to glutathione depletion in the liver. A number of other drugs, including even acetaminophen (Tylenol) in large doses, can have adverse effects on glutathione, one of the liver's major protective antioxidants. Recent research demonstrates that another component of milk thistle can similarly protect the liver from the toxic effects of a number of drugs that are metabolized in the body to produce hydrazines.

Oats

The green plant of the common oat (*Avena sativa*) has some surprising properties that may, in particular, benefit those who want to quit smoking. It may also prove useful in the treatment of dependence on opiate drugs, and perhaps other substances as well. The use of a tincture of *Avena sativa* to treat opium dependence was first reported on in the medical literature in 1925. It may have been used even earlier, however, by practitioners of Ayurvedic medicine (the traditional medicine of India) in the same capacity.

In the 1970s, the Indian researcher C. L. Anand reported, in the prestigious journal *Nature*, that he had come across a contemporary practitioner of Ayurvedic medicine who was successfully curing opium habits with a decoction of *Avena sativa*. An unlooked-for but quite welcome side effect of the herb was its ability to reduce the craving for nicotine, as well as opium. Several of those treated for opium dependence found that with the oat treatment, they no longer wanted to smoke.

Anand decided to conduct his own study in the United Kingdom to directly investigate any possible effects *Avena sativa* might have on nicotine craving. Nicotine dependence is one of the most powerful drug addictions there is, and so it seemed unlikely the herb would have much impact in a more carefully designed test.

Anand made an extract of *Avena sativa* using parts of the fresh plant picked just before harvest. His test subjects were twenty-six cigarette smokers (some healthy and some with chronic lung problems under treatment at Ruchill Hospital in Glasgow). All were still smoking at the time the study began. All were told only that they were to be part of a study in which a drug would be tested that might affect their smoking habits. They were told to make no conscious effort to alter those habits. The twenty-six were then randomly divided into two groups of thirteen each. The two groups were similar in smoking habits, age, sex, and other variables. No one was taking any other drug that would interfere with nicotine craving. One group received the herb for twenty-eight days, and the other group got only a lookalike placebo (no active ingredients) for the same period of time.

At the end of the twenty-eight days, the results were analyzed. In the placebo group, smoking had continued unabated. Whereas those in this group had been smoking an average of 16.5 cigarettes per day at the beginning of the study, they were smoking 16.7 cigarettes per day at the end of the trial. The results in the herb-treated group, on the other hand, were quite different—and quite extraordinary. Those in this group were smoking an average of 19.5 cigarettes per day at the onset and only 5.7 cigarettes per day at the end. Five in this group stopped smoking entirely; seven others cut back on their smoking by more than 50 percent; only one in this group experienced no reduction in nicotine craving. The reduction in craving that the others experienced persisted for the two-month follow-up period after the trial ended.

A few years after this report appeared, a group of pharmacological researchers in Scotland carried out some complex animal studies to further prove the seemingly miraculous properties of *Avena sativa*. By this time an antismoking clinic had been set up in Scotland, and *Avena sativa* was being used there, reportedly with good results.

The Scottish researchers, after concluding their animal experiments, reported that extractions of the herb definitely exhibit significant effects antagonistic to morphine (the opiate that was tested). It was also shown to reduce physical dependence upon morphine, when administered along with the drug. The herb was also found to antagonize one of the major nicotine effects in test animals. "It is tempting to speculate," these investigators concluded, "that the extract may also antagonize some effects of nicotine in man and that this may be the basis for the observation of Anand that *Avena sativa* reduced the craving for cigarettes."

So far the active elements in the herb that specifically antagonize morphine and nicotine have not been identified. A number of highly active substances have been isolated, but whether these include the antagonistic principles remains to be elucidated. They include an alkaloid, a glycoside, and two steroid saponins.

There have been reports that *Avena sativa* also has antidepressant and mild aphrodisiac effects. These reports need follow-up.

Valerian

Valerian (*Valeriana officinalis*) is a sedative herb that is quite useful in some detoxification regimens. Taken as a tea, it has calming effects. It can help quiet the stomach and soothe the nerves. It is a useful anti-anxiety adjunct. It may substitute, in a sense, for some of the addictive sedative drugs, making withdrawal easier.

6 Pharmaceuticals: The Detoxifying Drugs

DRUGS THAT QUELL CRAVINGS AND CLEANSE THE BLOOD, BODY, AND BRAIN

Use *drugs* to detoxify drugs and other chemical pollutants? That may seem contradictory and counterproductive at first blush, but there are, in fact, pharmaceutical substances that, when properly used, can be quite effective for this purpose. This is particularly true when these pharmaceuticals are used in conjunction with some of the more "natural" elements we have been examining.

The drugs you are about to become acquainted with are culled from a long list of pharmaceuticals that have been tried in the treatment of addictive and compulsive behavior, in detoxification and withdrawal, and in various blood-, body-, and brain-purifying regimens. These are the best and the most effective of the lot to date. They can have valuable effects in a wide range of situations, including addictions to nicotine, alcohol, cocaine, heroin, and other opiates; some of them can also help curb overeating and "binge eating" and can help reduce levels of blood cholesterol. One appears to be very effective in the treatment of radiation damage. Some have truly dramatic capabilities. (To find out how these substances are used in specific situations, see Part III.) With one exception, these are all prescription drugs and *must* be used only with a physician's consent and supervision.

Amantadine

Amantadine is considered, by those experienced with its use, to be a promising drug in the treatment of cocaine withdrawal. A number of well-designed studies and extensive clinical work have demonstrated that amantadine hydrochloride can significantly reduce cocaine craving. Amantadine (Symmetrel) is an approved drug for the treatment of Parkinson's disease and influenza A, but its effects on brain neurotransmitters suggested a possible role for it in treating cocaine addiction, and as noted above, studies have validated this suggestion. The regular use of cocaine inhibits dopamine, serotonin, and norepinephrine. Amantadine causes the brain to release reserves of these neurotransmitters. It does this in a speedy fashion—so quickly, in fact, that cocaine abusers usually experience a marked reduction in drug craving and other withdrawal symptoms within two hours of taking amantadine. Complete withdrawal has been reported within as little as seven days of amantadine treatment.

Amantadine thus largely displaces another drug that at one time looked promising but, in fact, had disappointing results in some anticocaine pharmaceutical studies. This drug is bromocriptine. Actually, it is still used in some clinics, but usually only as an adjunct to amantadine or in cases where amantadine alone fails to maintain cocaine abstinence after withdrawal. Best results with amantadine were achieved when it was properly combined with the amino acids tyrosine and tryptophan or the antidepressant desipramine. Amantadine's side effects are usually minimal.

Success rates as high as 95 percent have been reported for amantadine (augmented at times by some of the substances mentioned above). Success has been defined as complete withdrawal and continued cocaine abstinence (verified by urinalysis). So far there have been no long-term follow-up studies, and everyone involved in this work recognizes that, in many cases family, peer, and psychological support is necessary to prevent relapses. It is also recognized, however, that without successful withdrawal and inhibition of drug craving, psychological support alone is doomed to fail. Amantadine's ability to crush drug craving is highly significant. It is not the "magic bullet" in cocaine treatment, but it is an effective weapon, especially when used in conjunction with other substances, such as the antidepressant desipramine.

Antabuse

Antabuse (disulfiram) has been used for some time in the treatment of alcoholism. It is, in effect, an aversion therapy, since it makes drinking highly unpleasant. It does this by inhibiting the conversion of acetaldehyde, alcohol's major breakdown product, into acetic acid. Acetaldehyde, if not quickly converted into acetic acid, causes extreme nausea and other adverse reactions. A single dose of antabuse can produce these effects for up to two weeks if alcohol is consumed during that period. Antabuse by itself is seldom an effective treatment for alcoholism, but under certain circumstances and when used along with some other therapies, it can be helpful. Antabuse sometimes also proves beneficial in alcohol-triggered cocaine use.

Charcoal

Charcoal, because of its vast surface area, is one of the best filtration and absorption substances known. Charcoal is useful for filtering many impurities out of air and water. It can also be taken internally to help rid the body of various toxins and to help lower the cholesterol that clogs not only arteries but cells.

Clonidine

Clonidine has some significant ability to lessen the discomforts of alcohol and opiate addictions, but most of the current excitement over this drug relates to its effects on nicotine craving. In one recent double-blind, placebo-controlled study, seventy-one heavy smokers (defined as those smoking at least a pack of cigarettes a day) who had failed previous efforts to stop smoking were divided into two groups. One group got clonidine (which is usually used to lower blood pressure), and the other got a placebo for four weeks. Both groups got behavioral counseling. Neither the researchers nor the patients knew which group was getting the drug and which was getting the placebo—until the end of the study. It is this factor that makes a study double blind and minimizes the possibility of bias. At the end of that period, 64 percent of those getting clonidine were entirely abstaining from cigarettes. Only 29 percent of the placebo group was abstaining.

The success rate for women on clonidine was 72 percent, much higher than for the men. This is significant, because numerous studies have shown that it is generally more difficult for women to quit smoking than it is for men. The same dose was used in this study for both men and women. Since the men, overall, were significantly heavier than the women, it is possible they will experience greater benefit at higher doses.

The relapse rate for those who quit smoking is very high, and so it was no surprise that—six months after clonidine treatment ended— many of those who had quit smoking had now resumed the habit. But a very significant 27 percent of those given the four-week course of clonidine were still entirely abstaining half a year later. By comparison, only 5 percent of the placebo group was still abstaining. Further studies are under way to determine if a ten-week course of treatment will extend the drug's effectiveness. It is also possible that periodic "booster" treatments will enable many smokers to resist nicotine.

Clonidine, at doses used to control high blood pressure, can have a number of troubling side effects. But at the doses used in the smoking studies, side effects were mild and infrequent. Administering the drug via transdermal patch helps in this respect and also helps ensure compliance in taking the drug. The small skin patch affixes to the skin something like a Band-Aid, and the drug with which it is impregnated is slowly absorbed through the skin over a one-week period, after which a new patch is attached.

Clonidine holds promise because it actually seems to reduce the *craving* for nicotine. Most other antismoking substances developed or under development seem to work only on reducing the other— lesser—symptoms of nicotine withdrawal (anxiety, desire to eat, etc.). No one knows yet how clonidine works in this context, but it is known that it decreases norepinephrine outflow from the brain. The opiate drugs, and perhaps alcohol, are thought to increase that outflow. As noted above, clonidine has been used with some measure of success in easing withdrawal from heroin and other opiates. Clonidine, however, is not a "magic bullet" for smoking cessation and one study did not show the same dramatic results described above.

Doxepin

Doxepin is an antidepressant that, at lower doses, can be helpful in promoting sleep among those in drug withdrawal. Recently, a study suggested that doxepin might also be helpful in reducing the rigors of nicotine withdrawal. This study was launched as a result of spontaneous favorable reports from a few smokers using this antidepressant; they found they were able to quit without notable withdrawal symptoms. It does not appear that doxepin's antismoking effects are as remarkable as those of clonidine (discussed above), but this study further commends the judicious use of doxepin in some cases of withdrawal treatment.

Fenfluramine and Phentermine Resin

Fenfluramine (Pondimin) and phentermine resin (Ionamin) can both be useful in curbing food addictions when used properly. Fenfluramine curbs appetite through its effects on the serotonin neurotransmitters in the brain. Serotonin reduces brain activity that contributes to the desire to eat. Fenfluramine helps prevent the degradation of serotonin.

Fenfluramine has been shown to be significantly more effective than placebos in promoting weight loss in a number of double-blind studies. In one study, it was shown to be quite effective in quickly suppressing the craving for carbohydrate snacks. With prolonged use (three months), it also dampened intake of noncarbohydrate snacks. It was effective, as well, in curbing appetite for mealtime carbohydrates.

Phentermine resin can be used quite effectively in conjunction with fenfluramine. It is also an appetite suppressant, but it has amphetaminelike activity. Phentermine's "upper" effect can be neutralized, however, by fenfluramine's "downer" effect—and vice versa. The two can then work synergistically to suppress appetite without major side effects.

There are anecdotal reports, incidentally, that fenfluramine can assist with nicotine withdrawal. In any case, it is often a useful adjunct in nicotine withdrawal for use in women fearful of gaining weight once they give up smoking.

Lithium

Lithium, best known for its use in treatment of the manic-depressive syndrome, may be useful, at times, for controlling the mania associated with cocaine addiction. Recently, some evidence has emerged suggesting that lithium might also help alcoholics abstain from alcohol by suppressing the urge to drink.

Naltrexone

Naltrexone is a very potent opiate antagonist. At high doses it can completely block the opiate receptors, so that someone taking these drugs will feel no effect. Naltrexone is a remarkable drug in some other respects, too. There are preliminary findings that it can be very helpful in postconcussion syndrome and possibly useful, to some extent, in Alzheimer's disease.

In a double-blind study, eight of twelve Alzheimer's patients treated with naltrexone exhibited some improvement in memory. Naltrexone is known to block brain endorphins that suppress acetylcholine activity involved in memory functions. Other research with naloxone, a related drug, showed that it could improve memory in experimental animals. There have been mixed results in this memory work, however, and more study is needed.

Nicotine Gum

Nicotine gum (Nicorette) got something of a bum rap in some quarters—largely because it didn't live up to the "magic bullet" expectations some had for it. These people thought you could simply chew this nicotine-containing gum and magically lose all desire to smoke. It doesn't work that way, and its developers never said that it would. What it *can* do is make the pain and discomfort of cigarette withdrawal far easier to bear. And when used in a clinical, supervised setting, it can be very effective as an aid to those who genuinely want to quit smoking. An increasing number of clinicians and researchers also agree that a dose *double* that typically recommended (see Part III for specifics) can greatly increase the success rate.

In one recent double-blind, placebo-controlled Danish study in which heavy smokers were given twice the usual dose of Nicorette, excellent results were obtained. Some two years into the study, 33 percent of those getting the double dose were abstaining from smoking, compared with only 6 percent of those getting the usual dose.

Nicorette works by slowly releasing nicotine into the system. This acts as a replacement for the nicotine in cigarettes and removes the perils of drawing smoke into the lungs. When used properly, it gradually breaks some of the other habitual aspects of smoking. The nicotine in the gum is itself much easier to withdraw from than is cigarette smoking. But even if one were to stay on the gum indefinitely, this would be much safer than continued smoking.

A nicotine arm patch is expected to be released in the U.S. in the near future.

Piracetam

Piracetam (2-oxo-1-pyrrolidineacetamide) is a drug that is showing promise in the treatment of alcohol withdrawal. It has also been studied for its effects on memory and cognition, both of which, some believe, can be improved by this substance. Piracetam *does* help regulate and stimulate the cortical functions of the brain associated with reasoning, memory, and the like. There is some experimental evidence that this drug can abolish aggressive behavior caused by substances toxic to the brain. There is also evidence, from animal studies, that piracetam might improve learning ability and increase the energy of some brain cells, while also increasing their resistance to conditions of low oxygen.

In one study of piracetam's effects in alcoholics, the drug was found to be as effective in reducing the symptoms of withdrawal. Piracetam is neither addicting nor sedating.

In a more recent double-blind, placebo-controlled study, piracetam was tested to see how it might affect alcoholic psychoses (delirium and hallucinations, for example). The drug had previously exhibited useful activity in these states in open trials (uncontrolled studies). The piracetam-treated group did significantly better than the placebo group. And when the placebo group was crossed over to treatment with piracetam, it too showed marked improvement in reduction and resolution of psychoses. There were no significant adverse side effects from the drug. Piracetam is currently not obtainable in the U.S.

Fluoxetine (with a Note on Trazodone)

Fluoxetine (Prozac) is one of the most intriguing new drugs to come along in some time. It is showing promise in its ability to reduce cravings for both food and alcohol. It may have even broader application in a range of obsessive-compulsive disorders. It has been marketed as an antidepressant.

Prozac is a serotonin uptake inhibitor. As such, it conserves serotonin, an important brain neurotransmitter, in the places where it is needed most—in the synapses of the brain's nerve cells across which vital neurological signals flow. When serotonin-mediated messages are transmitted loud and clear, the chance for the kind of garbled brain messages that lead to destructive cravings seem to be minimized. This has been demonstrated in alcoholics and, more recently, in binge eaters (bulimics).

Binge eating was dramatically reduced in two studies designed to investigate this issue. In a Scottish study, seven of ten bulimics who got Prozac daily for three weeks halted their binging altogether; two others showed partial improvement; a third was nonresponsive. Almost identical results were obtained in a British Columbia study of ten bulimics, seven of whom stopped all binging within two weeks of treatment. Two others had partial responses, while a third patient was not helped.

Patients in these studies report that the drug seems to work by inducing a feeling of satiety or fullness. In some cases, the patients started to binge but then stopped after just a few bites, owing to a feeling of fullness and satisfaction. Larger, double-blind studies are now under way.

Prozac and similar serotonin uptake inhibitors may turn out to be some of the more important substances in the treatment of alcoholism as well as binging and overeating. Studies indicate that these substances, rather than just lessening withdrawal symptoms, actually cut back on the craving for alcohol—again, by inducing a feeling of satiety—*before* large amounts of alcohol are consumed. These drugs have also shown the capacity to *reverse* some types of alcohol-caused memory loss. Ironically, Prozac is not always the best antidepressant (the indication for which the drug was approved). When it fails to do the antidepressant job adequately, another antidepressant called trazodone is often useful. It has few side effects and can be used in conjunction with Prozac.

Superoxide Dismutase

Superoxide dismutase (SOD) is one of the cell's most potent detoxifiers of free oxygen radicals. Packaged in man-made lipid capsules called liposomes, this powerful antioxidant enzyme can penetrate into cells and produce remarkable protective and restorative effects in a number of situations. SOD's healing and purifying properties have already been demonstrated quite dramatically in the treatment of tissues and organs severely damaged by radiation treatments. Even long-established radiofibroses (tissue seemingly withered in a permanent way) have yielded to injections of liposomal SOD—often in two or three weeks. Typically, these SOD-treated fibroses regress by about a third or even more, and according to one report, significant softening and apparent renewal is seen in more than 80 percent of the cases. SOD is presently in clinical trials in the U.S.

7 *Food, Water, and Air: The Make-or-Break Elements*

"I FEEL AS IF I'M POISONED"

When Sandra first came to see me a few years ago, she was fifty-four years old. She had been a prominent and very successful businessperson as well as lecturer and media personality. I knew about her but had not heard any mention of her name for several years. Apparently, she "retired" when she was about forty-nine.

At our first meeting, Sandra sat down in my office, looked me straight in the eye, and said, "Doctor, I feel as if I am poisoned." She told me that she felt extremely tired all the time, that her memory was terrible, and that she suffered from aches and pains all over her body, among other things. It was this set of physical discomforts that had caused her to drop out of her career. She had seen several physicians. One placed her on medication for her "arthritic" pains. The medication didn't help alleviate the pains but did cause stomach problems, for which another medication was prescribed, one that provoked a drug reaction.

Sandra stopped *all* medication given to her by that physician and sought out the help of another doctor. This one focused on palpitations and skipped heartbeats and placed Sandra on new medication, which again caused a drug reaction. At that point, Sandra was referred to a cardiologist, who, on the basis of extensive testing, told her that her heart was fine and that she did not require any heart medications. She subsequently saw a gastroenterologist, who told her that her stomach and intestines were in good working order, and a neurologist, a rheumatologist, and an endocrinologist, all of whom gave her a clean bill of health within their respective specialties.

But because she continued to feel so poorly, she came to see me, referred by another physician. In interviewing Sandra, I felt confident that she was not a malingerer or hypochondriac. She felt sick and genuinely wanted to feel better. I took a detailed history of Sandra's eating and drinking habits and noted her breathing patterns. I concluded that she had indeed been poisoned.

Sandra had been poisoned by the very life-style that had led to her success, a life-style that included always eating on the run (a diet consisting of high cholesterol and high fat, as well as lots of sugars), drinking bad water, breathing bad air, getting little sleep, not doing any exercise, and becoming severely overweight. After the final "energy outage" that led to Sandra's early retirement, Sandra continued in many of her bad habits, making it impossible for her body and brain to cleanse themselves. What Sandra had done to herself, most of us are doing to one degree or another.

Sandra did change her diet, began drinking purer water, learned how to breathe correctly, took steps to clean up the air she was breathing in her home, started exercising, and lost most of her excess body fat. While doing this, she felt "the poisons draining" from her body. She has higher energy now and is back at work. But she has vowed to never again work with the same frenzy that she did in the past.

Good health and addictive behavior are incompatible. Sandra was a workaholic—a common and *toxic* addiction. She enjoyed living in the fast lane until her body gave out. Sandra's crash was quite similar to the crash of a cocaine addict. Not taking care of your health makes you vulnerable to addictive behavior of any type. One of the best protections we have against addictive behavior is *good nutrition*, including good air and water. These are the make-or-break elements. Let's look at each in turn: food, water, and air. Each can be either poisoning or purifying.

FOOD: FLOW AND FLUIDITY VERSUS THE FATAL ATTRACTIONS

Hippocrates, the father of medicine, said many years ago: *Let food be your medicine and medicine be your food.* It's about time we took this advice seriously. We now have enough information to state with certainty that the standard American diet (dubbed the SAD diet, appropriately enough, by nutritional researchers Sonja and William Connor) is not a good and healthy one. This diet is associated with elevated serum cholesterol levels, which make us vulnerable to hardening of the arteries that feed the heart, brain, and other tissues of our bodies. Heart attacks, strokes, other degenerative diseases, and death are possible consequences of this process. The good news is that we can now construct diets to ensure much longer, healthier, and happier lives based on some fundamental biochemical and physiological principles, some of which come from my own research. Let's examine these principles.

The basic units that make up our bodies are cells. There are brain cells, heart cells, muscle cells, blood cells, immune cells, and so on. The health of our bodies depends on the health of these cells. Central to the health and life of cells is the constant production of biological energy. This energy exists in a molecule called adenosine triphosphate, or ATP. ATP is mainly produced in small intracellular furnaces known as mitochondria. It is within the mitochondria that substances (derived from the carbohydrates, fats, and proteins we eat) "burn" in the presence of the oxygen that we breathe to form ATP. ATP is the energy that drives all life processes—such as heart beat, muscle contraction, the electrical activity of our nervous systems, etc.

Just as the burning of gasoline in an automobile is not a totally clean process and produces toxic exhaust fumes, so the burning of food-derived substances in the mitochondria is not a totally clean process, either; it also produces toxic exhaust products. These "exhausts" are the so-called free radicals, highly reactive substances that, if not detoxified, can damage cell membranes, nucleic acids, and other vital cellular constituents. Free radicals are major contributors to such diseases as cancer, atherosclerosis, arthritis, and other degenerative diseases associated with aging.

Key to the maintenance of optimal health and longevity of our cells (and hence of ourselves) is *maximizing* the amount of energy or ATP produced by our cells, while at the same time *minimizing* the production of free radicals as well as maximizing their detoxification. Here we must introduce the terms *flow* and *fluidity*. In order to maximize cellular ATP production, the foods we eat must smoothly flow through our guts (where they get digested), across the walls of the intestine, into the bloodstream, to all the tissues of the body. Once in the tissues, these nutrients must continue to flow smoothly across the cell membranes, into the cells, across the wall of the mitochondria. Oxygen itself must flow smoothly through our breathing tubes into the lungs, then across air sacs of the lungs into the bloodstream, where it is carried to the tissues, into the cells, and finally into the mitochondria. Interruption of any of these flows at any point can lead to decreased energy production, frank energy outages, and the death of cells, tissues, organs, and finally selves.

The flow of substances, including oxygen and those derived from food, across cellular and mitochondrial membranes depend upon the *fluidity* of those membranes. Membrane fluidity is a rather complicated concept. However, in broad strokes, it has to do with freedom of movement of molecules within the membrane. Putting it simply, the more fluid a membrane, the more easily molecules can flow through it; the less fluid or more rigid a membrane, the less easily molecules can flow through it. As membranes become less fluid or more rigid, they are less permeable to food metabolites and oxygen and, consequently, the cells are less capable of producing energy.

Cell membranes, as well as mitochondrial membranes, are made up of lipids—fatlike substances—and proteins. The lipids are primarily phospholipids and cholesterol, and the major phospholipid found in our cellular membranes is phosphatidylcholine. The fluidity of a membrane is roughly determined by the ratio of cholesterol to phospholipid. Membranes with high ratios are relatively *less* fluid than those with low ratios. Mitochondrial membranes, the most fluid of all membranes, have the lowest cholesterol-to-phospholipid ratio of any membrane. Factors that *decrease* cell-membrane fluidity or increase rigidity include increased cholesterol, increased saturated fatty acids, increased lipid peroxidation (rancidification caused by free-radical attack), and decreased phosphatidylcholine. Factors that *increase* cell-membrane fluidity include decreased cholesterol, increased unsaturated fatty acids, especially of the omega-3 (fish oil) variety, decreased lipid peroxidation, and increased phosphatidylcholine.

It should be clear from the above discussion that our diet is enormously important to the health of our cells. The absolute bottom line of optimal health and longevity is cellular health. What is good for the cell is good for the self. The standard American diet, the SAD, is a toxic diet, a membrane killer. It not only results in the accumulation of cholesterol and obstructive plaques in our blood vessels, but, at a deeper level, results in the accumulation of saturated fats and cholesterol in our cell membranes, making them less permeable to the nutrients and oxygen they need to make energy. What occurs at the cellular level is similar to what occurs at the level of the blood vessels. I refer to atherosclerosis. The SAD results as much in atherosclerotic cells as it does in atherosclerotic arteries. The consequences of cellular atherosclerosis are not pretty. They include decreased immune function, increased susceptibility to infection and cancer, dementia, and death.

The events leading to cellular atherosclerosis (as well as cellular atherosclerosis itself) are among the major factors that predispose us to addictive behavior. The reason for this is basic, but frequently overlooked. As your body and brain begin feeling poorly, tired, and less energetic, anything that can make them feel better, even for just a short time, becomes an attractive option. Enter alcohol, cigarettes, cocaine, opiates, fats, sugars, etc.—all of our fatal attractions—those things that may give us some short-term pleasure—and long-term pain. Many addictive substances are short-term membrane fluidizers—but used for any length of time, they have the opposite effect, causing membrane rigidity, more aches and pains, less energy and, overall, accelerated aging. Only proper diet can deliver both short- and long-term fluidity and the pleasure and youth that go along with them.

Having said all of this, What *is* proper diet? First, let's look at the SAD, which is *not* a good diet. The SAD derives about 40 percent of its calories from fat—mostly of the saturated variety—and about 45 percent of its calories from carbohydrate, with heavy emphasis on the refined carbohydrates or sugars. About 15 percent of its calories come from protein, mostly from animal sources, and it provides only 10 to 12 grams of dietary fiber daily. The SAD contains, on average, 500 milligrams of cholesterol daily.

The ideal diet is one that would: 1) optimally fluidize cellular membranes, particularly the mitochondrial membranes, allowing for free and uninterrupted flow of nutrients and oxygen into cells in order to maximize energy production; 2) prevent any obstruction to the free and uninterrupted flow of nutrients and oxygen through the blood vessels that feed all the tissues of our bodies; 3) minimize the production of the toxic free radicals and maximize their detoxification; 4) maximize the detoxification of any carcinogenic substance; 5) utilize the most efficient and economic energy sources—that is, foods that produce the greatest amount of biological energy with the least consumption of oxygen.

Such a diet would contain:

- no more than 20 percent of its calories as fat, with increased amounts of polyunsaturated and monounsaturated fatty acids and decreased amounts of saturated fatty acids.

- no more than 100 milligrams of cholesterol daily.

- at least 65 percent of the caloric intake as carbohydrates, mainly of the complex, unrefined variety. Carbohydrates are the most economic and efficient fuel, from a bioenergetics viewpoint. When they burn in the mitochondria to produce ATP, they require less oxygen to produce the same amount of ATP when compared to the burning of fat and protein metabolites. Consequently, they produce less "exhaust"—fewer free radicals. Complex carbohydrates allow for a slower release of the simple carbohydrates, which is important to prevent blood-sugar fluctuations, which can lead to hypoglycemia, itself a risk factor for addictive behavior.

- 12 to 15 percent of caloric intake as protein, with increased reliance on vegetable protein.

- 50 to 60 grams of dietary fiber.

This is similar to the diet the Connors pioneered, a diet they and other researchers have shown can reduce the risk of coronary heart disease by 40 percent. The Connors call this the new American diet, or NAD, which they contrast with the SAD. (See *The New American Diet*, Fireside, 1989.)

Healing Foods

We've now dealt with general principles for a healthy diet. Perhaps some of the most important discoveries in medicine these past few years have *not* been of the high-tech kind, which typically make media headlines, but have been those related to a number of foods that are exhibiting some extraordinary purifying healing properties. Let's look at some of them.

CRUCIFEROUS VEGETABLES VERSUS RADIATION AND CANCER

In 1950, two researchers named Lourau and Lartigue published a paper reporting on an unusual relationship between diet and biological response to X rays. They found that guinea pigs fed cabbage for some time before being exposed to dangerous whole-body X radiation did much better than guinea pigs prefed beets and then exposed to the same deadly rays. The cabbage-fed animals had a significantly lower rate of hemorrhage and death.

In 1959, two other researchers named Spector and Calloway published the results of their research inspired by the above study. They also subjected guinea pigs to whole-body X radiation and prefed the animals on different diets. The control animals were fed oats and wheat bran—and they all died within fifteen days of being irradiated. Animals that were fed raw cabbage along with the oats and wheat lived much longer. The experiment was repeated seven times to make sure the effect was real. The results were always the same. The investigators prefed a different group of guinea pigs with another member of the cruciferous vegetable family: broccoli. This was found to be even more protective. Best results were obtained when the vegetables were given both before and after irradiation. Spector and Calloway concluded that cabbage and broccoli are protective against the toxic effects of X radiation.

In 1979, Graham and Mettlin published the results of an epidemiological study on the relationship between intake of vegetables and the incidence of colon cancer in white men. The researchers found that the lowest incidence of colon cancer was in those men who reported eating the most vegetables. What was most interesting was that the vegetable that conferred most protection against colon cancer was cabbage. *Eating at least one serving of cabbage a week, according to this study, could lower the chance of colon cancer by over 60 percent.* Since the publication of this report, several other epidemiological studies have confirmed that increased intake of cabbage and other cruciferous vegetables lowers the risk of getting cancer of the colon. Further, there is evidence that eating cruciferous foods helps reduce the risk of cancers of the respiratory tract, esophagus, prostate, and bladder as well. A recent study in Norway indicates that people who consume cruciferous foods also have a significantly lower incidence of colonic polyps, which often precede cancer, than do those who eat little or no food from the cruciferous family.

Several substances have now been isolated from cruciferous vegetables that appear to have anticancer activity, as well as protective effects against radiation toxicity. Wattenberg and his colleagues pioneered this work. These substances include aromatic isothiocyanates and indoles. Among other things, some of these compounds enhance the body's mechanisms for the detoxification of carcinogenic agents.

The cruciferous vegetables rank very high as purification foods.

They protect against several types of cancer, they protect against radiation toxicity, and one Japanese study suggests that people who consume generous amounts of cabbage have the lowest death rate *from all causes*. The cruciferous family, known formally as the Brassicaceae family, includes several members: cabbage, broccoli, brussels sprouts, cauliflower, kohlrabi, rutabaga, and turnip. It is advisable to eat at least one of these vegetables *daily*. They are excellent steamed, cooked as side dishes, as Russian cabbage borscht, or, best, eaten raw or in salads. There are several types of cabbage that are available in most groceries: red cabbage, green cabbage, Chinese cabbage, bok choy, etc. Try to get the organic variety whenever possible, in order to avoid pesticide residues.

DIETARY FIBER: BLOOD AND BOWEL CLEANSER

By now virtually everyone has heard of dietary fiber. There has been a proliferation of advertisements on the cholesterol-lowering effects of some fiber-rich foods, mainly oatmeal and oat bran. What I call fiber consciousness is growing at a fast pace. This is good, since the standard American diet is generally low in fiber, and fiber has several positive health benefits. Dietary fiber is another major purifying food substance.

Dietary fiber, for the most part, is made up of polysaccharides derived from plant sources, which, in contrast to other dietary polysaccharides, such as starches, do not get digested in our small intestines. The various dietary fibers are often classified in two groups: soluble and insoluble. Basically, soluble dietary fiber dissolves in water, producing a gluey mixture. Insoluble dietary fiber does not dissolve in water. *Soluble* fiber is found in oat bran, oatmeal, rice bran, beans, apples, and in fruits and vegetables generally. Psyllium and guar gum, both rich in soluble fiber, are widely available commercially.

Consumption of *soluble* dietary fiber-rich foods in adequate quantities can significantly lower serum cholesterol levels. Three quarters of a cup of oat bran or three oat bran muffins or one cup of cooked dried beans *daily*, for example, can produce up to a 10 percent lowering of serum cholesterol in a few weeks.

Insoluble fiber, found in wheat bran, for example, promotes bowel regularity and is excellent for the prevention and treatment of constipation. Both insoluble and soluble dietary fiber may also help lower the risk of colorectal cancer. High-fiber diets are known to increase the stool quantity, which would dilute the concentrations of carcinogens in the bowel. Carcinogens may also bind to fiber and be excreted through the stool.

GARLIC AND ONIONS: BAD BREATH/PURE HEART

Garlic and onions have been staples of folk medicine for thousands of years. They have been reputed at one time or another to cure just about every disease under the sun. It turns out that this odoriferous duo may indeed have some very significant medicinal activity.

Some epidemiological studies indicate that the incidence of both atherosclerosis and cancer is lower among garlic eaters than among those who don't touch the stuff. Increased intake of garlic has been reported to lower serum cholesterol as well as decrease the tendency of blood to form clots. The greater the amount of garlic consumed, the greater the reduction in cholesterol. Garlic has also been reported to have antibacterial, antiviral (including against the influenza virus), antifungal, and anticancer activity. Research is ongoing to determine the active components of garlic that have these therapeutic effects.

Victor Gurewich, director of the Vascular Laboratory at St. Elizabeth's Hospital in Boston and professor of medicine at Tufts University, found that a medium-size yellow or white onion, or its juice, taken daily can raise high-density lipoprotein cholesterol (HDL) levels by up to 30 percent in those with abnormally low HDL levels. This finding is of enormous importance for several reasons. HDL cholesterol is "good" cholesterol and is protective against atherosclerosis. Even those with "safe" levels of total serum cholesterol may be at risk for coronary artery disease and its consequences if their levels of HDL cholesterol are low. Thus, any maneuver that can *increase* HDL levels is of utmost significance. The problem is that we do not know many ways of raising HDL. There are many drugs that lower cholesterol, but only a few of these raise HDL and, then, not by very much. The HDL-raising effect of onions is very impressive. In addition, onions, like garlic, help keep blood from forming dangerous clots.

HOT CHILI PEPPERS VERSUS "STAGNANT" BLOOD AND OBSTRUCTED AIRWAYS

Keeping our blood flowing through all our blood vessels without interruption is essential for the maintenance of good health. Hot chili peppers, like onions and garlic, inhibit dangerous clotting. A report in the *American Journal of Clinical Nutrition* suggests a strong association between the significant intake of hot chili peppers and the low incidence of often fatal blood-clotting diseases among the Thai people. The researchers found that capsicum (the scientific name of hot peppers) breaks down blood clots through enzymatic actions. Other reports support this finding. Significantly greater protection was found in Thais who consume capsicum several times a day than among Americans living in Thailand who consumed primarily American-style meals with little or no capsicum.

Irwin Ziment, professor of medicine at the UCLA School of Medicine, has found that capsicum is also a good decongestant and an excellent expectorant. An expectorant clears secretions from the breathing tubes. Another flow that is central to good health is the movement of air into and out of our lungs. The continuous removal of mucous secretions from our airways is crucial for the maintenance of this flow. Smoking is the most common cause of mucous plugging, the symptoms of which are coughing, breathing problems and, frequently, infection. Capsicum may be useful for both the treatment and prevention of bronchitis.

Capsaicin is the active principle of capsicum and appears to be the substance that clears lung secretions. When capsaicin was given to experimental animals before exposing them to cigarette smoke, it prevented the swelling and constriction of airways that is typically caused by cigarette smoke and some other respiratory irritants. Capsicum, garlic, and possibly onions may help prevent destruction of the lungs by cigarette smoke and other air pollutants.

Many people are afraid to eat hot, spicy food because they have heard somewhere that it can cause inflammation of the stomach or ulcers. While it is true that hot peppers can upset *some* stomachs, there is no evidence at all that hot peppers damage the stomach or small intestine. A recent study reported in the *Journal of the American Medical Association* used videoendoscopy (continuous visualization of the gut) to investigate the effect on the lining of the stomach from eating these foods. The authors conclude that "ingestion of highly [capsaicin] spiced meals by normal individuals did not cause endoscopically demonstrable gastric or duodenal mucosal damage . . . We conclude that although capsaicin-containing spices increase gastric distress, they add to the flavor and enjoyment of eating and do not appear to cause mucosal damage." Another study has shown that the healing of duodenal ulcers is as rapid in those who habitually eat large amounts of chilies daily as it is in those who avoid them.

FISH: THE GOOD FATS

Not all fat is bad for you. There is "good" cholesterol, the HDL kind, and "bad" cholesterol, the LDL kind. Likewise, there is "good" fat and "bad" fat. Some of these good fats are found in fish. Despite a diet high in fat and cholesterol, many Eskimos have a remarkably low incidence of atherosclerosis and heart attacks. Greenland Eskimos, whose diet consists primarily of fish, seal, and whale meat, have low blood levels of triglycerides and cholesterol, high levels of HDL cholesterol, and decreased stickiness of their platelets, making their blood less likely to clot. Japanese living in coastal villages of Japan where fish is their major dietary staple have similar findings.

It turns out that the seafood consumed by the Eskimos and Japanese is rich in omega-3 polyunsaturated fatty acids. These fatty acids have come to be known as fish oils, and the one believed responsible for most of the health benefits is called eicosapentaenoic acid, or EPA. Another omega-3 found in fish is docosahexaenoic acid or DHA. EPA itself has been found to lower LDL-cholesterol in those with elevated serum triglycerides. Recent studies indicate that fish oil protects the lining of blood vessels from destruction by free radicals. Fish oil also increases cellular membrane fluidity. So the more fish you eat, the more fluid you can expect to become.

Fish that are highest in omega-3 fatty acids are mackerel, salmon, bluefish, tuna, sturgeon, and herring. It is usually assumed that fatty ocean fish provide the best source of omega-3 fatty acids. However, some freshwater fish are also quite rich in these oils. They include trout, whitefish, chub, sucker, and lake herring. One of the richest sources of omega-3 oil is the deepwater trout, which contains up to three times more than Chinook salmon.

FERMENTED FOODS VERSUS A POLLUTED WORLD

Fermented foods are prepared by the action of bacteria or yeast. Some popular fermented foods are those prepared from milk and soybeans. Fermented foods from milk include kefir, yogurt, and acidophilus milk. Those from soybeans include miso and tempeh. Several types of bacteria are used in the fermentation process. Most of these bacteria produce lactic acid, imparting a sour taste to the completed product.

Anecdotes abound regarding the health-promoting effects of the above-listed fermented foods. Miso is thought by some to prevent radiation sickness. This claim originated in the observation that those surviving the Nagasaki atomic bomb blast were regular consumers of miso soup. Some Japanese scientists believe that the putative radiation protector in miso is a molecule called picolinic acid, which is capable of binding to such substances as strontium. Miso is also thought to neutralize the toxic effects of smoking and air pollution. Daily consumption of miso soup may reduce the risk of stomach cancer among Japanese.

There is evidence that yogurt has beneficial health effects. Yogurt may enhance immunity. A study performed by researchers at the United States Department of Agriculture compared two groups of rats injected with large doses of Salmonella. One group had been fed yogurt prior to injection; the other group, milk. The rats fed yogurt did not get nearly as sick as those fed milk, and fewer of them died. In a study performed in Romania, yogurt appeared to protect mice against influenza. Yogurt has been used to treat diarrhea that is secondary to bacterial infection or that is associated with antibiotic use, ulcerative colitis, and diverticulitis. Yogurt does contain some substances that have antibiotic activity. Recently, Italian scientists have shown that yogurt has immune-enhancing effects in experimental animals and humans. There is some evidence that yogurt and acidophilus milk are protective against colon cancer.

MUSHROOMS: ANTIVIRAL, IMMUNE-BOOSTING, CHOLESTEROL-LOWERING

Shiitake mushrooms, prized in Japan, are now available in the United States either fresh or in dried form. This mushroom has demonstrated both antiviral and immune-stimulating effects. Lentinan, a polysaccharide found in the mushroom, is being investigated as an anti-AIDS drug. The mushrooms also lower serum cholesterol. The Chinese black tree fungus, a mushroom also known as mo-er, has been reported to prevent clotting of the blood. It appears to have this effect by preventing platelets from sticking to each other.

GREEN TEA AGAINST CANCER AND POLLUTANTS

Green tea, particularly the Japanese green tea known as *Camellia sinensis,* appears to contain some substances that may confer important health benefits. Japanese who are green tea drinkers have significantly lower rates of stomach cancer than those who either do not drink this beverage or use it sparingly. Some components have been extracted from green tea that protect against cancer in experimental animals.

These components also appear to prevent the formation of nitrosamines, substances known to cause stomach cancer. Green tea may, additionally, protect against radiation damage. Substances isolated from green-tea leaves, called catechins, may help prevent oral cancer in those who use snuff and chew tobacco. Clinical studies are being pursued to determine if this is indeed the case. Catechins are thought to block the deposition of strontium 90 in bone.

WATER: FLUSH OUT THE POISONS WITH THE PURE STUFF

Water is an essential and major nutrient. When the water we consume is inadequate or impure, every cell in our body suffers, as does every bodily and mental function. As with impure or inadequate diet, this is just the sort of situation that increases our vulnerability to addictive behavior. When our bodies and brains cannot delight in their own biology, then they will look to other sources for pleasure and health.

Many of us do not consume adequate amounts of water. As we age, our thirst drive diminishes and so we drink less. I have seen miraculous changes in many of my older patients when they start paying attention to their water consumption and begin getting optimal amounts. Some find they have to *double or even triple* their water intake. Dehydration is one of the commonest causes of acutely altered mental states in the elderly. Their water consumption and slow dehydration is often overlooked.

Drinking plenty of pure water is particularly important in *any* detoxification program; this is vital in order to flush out noxious substances. But what is plenty? The formula to determine this is fairly simple. Whatever goes out must be put back in. Average adult daily output of water is about two and a half quarts. This represents water lost through urination, defecation, perspiration, and respiration. A number of things can result in far greater water output, such as excessive urination, extensive burns, vigorous exercise, and excessive sweating. Given an average loss of about two and a half quarts daily, we must take in at least that amount each day. That's the equivalent of ten 8-ounce cups daily. The food we eat also contains water—and you can count on getting about three cups of water a day in your food. Metabolic water (the kind you make in your cells) should provide another cup. That leaves 6 to 8 cups per day you'll need to drink in the form of water, juices, and other beverages. If you are exercising a lot, you'll need to drink quite a bit more.

Make sure that at least half of your daily water intake is in the form of pure, unadulterated water—and more, if possible. Milk (no-fat or 1 percent fat) and pure fruit juices are good sources of water. Fruit drinks, on the other hand, are usually loaded with sugar and, sometimes, many other additives—check labels. Seltzers are a better choice than the typical sodas. Alcoholic drinks don't count at all. They usually require even more pure water—to partially detoxify the alcohol.

How do you get pure water or something approaching it? More than a thousand different organic chemicals have been found in our drinking water. In addition, many water supplies are laden with numerous inorganic substances such as lead, cadmium, arsenic, etc. Many of these toxins have cancer-causing and immune-impairing properties. As noted in Part One, the Environmental Protection Agency estimates that at least 40 million Americans are regularly drinking water with unsafe lead levels.

You can have your tap water tested for lead by calling your local health department and getting the necessary information on how to go about it. Alternatively, look in your Yellow Pages under "Environmental" or "Water Testing." These tests are quick and usually inexpensive.

There are several devices you can use to clean up your water. One of the simplest and least expensive is an activated charcoal filter that you can install on your kitchen tap yourself. Or you can get a pitcher-type filter that requires only that you run tap water into it. These filters get rid of most of the lead and a number of other harmful substances. The filters should be changed according to the manufacturer's recommendations. Water Pik, Brita, and Secus make good, inexpensive filters for home use. More complicated systems are also available. One called the Seagull IV is installed under your sink and utilizes a complex filter made from powdered carbon bonded together with other materials. This filter removes chlorine, chloramines, bacteria, asbestos, and heavy metals, including lead and radioactive debris. The Culligan-Aqua-Clear System and its clones are comprised of three parts: a particulate filter for removal of small particles; an activated charcoal filter, which removes chlorine, chloramines, other substances that affect taste and odor and lead; and a reverse osmosis unit, which reduces levels of impurities such as heavy metals (lead, mercury, etc.) and sodium. This unit is also installed under your sink.

Your grocery store or supermarket has several different types of bottled water available. Spring waters are somewhat risky if you are not certain where they come from. Many bottled waters that use the word *spring* in their names are actually drawn from rivers, streams, and even municipal taps. Distilled waters are probably a better choice for home consumption—and are usually cheaper, too. Be aware, however, that even distilled water can become contaminated if it sits on the store shelf or in your home too long.

Recommendation: Check out the Brita. It usually costs under $30, with filters you replace about once a month—for $6 to $10, depending on where you buy them. It's a good purifier and has fared very well in comparative tests.

AIR: FOR THE PURE HIGH

Isn't it interesting that the first users of cocaine did so in order to help them breathe better? I refer to the Indians who lived high up in the Andes, where oxygen is quite sparse. They ate the coca leaf to stimulate their respiration and give them more energy.

These days, many of us are breathing air that's frighteningly impure. In fact, there are several cities where the air is so polluted that people should not be living in them, and if they stay there, they won't. Mexico City is the most famous example, but Los Angeles is very quickly getting there. It's difficult to breathe when the air is bad, more so if you have any respiratory problem, such as asthma. Chronic tiredness is common in areas where the air is bad—indoors and out. A plethora of problems is associated with breathing impure air, ranging from chronic fatigue, multiple allergies and sensitivities, and frequent infections to memory disturbances and deafness. It has even recently been shown that breathing polluted air in noisy areas—and, as most city dwellers know, there are lots of places like that—can cause permanent hearing damage! For many of us, the air situation is much worse than it is for those living high up in the Andes. Perhaps that's one reason people who try cocaine want to try it again—and again. It helps them—at least initially—breathe better and have more energy.

Again, we see the same situation—a poor health condition, impure air—placing us at increased risk for addictive behavior. As a patient of mine once said, "When you feel bad, anything that makes you feel better you can get addicted to." Unfortunately, most go for the quick fix. There is nothing as important to our health as breathing. We can live for a few weeks without food, for about a week without fluids, but we cannot live for more than four minutes without oxygen. *Anything* that affects our breathing affects our health—and does so globally, affecting every aspect of mind and body. At least $9 billion a year is spent on health bills in Los Angeles alone because of its polluted air.

What can we do about the bad-air epidemic? For starters, I would recommend living in an area, *if possible*, where the air is good; such places *do* still exist. Most of us, of course, can't pull up stakes and move. But there *are* other things we can do. If you're a smoker, getting free of that addiction (see Part III) is the first—and vital— step. For all of us, the goals should be to try to surround ourselves with a blanket of the purest air possible and then to keep our airways as unobstructed as we can so that air can freely flow into and out of our lungs without interruption.

If you are concerned about the quality of your outside or inside air, there are several ways of getting information that can help you. Contact the Consumer Product Safety Commission (800-638-2772) or your state health department or regional office of the Environmental Protection Agency (EPA). Look under "Environment" or "Laboratories" in the Yellow Pages for local independent laboratories that can explain testing procedures for particular pollutants that may be found in your home. The American Council of Independent Laboratories, 1725 K Street, N.W., Washington, D.C. 20006 (202–887–5872), may also be able to recommend a testing laboratory. The home is assessed for presence of any harmful air contaminants as well as for ventilation efficiency or flow rate of fresh air per occupant. An acceptable rate of fresh air supply per person is 24 to 25 cfm (cubic feet per minute).

There are a number of air-purification devices available. These can be helpful for those living in poorly ventilated areas and/or for those who are sensitive to odors or particulates (e.g. perfumes, dust, dander, etc.). If you have a window in your home or office, opening it even a crack can make a significant difference. Many believe that air conditioners are air purifiers. *They are not.* Air conditioners cool and remove moisture from the air. Their filters collect large particulates, such as dust, and *must be cleaned regularly* to prevent blowing these pollutants back into the air.

Some air purifiers consist of a prefilter, which removes large particles; an electrostatic precipitator, which puts a charge on smaller particles (dust, pollen, smoke, bacteria), which are then deposited on collecting plates; and an activated charcoal filter, which removes odors (perfumes, cosmetics, body odors). The electrostatic precipitator requires frequent cleaning and gives off a small amount of ozone. The filter can be quite noisy, especially when it gets dirty. Other units consist of a high-efficiency particulate air (or HEPA) filter instead of the electrostatic precipitator. HEPA filters are generally more efficient, do not produce ozone, and filter air at high levels of efficiency for long periods without need of cleaning or complex maintenance. In addition to activated charcoal filters, activated alumina filters are available in some air-purification units. Activated alumina is better than activated charcoal for removing formaldehyde, ammonia, and nitrogen and sulphur oxides.

To keep your breathing tubes clear and your respiratory system in optimal condition, good dietary habits are crucial, as is the adequate intake of pure water. Remember, too, that hot (spicy) foods are excellent for removing secretions from the airways, keeping them open for the passage of oxygen. Those with inhalant and food sensitivities and allergies often have clogged airways. (See Part III for programs on how to deal with these problems.)

8 Light: Healing Rays

ALCOHOLICS SEE THE LIGHT

Some of you may have heard of SAD—seasonal affective disorder. SAD, as the name suggests, is a form of depression. In this case, it is a depression that usually occurs during the dark and gloomy days of winter, especially in more northerly climates, where the days are particularly short. Scientists who study SAD often compare it with jet lag (only much more prolonged and extreme), in that it seems to be characterized by disordered circadian rhythms. These circadian rhythms are our biological clocks. When these clocks get out of proper synch, all manner of hormonal and other physiological upsets occur that affect our bodies and minds. These disturbances can increase our susceptibility to infection and other illnesses, can rob us of energy, and disturb our brain chemistry in numerous ways.

People who suffer from SAD have difficulty with light adaptation. Their biological clocks fail to make the needed adjustments as winter comes on, and consequently, their brains think that when it gets dark (as early as 4 or 5 P.M. in some areas) it is actually much later than it is. If they go to bed at 10 or 11 P.M., it is the same as a normal person's going to bed at 2 or 3 A.M. Obviously, they tend to awaken for work still feeling exhausted.

The treatment, which has been quite helpful in most cases, is artificial lighting four to six times greater than that found in a typical well-lit office or other workspace. Exposure to 2,000- 3,000-lux fluorescent lights for a couple of hours early each morning (often beginning around 6 A.M.) can often reset the biological clock and dispel the depression within a few weeks. Booster doses of light, as needed thereafter, usually keep the individual on an even keel.

The SAD problem is a big one. Up to 25 percent, or even more, of the population may suffer from SAD, according to some studies. Women are more often victims of this disorder than men, but it affects both sexes and all ages. And there is now evidence that even in places like Southern California, many suffer episodes of SAD owing to foggy and smoggy periods. There is also evidence that those prone to substance abuse may be suffering from SAD, though it is not clear yet whether SAD predisposes to substance abuse or vice versa. It is possible that each contributes to the other in different circumstances.

In any case, a group of psychiatrists and neurologists report finding a number of similar factors at work in SAD and alcohol withdrawal. Accordingly, they launched a pilot study to see whether light therapy could make withdrawal from alcohol any easier. Their test subjects were 20 male alcoholics whose withdrawal symptoms were particularly severe. Ten got the intensive light treatment, and the other ten acted as controls, getting only normal light.

The results were quite positive. The group treated with intensive light (3,000 lux from 6 A.M. to 10:30 P.M. over a two-day period) was found to benefit in a number of ways. They scored significantly higher than the controls in terms of ability to concentrate, memory, and mood. They also required far less anxiety-allaying medication than did the controls—about five to ten times less.

"Seeing the light" may prove helpful in other situations of drug dependence as well. And it may significantly reduce the need for sedating, anti-anxiety, and antidepressant drugs in detoxification and withdrawal regimens. It is possible (and this hypothesis should certainly be tested) that light therapy may also reduce the *craving* for alcohol and other drugs in some individuals.

9 Exercise, Relaxation, and Stress Management

PURIFYING EXERCISE VERSUS EXERCISE ADDICTION

That we live in a high-stress world is now one of the givens of our time. The intense stress of daily life has contributed significantly to addictive, compulsive, and other unhealthy behavior. The challenge is to find effective ways to relieve the pressure and detoxify the stress. Exercise, including proper breathing and relaxation techniques, is one of the most effective ways of achieving this. Done correctly, exercise can help *prevent* addictive behavior—and it is extremely valuable in the *treatment* of addictions. It has potent detoxifying capabilities.

EXERCISE: WHEN LESS IS MORE
(THE CASE OF MARILYN)

Exercise is excellent for the prevention and treatment of addictive behavior *if done in moderation*. Exercise itself can become addictive if done in excess or with improper technique and/or inappropriate motivation. Let me explain what I mean by this with a case history. Marilyn was referred to me by a clinical psychologist. When I first saw her, she was twenty-six years old and was studying for her doctorate in physics. Her problem was multiple drug addiction. When she was about twenty-four, Marilyn began using cocaine. She said it made her feel more energetic, and sharpened her mind. She attributed her success in school to its use. It was true that she was doing well in school, but she had done well before she began using cocaine. In fact, she had graduated first in her (undergraduate) college class when she was twenty. Her cocaine use rapidly escalated as she began her graduate studies. For the first time in her life, Marilyn had insomnia and began using alcohol and barbiturates to knock herself out. Very soon, she was addicted to three drugs—cocaine, alcohol, and barbiturates. Make that four: She also smoked two packs of cigarettes a day. Her diet consisted of greasy fast foods and, typically, six to eight sodas daily. She never ate breakfast. She never exercised.

Marilyn's psychologist and I joined forces to design a purification program—similar to what you will learn about in Part III—consisting of diet, nutritional supplements, amino acids, herbs, a specific antidepressant, exercise, meditation, breathing techniques, therapeutic massage, and psychological counseling. Marilyn responded very favorably. Within a week she was off cocaine, alcohol, and barbiturates and even began cutting down on her smoking. She stopped smoking altogether after another week. At the end of four weeks, she said she no longer had any uncontrollable cravings—except one, a new one.

Marilyn said she couldn't get enough exercise. She proudly announced that she was already "far, far beyond" the exercise goals we had set for her. She had started out, following our recommendations, walking a couple miles a day and within three weeks was running ten miles daily and had signed up for a marathon! What Marilyn had done was to transfer all of her compulsive drive to running. She had, in fact, become addicted to running and in very short order.

Was this bad? Yes, as it turns out, and not only because Marilyn was risking physical damage by trying to transform her body from a rock to a rocket virtually overnight; the real danger was that she had not really gotten "clean." The brain makes its own opiates, called endorphins, and these are released during exercise. The more vigorous the exercises, the greater the release of endorphins. For those who are *not* addiction-prone, there is usually little danger in this; in fact, it can be a way of enjoying the delights of our biology again, provided it is not overdone. In Marilyn's case, however, her body was not accustomed to doing *any* exercise, and in response to the enormous exercise "load" she was placing on it, her brain was working overtime to supply opiates to deal with the stress.

It is all too easy, unfortunately, for an addiction-prone person to slide from one addiction to another. I explained all of this to Marilyn and modified her program, including the amino-acid regimens that affect brain neurotransmitters. She responded favorably again, this time moderating her exercise drive. She has not signed up for any more marathons, has finished her doctorate with honors, and has been drug-free now for nearly three years. She remains vigilant, however, as she must for life, and continues to live a healthy existence.

There is no doubt that appropriate exercise has very significant health benefits. It helps protect against heart disease and cancer, decreases stress, increases energy, promotes good sleep, and helps dispel depression, among other things. There is likewise no doubt that *lack* of appropriate exercise speeds up the aging process both physically and mentally. That "appropriate" exercise, in most cases, is moderate exercise is becoming increasingly clear. This contrasts with the view, prevailing up until very recently, that in general, the more exercise the better.

Beginning in the 1970s, we witnessed an epidemic of overexercise. "No pain, no gain" was the theme song of the heavy breathers. Pushing to the max was thought by many to be their passport to immortality, or at least to much longer and more vital lives. Then, in the 1980s, reports began appearing in the medical literature documenting some of the adverse effects of the fitness revolution. The real shocker was a Stanford University School of Medicine study reported in 1986. This major study revealed that those who exercise strenuously on a long-term basis are about as likely to die prematurely as those who do not exercise at all or who exercise very little. This conclusion was based on a long-term study that followed 17,000 Harvard University alumni. The people who consistently *do* live longer, this study found, are those who take the middle ground and do *regular moderate exercise,* such as walking and climbing up and down stairs.

Many studies have now shown that regular strenuous running greatly increases the risk of developing serious musculoskeletal problems such as damaged feet, ankles, knees, and hips. A few reports reveal that a significant percentage of marathoners suffer from iron-deficiency anemia, as well as gastrointestinal bleeding. Rigorous aerobic exercisers suffer from more asthma, allergies, and respiratory infections that those who do more moderate exercise. (Moderate aerobic exercise can actually benefit asthmatics.) Some studies show that marathoners have depression of some elements of their immune system, such as their natural killer cells. Moderate exercise, on the other hand, can *boost* immunity.

THE BENEFITS OF WALKING

One of the best exercises is walking. Walking can reduce tension and anxiety *immediately*, and it can get you into excellent aerobic condition very quickly. A little stroll five times a week is all it takes. Walk for one hour a day—building up slowly to that level—five days a week, quickening your pace a little as you go along. If you have any serious heart or joint problems, discuss this with your physician prior to starting this program.

Get a good pair of walking shoes. If possible, vary your route a little each day, to keep things interesting. Don't walk near heavy traffic if you can help it. Join walking or hiking groups when you feel up to it. Walking gives you time to look around and see things, to think, to talk, to feel, even to create. It becomes much more difficult to light up that cigarette once you get into the walking habit. In fact, walking is good for any addiction.

Stretch for five to ten minutes before setting off on your walk each day, as well as afterward. Shop around for a book on stretching exercises. There are several good ones. Concentrate on exercises that gently increase the range of motion of your neck, shoulders, arms, legs, and back. Here's one you can try right now. Very slowly, turn your neck to the left, trying to touch your left shoulder with your chin. Don't move your left shoulder toward your chin and don't stretch your neck beyond the point where it begins to feel uncomfortable. Now, cup your left hand around the left side of your chin so that your chin snuggles into the palm of your hand. Push your left hand against your head but try to keep your neck from moving. That is, try to resist the force of your hand attempting to turn your neck to the right. Do this for a count of ten. Take your hand away and turn your neck back to the center. Stretch your neck to the left again. You will probably now find that you can stretch it a little farther than you did the first time. Repeat the same steps on the right. This is an excellent stretching exercise to do every day. It will increase the flexibility of your neck. The idea is to increase flexibility in *all* the joints of your body.

When you first start walking, aim to get your heart rate up to about 60 percent of your *maximal* heart rate (MHR). Your MHR can be calculated by subtracting your age from 220. Then take 60 percent of that number to determine your goal heart rate. For example, if you are forty years old, then your MHR is 220 minus 40, or 180 beats per minute. Sixty percent of that is 108 beats per minute. You can check your heart rate at your radial pulse, which is located in the wrist near the base of your thumb—or by pacing two fingers gently over the carotid artery in your neck.

Try to walk a little faster each day, until you get your heart rate up to 80 percent of your MHR. *Take your time getting there.* Don't push yourself to the point of breathlessness and try *never* to walk so fast that you cannot maintain a conversation without great difficulty while continuing to walk. Don't worry if you *can't* get your heart rate up more than 60 percent of your MHR. Even at this rate, you will still reap significant health benefits if you walk at least five times a week.

Fast striders can walk about four miles in an hour. A runner can cover that distance two to three times as fast. Distance, however, is more important than pace. *The caloric expenditure from walking one mile is about the same as running one mile.* Always try to swing your arms while walking. Walking with hand weights gives a slightly greater caloric expenditure and is also good for the heart, but if you find these weights uncomfortable, don't use them. You want to make your daily walk a totally enjoyable experience.

Many who are in drug-rehabilitation programs find brisk daily walks extremely helpful. The Betty Ford Center for alcohol and drug rehabilitation uses the daily stroll as a therapeutic tool. And researchers at the University of North Carolina have found that aerobic exercise, such as walking, definitely reduces the depression and anxiety experienced by alcoholics as they disengage from their addiction and as they attempt to maintain recovery.

RELAXATION AND STRESS MANAGEMENT: THE IMPORTANCE OF BREATHING PROPERLY

I'm sure there have been many times when you felt nervous, worried, or depressed and someone told you with good intentions, "Don't worry—relax." We've all had that experience. But *how* do we relax? Proper exercise, as we've just discussed, is one way. Therapeutic massage and meditation are others. But basic to *all* relaxation techniques is *proper breathing*.

Very few people breathe correctly. If medicine paid more attention to that fact, we could reduce illness dramatically. The benefits of walking and other moderate aerobic exercises are due, in large part, to improvement in breathing skills. *Breathing properly is unquestionably the single most important thing we can do to improve our health. It is also the most fundamental and important thing we can do to prevent and treat any type of addictive behavior.*

Remember that the bottom line for all health is *cellular* health. If we could continually keep all of the cells of our body maximally energized and at the same time maximally protected from toxic free-radical activity, we could almost certainly extend our life span dramatically. We'd also enjoy optimal physical and mental health. The key to this is getting optimal amounts of oxygen into our cells. We've discussed the importance of food, water, and air in this process. How we breathe is even more important.

Most of us breathe so that we expand only the upper chest. This is the old military mode of breathing, which emphasizes sucking in the gut and expanding the chest as you inhale. What this does is suck air into the *upper* lungs. This is bad, because the blood vessels that perfuse the lung are concentrated in the lower part of the lungs, and we need to get the oxygen down there where more of it can be picked up by the blood and transported to the cells. To maximally ventilate the lower lungs, we must learn how properly to use the most important muscle in our body—the diaphragm.

When we *breathe in* properly, the diaphragm contracts and descends, the abdomen protrudes, and the ribs fan out. *Never* suck in your gut while inhaling. When we *breathe out* properly, the diaphragm relaxes and ascends, the stomach flattens, and the ribs pull in. Here are some exercises to help you master diaphragmatic breathing; you should practice these daily. Ideally, they should be performed wearing comfortable clothing, in a quiet place. Once you get the hang of them, which you should be able to do very quickly, you can use them under other circumstances, such as while driving, sitting at a desk, whenever you feel anxious or depressed—before giving a speech, and so on.

Lie down on your back on the floor; lie on a mat if that makes you more comfortable. Bend your knees up and move your feet about eight inches apart, with toes turned slightly outward. Make sure your spine is straight. Place both hands, spread out, palms down, on your sides, with the index fingers pushed up right under the lower ribs and the thumbs touching the lower ribs in the small of your back. The other fingers rest on the upper abdomen. In this way you can feel the movement of your diaphragm and make sure that it is working correctly.

Shut your eyes, try to clear your mind of any immediate concerns, schedules, and so on, and begin to concentrate on your breathing. As you inhale, you should feel your hands rise and then fall when you exhale. Don't let your breastbone rise appreciably while you are inhaling. Your breathing rate will be four to six breaths per minute. Exhalation should take somewhat longer than inhaling—about one and a half times as long. Count to four slowly, during inhalation, pause for a moment, then count to six slowly, during exhalation. Pause for about three seconds before you inhale again. Before long this will become natural, and you will be able to cease counting. Breathe through your nose throughout this exercise. Make sure, of course, that your nose is clear (use a decongestant if necessary) and that the air you are breathing is as pure as possible. This exercise is good to do for ten minutes upon arising and ten minutes before retiring. You can also use it as a meditation exercise, and it can be done at any time during the day.

A variation of this exercise is done while sitting. It's best to practice this while sitting in a comfortable chair with a firm, straight back. Keep your head, neck, and back straight and place your hands on your knees, palms up or down, whichever you find more comfortable. Don't cross your legs. Keep your feet flat on the floor. Clear your mind of any concerns and concentrate on your breathing. Always breathe through your nose.

Breathe in and out four to six times per minute, exactly as in the previous exercise, and pause before each inhalation. To check if you are breathing correctly, place both hands spread out palms down on your sides so that your index fingers are right up under the lower ribs on the front and your thumbs are touching your lower ribs in the small of your back. The other fingers rest on the upper abdomen. If you are doing the exercise correctly, you'll feel your hands move forward when you inhale, as your abdomen protrudes. This exercise can be done while driving (it is especially calming while waiting in traffic), while you are working, and even can be done standing up. The goal is to try to breathe diaphragmatically most of the time. It will soon become second nature, and you'll be amazed at how much better it makes you feel.

Nasal Cycles and Obstacle Breathing

For thousands of years, practitioners of yoga have been performing a breathing exercise known as nasal-cycle breathing. Many find this exercise very calming, and it is helpful in the treatment of drug dependence. To practice this form of breathing, sit in a comfortable chair with your head, neck, and back in a straight line. Do not cross your legs. Exhale completely. Close your right nostril with your right thumb and then inhale slowly and completely through the left nostril. Now exhale through your left nostril. At the end of the exhalation, close the left nostril with the left thumb, inhale and exhale through the right nostril, slowly and completely, as before. Continue to repeat this cycle, alternating from side to side. Breathing rate, as in the other exercises, should be four to six times per minute and there should be a pause before you start each new inhalation. Try to perform this one for ten minutes once or twice a day. It is an excellent meditation exercise and one that you can use to bring down your level of stress. There are some studies indicating that nasal-cycle breathing can favorably regulate the electrical activity of the brain.

Here's an exercise or meditation that I find particularly helpful to reduce tension. This can be done either lying on a mat, as in the first exercise, or while sitting in a chair, as in the second exercise. Begin by taking in deep breaths through your nose, but instead of breathing out through your nose, slowly exhale through *pursed* lips. This is a form of obstacle breathing. Do this for a few minutes. Now, locate an area of your body that is particularly tense or rigid. Select just one area at a time and, as you very slowly and deeply breathe in, imagine that area becoming even *more* tense. Focus on this until the area is almost painful. Then, as you slowly breathe out (remember to do this through pursed lips), gradually release the tension you have created in that area; as the tension dissipates, feel the warmth and fluidity that washes in. Continue this until you have breathed life into all of your trouble spots.

PART
III

THE
PURIFICATION
PRESCRIPTIONS

1 *Alcohol*

THE HUMAN SIDE: THE CASE OF MRS. J

Mrs. J was fifty-three when she first consulted me. She was frank about her alcoholism. She stated that she had been an alcoholic for ten years and had "drunk quite a lot" for fifteen years. Alcohol had cost her one marriage, several jobs, the affection of two of her children, and was now threatening her current marriage.

As I took a detailed history, it became apparent that a number of factors had contributed to Mrs. J's alcoholism. She had a history of chronic allergies and fibromyalgia, a still puzzling but fairly prevalent disorder (more common to women than men) characterized by diffuse aching in various muscles and bones, stiffness, pins-and-needles sensations, poor sleep patterns, fatigue and, sometimes, irritable bowel syndrome, tension headaches, hypersensitivity to loud noises, and occasional swelling of the hands. Mrs. J suffered from most of these symptoms intermittently and, in addition, was beset by numerous food sensitivities and respiratory allergies.

These are precisely the kind of chronic, nagging problems that, if they don't actively drive a person to drink, at least help predispose the sufferer to alcoholism. Mrs. J, like so many other alcoholics I've seen, initially used alcohol to try to self-treat her medical problems. Of course, she wasn't aware she was doing this. She only knew that she felt better when she'd had a few drinks. The history I took, however, revealed a definite association between these disorders and Mrs. J's drinking, an association that persisted.

The simple fact—frequently overlooked by society—is that people who drink a lot usually do so because they hurt one way or another. Alcohol—like most addictive drugs—is a *short-term* revitalizer—right down to the cellular level, where it has an *initial* membrane-fluidizing effect that boosts energy. The addiction to alcohol, as noted in Part I, is the result of a chance or misguided quest for wholeness and health, *not,* in the overwhelming majority of cases, a conscious quest for oblivion on the one hand, or mindless pleasure on the other. The drinker just wants to feel better, less depressed, more energetic, more *normal.*

Mrs. J remembered developing "a really obnoxious nonstop postnasal drip" a couple of years before her drinking became compulsive. She consulted many physicians about the problem and was treated with everything from antihistamines to antibiotics for a problem that simply wouldn't relent.

"The only time my throat felt good," she said, "was when I was eating or drinking something tart or with a tingle to it." Mrs. J, not unexpectedly, began to gain weight—and found herself drinking a lot of citrus juice, something she'd always liked anyway. Unfortunately, her postnasal drip and scratchy throat not only persisted; they worsened.

Mrs. J was already drinking quite a lot of something else—white wine and, later, gin—when she abruptly realized one day that she was less bothered by her sore throat. At about the same time, she also noticed that whenever she decided "to go easy" on the booze, the postnasal drip seemed to worsen—along with a lot of other problems alcohol seemed to be putting to sleep. The resolution to "go easy" weakened, and arose less and less frequently. By then, Mrs. J was well down the road to addiction.

We can't say with certainty that a patchwork of aches and pains that wouldn't go away *caused* Mrs. J's alcoholism. But there is no doubt whatever, in my mind, that the relief from those persistent aches and pains that alcohol delivered (where all else seemed to fail) is what *kept* Mrs. J drinking—until she was addicted and could not stop, without incurring even greater pain.

Rather than look for the most complicated moral and metaphysical "reasons" for alcoholism, it's time we pay heed to what I tell my patients are "the little details." Yes, those chronic afflictions, however "insignificant," that when neglected can add up to real monsters. When my new patients, schooled in the language learned from the practitioners who have failed them, ascribe their alcoholism to "genetic predisposition," bad toilet training, or an unhappy marriage, I say, "Yes, all those things *may* have contributed, but tell me, do you suffer from allergies, chronic pain, depression you can't explain?" and so on.

It is quite evident to me that had Mrs. J received timely and effective treatment for her fibromyalgia and what turned out to be a specific food sensitivity (to citrus—the very thing she craved!), Mrs. J—and many others like her—would not have become alcoholic. Far more alcoholism than most in the medical profession are willing to admit is the product of inadequate or failed medicine.

Mrs. J had made several efforts to quit drinking by the time she first consulted me. These ranged from cold-turkey efforts undertaken entirely by herself to supervised treatment at detoxification centers. She had joined AA some years earlier but had abandoned it along with one of her brushes with abstinence.

As I reviewed with Mrs. J what had been tried in the past in the way of cleansing her system of alcohol and the craving for alcohol, I recognized the same treatment approaches I've seen fail so many times before.

The biggest shortcoming in all of these approaches is the failure to take into account and clean up all of those little details I spoke of. The present medical method is a mechanical and linear one, not an interactive one, and consequently, it is ill-equipped to deal with more than one or two variables at a time. It is a method that is always searching for *the* cause, rather than the *causes*. There is a real resistance among most physicians to work with several therapeutic modalities at the same time. And there remains in this method the outdated and therapeutically stultifying separation of mind and body that leads to so much worthless psychologizing.

I told Mrs. J that my approach to treating alcoholism was quite different. It consists of a program that quickly sets the body (including the brain and "mind") on a path of health, one that pays particular heed to sorting out the kind of biochemical defects and, in some cases, outright chaos that, in terms of alcoholism, "set up" the individual in the first place. It is designed to achieve—in the *long term*—all of the benefits that alcohol (and other addictive drugs) deliver on a *short-term* basis only. It is a program of diet, supplementation, exercise, and judicious and forward-looking pharmacological intervention that not only purifies and detoxifies but also discourages any recurrence of destructive cravings. It is a creative and interactive program that can detoxify in one week and help inoculate against recurrence in five weeks.

You've already learned, in Part II, about the individual elements of these programs. Now, in the sections that follow, you'll see how several of these elements are used in the treatment of alcoholism. In Mrs. J's case—and hers is typical of many—the results have been rewarding. The program vanquished her food sensitivities (which had grown in number, due in part to alcohol-induced metabolic disturbances) and diminished many of her fibromyalgia symptoms. The recommended amino acids, breathing exercises, light therapy, and herbs were particularly useful in Mrs. J's case.

She detoxified without need of hospitalization within a week, continued with the postdetoxification program for another four weeks, and has now incorporated many of the elements of the program into her daily life, particularly the dietary and exercise recommendations. She uses the herbs, amino acids, and relaxation techniques to control cravings, anxiety, and muscular tension.

Two years postdetox, Mrs. J remains alcohol- and drug-free. Her marriage has been restored and is "happier than ever," she has reconciled with her children and is working at a rewarding job. The bottom line: "I haven't felt this well since I was sixteen."

THE NATURE OF THE ADDICTION

LIGHT, MODERATE, AND HEAVY DRINKING DEFINED

Alcoholic beverages, produced by the fermentation of foods, are widely available in the form of beer, wine, and distilled spirits. In a strict chemical sense, alcohol refers to a family of compounds that all share a common structural component called hydroxyl group, or OH. Alcohol, as used in this context, refers to one member of the family, ethanol.

The ethanol content of the different alcoholic beverages vary, as follows: Beer is typically 4 percent alcohol by volume; wine, about 12 percent; and distilled spirits, usually 40–50 percent. *Proof* is percent alcohol multiplied by two. Thus, a liquor that is 40 percent alcohol is 80 proof. Twelve ounces of beer is equal, in terms of alcohol content, to 4 ounces of wine or 1¼ ounces of liquor (one shot). Each of these quantities is considered to be one standard drink.

Someone who drinks from one to nine standard drinks, as defined above, weekly, spread out over the week, is a *light drinker*. A *moderate drinker* is one who drinks from ten to thirty standard drinks weekly, again spread out over the week. A *heavy drinker* is one who drinks more than thirty standard drinks weekly. These are only rough guidelines, and they should not be construed to mean that it's *always* okay if you are only a light drinker. This is not the case. *Any* drinking can be risky, if, for example, you are pregnant.

YOU ARE ADDICTED WHEN . . .

You are addicted to alcohol when your body and mind crave it and you get sick when you stop drinking it for any period of time. People are often addicted without actually knowing it or recognizing it. When I was a jazz musician in the 1950s, many of my fellow musicians were addicted to a variety of substances. I remember one great musician who would have six to eight drinks before he played. When I expressed concern, he would tell me not to worry, that he could stop whenever he wanted to; but he never did, not until it killed him.

The so-called CAGE questionnaire is a quick and simple screening test to identify those who are either addicted to alcohol or who are at high risk of becoming addicted. CAGE is a mnemonic (memory aid) for the first letters of key words in each of four questions. The questions are:

1. Have you ever felt you ought to *Cut* down on your drinking?

2. Have people *Annoyed* you by criticizing your drinking?

3. Have you felt bad or *Guilty* about your drinking?

4. Have you ever had a drink first thing in the morning (*Eye* opener) to steady your nerves and get rid of a hangover?

Two or more yes answers indicate probable alcoholism. Even one yes answer suggests a possible problem. How did *you* do? You don't have to be a *continuous* heavy drinker to qualify as an alcoholic. Alcoholics can also be weekend binge drinkers and those who drink a lot intermittently—that is, for a few weeks or months at a time.

How does one get addicted to alcohol? The answer to that question, as far as we can answer it at this time, takes us on a circuitous journey through all of medicine and psychology. Let's try to abbreviate it. Alcohol dependence or addiction, commonly referred to as alcoholism, is a biochemical disorder that afflicts those who are vulnerable to it due to interactions between their genes and their environment. The environmental component includes the aggregate of all social, economic, and physical factors (such as climate and diet) that influence the individual's life. The genetic component is an inherited vulnerability. There *is* a higher incidence of alcoholism in children who come from alcoholic families. But that doesn't mean that all children of alcoholics are doomed to become alcoholics themselves. Their genetic endowment may indeed put them at greater risk, but the *expression* of our genes is governed to a significant extent by our environment. This means that children of alcoholics may never become alcoholics, even if they have inherited the genetic propensity for this disorder, if the genetic-environmental interactions are such that the genes are not expressed. Leading a healthy life—following a good diet, exercising, breathing properly, and knowing how to relax— will help ensure that sleeping "alcoholic genes" *remain* asleep.

On the other hand, those who do *not* come from alcoholic families, it should be noted, can develop the addiction if *they* do not lead healthy lives. Even when the hereditary factors are very weak, the environmental factors can still conspire to create a new alcoholic.

The addictive process goes something like this. You start drinking, and the alcohol makes you feel good. Even though, pharmacologically, alcohol is a brain depressant, it has stimulatory properties at low doses. With one or two drinks you may feel mildly euphoric, warm, and less tense and anxious. Alcohol has the seductive ability to cause selective memory loss for those things that often cause stress or physical and social discomfort. Another few drinks can literally knock you off your feet, leading to sedation and frank intoxication.

As you continue to drink, you will need to drink ever increasing amounts to produce the same euphoric, relaxing, sedating effects. This phenomenon is called *tolerance*. After continued heavy drinking, any effort to significantly reduce or stop drinking can lead to symptoms of what is called the *abstinence syndrome* or *alcohol-withdrawal syndrome*. The syndrome will be described shortly; its symptoms are all quite unpleasant. One way of "treating" this syndrome is with alcohol. Most alcoholics self-treat in this manner. Thus, the vicious cycle of alcoholism becomes evident—a cycle enforced by both positive and negative feedback. The positive reinforcement is the pleasure, however brief, drinking delivers; the negative reinforcement is the pain, persistent and terrible, that abstinence brings.

ALCOHOL'S EFFECTS IN THE BRAIN

The actual effects of alcohol in the brain are being widely studied. It is clear that alcohol affects many of the brain's neurotransmitters and neuropeptides. These substances are chemicals that carry messages from one part of the brain to another. When these messages get garbled or lost, the results can include anxiety, feelings of unease, paranoia, mental dullness, memory loss, abnormal body movements, depression, etc. Alcohol particularly affects the neurotransmitters dopamine, norepinephrine, gamma aminobutyric acid (GABA), serotonin and acetylcholine, as well as the neuropeptide endorphins, enkephalins, glutathione, corticotrophin-releasing factor or CRF (involved in regulating cortisone levels), somatostatin, vasopressin, and the steroid hormones found in the brain. Several of these neurotransmitters and neuropeptides mediate the addictive effects of alcohol.

Serotonin appears to be an especially important factor in alcoholism. This neurotransmitter is involved in the modulation of tension, mood, perception of pain, attentiveness, and sleep, among other things. Alcohol may have short-term serotonin-boosting effects, but prolonged use can result in decreased functioning of serotonin systems in the brain. There is data on both animals and humans to support this conclusion. Mice and rats that are genetically bred to prefer alcohol have been found to have significantly lower than normal serotonin activity in certain brain regions. And human alcoholics have been found to have lower levels of serotonin in their blood and platelets and lower amounts of a metabolite of serotonin in their cerebrospinal fluid. Drugs have now been developed that increase serotonin concentrations in certain brain regions. These drugs are capable of significantly reducing alcohol intake in both laboratory animals and humans. L-tryptophan itself, the amino-acid precursor of serotonin, has been shown to reduce alcohol intake in animal experiments.

There is a center in the brain where another neurotransmitter, dopamine, mediates pleasurable sensations. Several addictive drugs, including alcohol, may produce their initial pleasurable effects, at least in part, by increasing the activity of dopamine in such regions. But again, repeated heavy use of alcohol seems to have the opposite long-term effect, *decreasing* dopamine activity, so that more and more alcohol is needed to produce the pleasure. This is the phenomenon of tolerance we discussed above.

Another neurotransmitter, GABA, modulates tension and sleep.

GABA activity also appears to be involved in some of the effects of alcohol, particularly in reducing anxiety and causing sedation. Once more, however, these are short-term benefits. Continued heavy use of alcohol *depresses* GABA activity. This has been seen in experiments with animals and with human alcoholics.

The enkephalins and endorphins are opiatelike neuropeptides produced in our brain; they modulate perception of pain, mood and, most likely, various cravings. There is some evidence suggesting that these substances are abnormally diminished in the brains of those who consume a lot of alcohol. Heavy drinkers have decreased endorphin levels in their cerebrospinal fluid and decreased enkephalin levels in their blood. There is speculation, based on some animal research, that a metabolite of alcohol, in combination with dopamine, may bind to enkephalin and endorphin-binding sites and produce a (short-term) opiatelike sense of well-being. In the long term, however, alcoholism most likely depletes the brain of its enkephalins and endorphins.

Any substance that could prevent the breakdown of these neuropeptides might be expected to play a useful role in the treatment of alcoholism. And, in fact, D-phenylalanine, which inhibits the breakdown of enkephalins, was shown, in one recent study, to decrease alcohol intake in mice genetically predisposed to alcohol preference.

IMMUNOLOGICAL AND METABOLIC EFFECTS OF ALCOHOL

It should be clear by now that alcohol affects many of the brain's neurotransmitters and that any successful treatment of alcoholism will depend, in part, upon a restoration of normal neurotransmitter activity. But to understand how best to treat alcoholism it is important that we discuss the metabolism and immunological effects of this drug, as well.

The liver is the major organ of alcohol metabolism. One of the major products of that metabolism is acetaldehyde, a highly toxic substance, a free-radical generator that produces tissue damage and depletes cellular glutathione, a major defender against free-radical damage. Other negative consequences of alcohol metabolism include oxygen-starved liver cells, increased production of lactic acid, increased production of fatty acids and accumulation of fat in the liver, decreased production of biological energy, and decreased production of glucose leading to alcoholic hypoglycemia, common among alcoholics.

Alcoholics, in addition to being severely malnourished due to metabolic chaos, often have badly impaired immunity and are at greatly increased risk of infections and cancer. They are also more prone to food sensitivities. Alcohol has a toxic effect on the mucosa of the gut, causing what is called the "leaky" gut. Undigested molecules of food pass through the gut in this condition, causing allergic and sensitivity reactions. Grains, such as wheat and corn, may cause problems. Some alcoholics develop increased sensitivity to milk due to an inability to digest milk sugar (lactose). This condition is known as lactose intolerance. Alcohol-induced food sensitivities produce such symptoms as abdominal pain and bloating, diarrhea, and nasal congestion. Some are sensitive to substances within alcohol itself. The hangover is usually due to these sensitivities, which can result in headache, nausea, and vomiting.

TREATMENT

DETOXIFICATION (WEEK ONE)

Detoxification is the process of ridding the body of contaminants, in this case alcohol. Abstinence from alcohol, in those who have been heavy drinkers, produces the alcohol-withdrawal syndrome. The syndrome ranges in symptoms from headaches, body aches, nausea, vomiting, and a flulike state to profound anxiety, tremulousness, seizures, fever, very fast heart rate, psychosis and, sometimes, death. The intensity of symptoms usually depends on the length of time one has been a heavy drinker. Those who have been drinking heavily for short periods of time—weeks or months—are much less likely to suffer severe withdrawal symptoms than those who have been addicted for long periods of time.

For a chronic heavy drinker, even any decrease in alcohol intake will bring on some of the symptoms of alcohol withdrawal. Sometimes, in fact, the symptoms are experienced even *without* any reduction in intake. What is happening here is that less alcohol is getting to the brain. The alcoholic ultimately responds to this situation by drinking *more*—self-treating withdrawal symptoms (unrecognized as such) with alcohol. There is probably nothing that contributes more to *sustained* dependence on alcohol than this reaction to the body's efforts at withdrawal. It is crucial that the alcohol-addicted individual recognize that the physical and mental depression he or she seeks to treat with alcohol is in fact *caused* by alcohol.

Severe withdrawal symptoms often occur in chronic heavy alcohol users from six to forty-eight hours after their last drink. These symptoms can include tremulousness, sweats, convulsions, disorientation, hallucinations, irritability, nausea, vomiting, and depression. Hallucinations are usually of the auditory type. Many hear voices, often those of family or friends, discussing the alcoholic in a critical way.

The most severe (and fortunately rarer) syndrome of alcohol withdrawal is the infamous DTs, or delirium tremens. When this occurs, it usually has its onset from forty-eight to ninety-six hours (two to four days) after the last drink but may occur, although much less frequently, up to twelve days after the last drink. DTs consists of profound disorientation (confusion), severe agitation, tachycardia (very fast heart beat), fever, and profuse sweating. The condition is typically accompanied by deficiencies in the minerals magnesium, potassium, and sodium; the vitamins thiamine, folic acid, and others; severe dehydration; and occasionally, by serious infections of the abdomen, lungs, and brain. Delirium tremens is a serious, potentially life-threatening, disorder and must be intensively treated in a hospital. *Many alcoholics enter the hospital for other reasons (surgery, heart attack, etc.) and never discuss their heavy drinking with their doctor. Many have died unnecessarily, from untreated DTs, because of this.*

Detoxification of alcohol takes, typically, from three to seven days, depending on the severity of the alcohol withdrawal reaction. A mild withdrawal syndrome usually can be treated in an outpatient setting. More severe withdrawal syndromes require hospitalization. How do you know if you will have only a mild withdrawal reaction? The following are some guidelines. (These should be reviewed with your physician.)

1. You are motivated to stop drinking and, with the exception of nicotine and/or caffeine, are not addicted to any other chemical substance.

2. Your heavy drinking has been relatively short—no longer than a few weeks.

3. You have no history of alcohol-withdrawal seizures or DTs.

4. You have no other medical problem that requires hospitalization.

5. You have a buddy (wife, husband, boyfriend, girlfriend, etc.) who will keep a close eye on you and, if necessary, contact your

physician, whom you should see *daily* during your alcohol detoxification.

If you qualify for outpatient detoxification, I recommend the following treatment plan. Review this with your doctor before starting and have him or her review the relevant sections of the book related to any point he or she may not be familiar with.

Medical Tests

You should have a chemistry panel to determine electrolytes, kidney and liver function, magnesium and calcium levels, uric-acid status, and total cholesterol, HDL cholesterol, and LDL cholesterol levels. You should have a complete blood count and thyroid-function tests, including TSH—thyroid stimulating hormone. Tests for iron, total iron binding capacity and serum ferritin (to determine iron stores), as well as a drug screen (including alcohol level) should be performed. These tests will alert your doctor to any major relevant complication of your addiction.

Pharmaceuticals

These are to be used only if you have had alcohol-withdrawal symptoms, such as agitation, mild confusion, tremulousness, nausea, and vomiting in the past. These are often not necessary if the patient is not a regular, long-term heavy drinker. If required, the drugs of choice are *chlordiazepoxide* (Librium) *or lorazepam* (Ativan). Librium is given at 25 milligrams four times daily for three to five days and then stopped. Ativan is given at 1 to 2.5 milligrams four times daily for three to five days and then stopped.

The risk of convulsion is greatest during the first three days of detoxification, and if your physician or buddy witnesses or you witness withdrawal symptoms such as agitation and tremulousness, then it is advisable to receive an intramuscular injection of phenobarbital. If a seizure does occur, even though it may look terrible, remember that it is *not* life threatening and is unlikely to occur again. If your doctor believes it is a sign of more serious withdrawal problems, however, he or she will make the decision with regard to hospitalization. *An alcohol-withdrawal seizure does not require long-term seizure medication.* Unfortunately, there are many who are still on seizure medications *years* after their only alcohol-withdrawal seizure!

Vitamins and Minerals

- Thiamine, 100 milligrams, intramuscularly every day for three days. Given by your physician.

- Magnesium sulfate, 1 gram, intramuscularly every day for three days. Given by your physician.

- Plus the following amounts of oral vitamins and minerals. Make sure that the formula that you use is hypoallergenic (check labels). Take with food:

Vitamin	Recommended Daily Dose
vitamin A	2,500–5,000 IU
beta carotene	15–30 milligrams (mg)
vitamin B_1 (thiamine)	100 mg
vitamin B_2 (riboflavin)	1.7–10 mg
vitamin B_3 (niacin)	20–100 mg
pantothenic acid	10–50 mg
vitamin B_6 (pyridoxine)	2–25 mg
vitamin B_{12}	6–100 micrograms (mcg)
folic acid	800–1,000 mcg
biotin	100–300 mcg
vitamin C	60–1,000 mg
vitamin D	200–400 IU
vitamin E	30–400 IU
vitamin K	100–200 mcg

Mineral	Recommended Daily Dose
calcium	250–1,000 mg
magnesium	300–500 mg
zinc	15–30 mg
iron	10–15 mg*
manganese	2–10 mg
copper	2–3 mg
selenium	50–200 mcg
chromium	100–200 mcg
iodine	50–150 mcg
molybdenum	50–200 mcg

* If your laboratory studies indicated that you have elevated iron stores (measured as elevated serum ferritin) and/or elevated serum iron (this occurs in alcoholics as a result of alcoholic liver disease), then *don't* take supplementary iron.

Amino Acids

The amino acids nourish the brain with nutrient precursors of some of the neurotransmitters. They are used here to decrease alcohol craving and help with anxiety and insomnia.

L-glutamine helps many, but not all, alcoholics decrease alcohol craving. A leading alcohol researcher, Joseph Beasley, recently found that the addition of L-glutamine lowered alcohol craving in a significant number of alcoholics who had failed many attempts at detoxification and rehabilitation. Take 3 grams daily in divided doses on an empty stomach. That is, take 1 gram with water about an hour before eating, three times a day. If you are taking Librium or Ativan, don't start the L-glutamine until you are off these drugs. L-glutamine's effect in reducing alcohol craving may be due to conversion to, among other things, the brain neurotransmitter GABA.

Food and Fluids

The goals here are to properly nourish your brain and body, to establish a healthy diet, to correct and/or prevent hypoglycemia, and to improve your immune system and avoid foods and food additives that will make you feel ill and will fuel addictive behavior.

THINGS TO AVOID

Avoid sugar. Avoid coffee or any caffeinated beverages. (Decaffeinated coffee or tea is okay.) Avoid any foods that you are sensitive to, such as wheat and corn. Later on you may reintroduce these foods into your diet *one at a time*. If you then develop symptoms (abdominal discomfort, gas, diarrhea, nasal congestion, headaches, etc.) from these foods, you'll probably need to eliminate them permanently from your diet. Avoid food additives whenever possible, especially sulfiting agents and monosodium glutamate (MSG). For those who eat out and are not sure if sulfiting agents are added to the foods, a 1,000-microgram sublingual tablet of vitamin B_{12} (available in health-food stores) is advisable before eating. The B_{12} will largely neutralize the sulfites. Some people are sensitive to milk and milk products because of intolerance to lactose (milk sugar). Those individuals should either stay away from milk and milk products (although many can handle yogurt without problems) or add the enzyme lactase (Lactaid), now widely available, to these products. In fact, milk is now available with the enzyme already added.

Avoid egg yolks, lard, butterfat, and organ meats such as liver, kidneys, heart, brains, and gizzards. These foods are high in saturated fats and cholesterol. Avoid also high-fat milk, cream, butter, fatty cheeses, fried foods, candy, cookies, chocolate, and most cakes.

WHAT TO EAT INSTEAD

After reviewing the above, you may wonder, What's left? The answer is, A lot. What you will be doing, among other things, is reeducating your palate to develop tastes for foods that will make your body, brain, and mind healthy and that you will find delicious at the same time. This process will also help you lose your taste for alcohol. Review Chapter 7 of Part II for more diet specifics and suggestions.

Increase your consumption of carbohydrates. Emphasize the *complex*, unrefined carbohydrates. Keep your intake of *simple* carbohydrates (sugars) down as low as possible.

Start decreasing your saturated-fat intake. Increase amounts of polyunsaturates and monounsaturates.

Your protein intake should amount to 12 to 15 percent of your total calories, with increased reliance on vegetable protein, less on animal protein.

Begin increasing your dietary-fiber intake.

Drink 6 to 8 cups of water daily and ensure that the water is as nearly pure as possible. You can add a lemon twist or lime to your water to give it some flavor.

Eat more beans and grain products (with the exception of those that you may be sensitive to for the time being) as protein and fiber sources.

Increase the amount of fish in your diet. Eat poultry and fish in place of fattier red meats.

Substitute soft margarine for butter. Use vegetable oils (with the exception of palm and coconut oils) instead of lard.

Use no-fat, 1- or 2-percent-fat milk in place of whole milk (which is 4 percent fat).

Use low-fat cheeses and egg substitutes.

Eat more fruits and vegetables, with emphasis on the cruciferous family (cabbage, broccoli, cauliflower, brussels sprouts, kohlrabi), dark green leafy vegetables, carrots, pumpkins, spinach, peaches, cantaloupes, sweet potatoes, winter squash, pumpkin, citrus fruits, and tomatoes.

Cut down on salt and use some of the new herbal seasonings and salt substitutes instead.

Most important: Eat three meals a day: breakfast, lunch, and dinner, and have a light snack between meals.

Remember to include such items as garlic, onions, chili pepper, seaweed, tofu, miso, tempeh, and yogurt in your diet. (Again, see Chapter 7, Part II, for specifics.)

Here's a diet that works well for many undergoing detoxification:

DAY ONE

Breakfast: A glass of orange or grapefruit juice—fresh, if possible; three pieces of fresh fruit; 1 cup of noncaffeinated tea or coffee.

Lunch: A glass of orange or grapefruit juice. Four to 6 ounces of low-fat cottage cheese (mix some fresh fruit into the cottage cheese); 1 cup of noncaffeinated tea or coffee or 1 glass of water or seltzer.

Dinner: A bowl of chicken soup with rice, vegetables, and a few small pieces of chicken. A serving of fruit; a cup of Jell-O; 1 cup of noncaffeinated tea or coffee or 1 glass of water or seltzer water. You may want to add lemon for flavor.

Snacks can include carrot sticks, celery sticks, and apples.

Drink 6 to 8 glasses of water spaced throughout the day.

DAY TWO

Same as Day One. Keep it light.

DAY THREE AND AFTER

The following can be included in your diet from this point on:

Animal products: daily intake of 6 ounces of fish, calamari, clams, scallops, or 4 ounces of poultry (chicken, turkey, etc.), game meat (such as venison), veal, lobster, crab, shrimp, or 6 to 8 ounces of low-fat cottage cheese. Combinations of any of these to add up to the total amounts suggested are acceptable.

Vegetables: 2 to 4 cups daily.

Fruits: three to five servings of fresh fruits daily.

Beans: Try to eat a cup of beans daily. Beans include lima, navy, pinto, soy, chili, lentils, refried.

Whole grains and potatoes: (Avoid wheat and corn products if you are sensitive to them.) Eat two to five servings at *each meal.* These can be breads, rice products, oats, cereals (except wheat and corn cereals if you are sensitive to them).

Snacks: These can include vegetables, fruits, rice cakes and wafers, bread with margarine. Remember that snacks are very important. *One* of the reasons for eating three meals daily (plus snacks) is to keep food cravings down.

Herbs

The herb valerian has a calming effect in many who use it. A tea brewed from the roots of the herb is frequently helpful in drug detoxification. During the alcohol-withdrawal period, the tea can be used *every two hours* as necessary to reduce anxiety and nervousness. It is often helpful for insomnia as well. Valerian-root extracts, or teas made from the valerian root, should not be used at the same time as Librium or Ativan.

Light

Exposure to full-spectrum lighting can be helpful in alcohol (and other drug) detoxification. (See discussion in Part II.) The most widely used full-spectrum light is the Vita-Lite, which is available as separate light bulbs or in units (see Resources section). Halogen lights, now widely available, also emit fuller spectrum lighting than "normal" room lights, but they get very warm. Those undergoing alcohol detoxification can benefit from continuous exposure, during the first three days, to full-spectrum lighting (either naturally, i.e., from the sun, or artificially) from early in the morning (about 6 to 7 A.M.) to late evening (about 9 to 10:30 P.M.). Thereafter, the "dosage" can be reduced to a few hours a day for the next few weeks. Many will want to continue exposure—especially during dark winter months.

Exercise

An exercise program should begin at the very start of alcohol detoxification and continue from that point on. Even on the first day, do about ten minutes of stretching of your neck, arms, back, and legs followed by a slow walk for about thirty minutes to one hour. Do this with your buddy. Do not overexert yourself. Take the stroll during daylight, preferably very early in the morning, to get the full healing effect of the light. During this first week, don't bother about how fast you can get your heart rate up to is or how much distance you have covered. The idea is just to get into it without putting any additional pressure on yourself. In fact, the walk is to get the pressure *off*.

Following the walk, you may want to do some more stretching exercises.

Another thing. Try to walk where the air is pure. Many alcoholics are particularly sensitive not only to foods and food additives, but to impure air as well.

Relaxation and Stress Reduction

Relaxation and stress reduction are crucial in helping to break the vicious cycle of alcohol addiction. And central to all forms of stress reduction is knowing how to breathe correctly. (Review Chapter 9, Part II.) You also need to ensure that the air you breathe is as pure as possible. This is particularly important for alcoholics, who are often highly sensitive to impure air (often without knowing it). See Chapter 7, Part II and the Resources section of this book to determine how you can best improve the quality of the air you breathe. I cannot overemphasize the importance of this.

If you have problems breathing because of sensitivities or allergies, relaxation is going to be difficult. But here are a number of things you can do about this stressful problem. Of course, cleaning up the air is by far the most important thing. The use of Nasalcrom, which is the nasal inhaler containing the antiallergy substance cromolyn sodium, is frequently helpful. This is a prescription drug and is used by taking two whiffs in each nostril four times a day for about two weeks, then twice a day for another week, and finally using a maintenance dose of two whiffs in each nostril before retiring. Quite often, people don't sleep well because they have problems breathing at night. This will help.

Now, try some of the breathing exercises described in Chapter 9 of Part II. They were designed for relaxation and stress management. Therapeutic massage and hot baths and showers are also helpful. These techniques soften up rigid muscles.

Support Groups

Your physician and your buddy or buddies will be invaluable as you go through alcohol detoxification. Many find support groups very helpful. There are several of these now, the most famous being Alcoholics Anonymous, or AA. The philosophical basis of AA, as well as all of the Anonymous support groups, is the so-called Twelve Steps. *New York Times* reporter Nan Robertson, who belongs to AA, summarized the Twelve Steps as follows: "We admit we are licked and cannot get well on our own. We get honest with ourselves. We talk it out with somebody else. We try to make amends to people we have harmed. We pray to whatever greater Power we think there is. We try to give of ourselves for our own sake and without stint to other alcoholics, with no thought of reward." Many are helped by AA. Some are able to make it without AA, relying on the support system of friends, family, and a caring physician. There are also support groups that do not have the "greater Power" or religious aspects associated with them. The various support groups are listed in the Resources section.

POSTDETOXIFICATION (WEEKS TWO TO FIVE AND BEYOND)

Now that the alcohol is out of your body, how do you keep it out of your mind? There are four general conditions that make recovering alcoholics vulnerable to drinking urges: *hunger, anxiety and irritability, tiredness,* and *depression.* It is important to understand this and know how to handle each of these situations as they arise. It is equally important to understand how to identify these conditions, that is, to know what's going on with your body, mind, and emotions. It is not uncommon to get the body's messages mixed up and feel hungry, for example, when you are actually tired. The result is that you wind up with a craving for food that can turn into a craving for alcohol when what you should be doing is getting some rest. The following program will help you help your body satisfy its true needs.

Pharmaceuticals

If, as you enter your postdetoxification period, you begin experiencing difficult-to-resist cravings for alcohol, discuss with your physician (whom you should still be seeing at least weekly) the use of the serotonin uptake inhibitor *fluoxetine* (Prozac). This drug is approved by the FDA for the treatment of depression. A physician, however, can use any FDA-approved drug for any indication he or she believes appropriate. Of course, it is essential that the physician explain to the patient what is being prescribed, what the possible side effects of the drug are, and so on. Prozac, clinical experience demonstrates, may be effective in weakening alcohol craving, and if it works, it does so very quickly. This contrasts with its antidepressive effect, which typically takes a few weeks to kick in. Prozac has also been effective in the treatment of other types of compulsive behavior.

I suggest starting with one tablet (20 milligrams) in the morning for two days. A few get "wired" at this dose, while it makes some others feel tired. If you tolerate Prozac well, without any significant side effects, increase the dose to one in the morning and one at lunchtime. If the drug dampens or abolishes your craving for alcohol, I recommend continuing it through the most vulnerable part of your postdetoxification period, which is the next four to six weeks. At that time, you should discuss its possible continued use with your physician. If you do experience the side effects mentioned above with the one tablet in the morning, continue it for another few days to see if there is any reduction of the side effects. Some who develop tiredness from the drug find they can handle it better if they take one to two tablets in the evening. It helps them sleep better and still reduces alcohol cravings. Those who continue to feel "wired" from the drug, however, should stop taking it. Likewise, those who do not experience significantly decreased alcohol craving, after taking the drug for two weeks, should discontinue it.

Some may find that Prozac works great, but they have problems sleeping. For those on Prozac who have trouble sleeping, I recommend a small dose of *amitryptiline* (Elavil) or *doxepin* (Sinequan) just before retiring. A 10–25 milligram dose is usually sufficient. Although both of these drugs are also classified as antidepressants, they do not have significant antidepressant activity at these low doses. They will, however, help you sleep and can safely be taken with Prozac. None of these three drugs is addictive or subject to dependency or tolerance. However, they should never be discontinued abruptly.

Disulfiram (Antabuse) has been used for many years in the treatment of alcoholism, with mixed results. By itself, it has no effect in reducing alcohol craving. It works by making the person violently sick if he or she drinks alcohol. This is called aversion therapy—a kind of negative feedback. There are a lot of drawbacks to Antabuse. It causes acetaldehyde to accumulate in the liver and then to spill over into the blood, where it reaches all parts of the body. Acetaldehyde, as previously noted, is a very toxic substance. Antabuse can cause liver damage and can lower blood pressure. It should not be used by those with serious liver disease, a history of stroke or heart attack, those with difficult-to-control diabetes, and those with heart disease.

Note that Antabuse stays in the system from three to ten days, and sometimes even longer. So anyone who has taken Antabuse and stopped will still get sick during this time period if he or she drinks *any* alcoholic beverage. Antabuse should only be used as a temporary solution. If, after trying everything else suggested here, you still need help to keep from drinking, then taking 500 milligrams of Antabuse daily for one week, followed by 250 milligrams daily for a few more weeks, could be helpful.

Gas and abdominal pain, distension, and diarrhea are symptoms many alcoholics experience due to increased food sensitivities. Eliminating such foods as wheat, corn, and milk products from the diet is one approach to deal with this. If these symptoms still persist, then the following maneuvers can be tried.

Take two to four capsules of *activated charcoal*, as necessary, for the abdominal gas and gas pains. Charcoal capsules can be obtained in a pharmacy or health-food store, and although they color the stool black, they have no significant adverse side effects. A few tablets of pancreatic enzymes with each meal may also be helpful. These, too, can be purchased in a pharmacy or health-food store. Fermented milk products, such as yogurt, taken daily can help restore a normal intestinal flora and possibly help in the healing process of the "leaky-gut" syndrome common in alcoholism. Fermented milk products contain lactic acid, which causes their sour taste. Lactic acid has healing properties for dry skin and may have similar healing power in the intestine.

Oral *cromolyn sodium* has been found in several studies to significantly help with food allergies or sensitivities. The problem is that it is not approved in the U.S. for that indication. However, powdered cromolyn sodium is available in the U.S. as a capsule, called Gastrocrom, for use in the treatment of the rare disorder mastocytosis. To use it orally, dissolve the contents of one to two capsules in ½ cup of warm water and drink this one-half hour before meals. It doesn't have any significant side effects. Of course, all of this needs to be done with the blessing of your physician. This is a prescription drug.

Vitamins and Minerals

See the discussion in the Detoxification section. The formula is the same.

Amino Acids

See the discussion in the Detoxification section.

Food and Fluids

See the discussion in the Detoxification section.

Herbs

See the discussion in the Detoxification section. Use of valerian can continue to be quite helpful during the postdetoxification period. Milk thistle (*Silybum marianum*) has been shown to protect against alcohol-induced free-radical damage to the liver. The active substance in this herb, silybin, is a bioflavonoid. Silybin itself is not available, but milk-thistle extracts can be found in many health-food stores. (Also see Resources section.) This herb may also help protect against liver damage in those taking Antabuse.

Light

See the discussion in the Detoxification section. Full-spectrum lighting can continue to be very helpful in the postdetoxification period. I recommend two hours of exposure in the early morning each day.

Exercise

See the discussion in the Detoxification section. Walk at least an hour a day. Try to follow this schedule:

WEEK ONE: Try to walk one mile in one hour daily.

WEEK TWO: Try to walk one and a half miles in one hour daily.

WEEK THREE: Try to walk two miles in one hour daily.

WEEK FOUR: Try to walk two and a half miles in one hour daily.

WEEK FIVE: Try to walk three miles in one hour every day.

Subsequent weeks: Try to build up your walking speed to three and a half to four miles in one hour daily, if possible. Walk at least three days every week. Better yet—five days; and best—every day. Make sure to discuss this exercise program with your physician before starting it.

Relaxation and Stress Reduction

See the discussion in the Detoxification section.

Support Groups

See the discussion in the Detoxification section. Continuous participation in support groups such as AA is essential to the success of your program.

Sleep

Sleep is the great restorer. It may seem a waste of time to some, but if we don't have a good night's sleep, we will waste even more time. Establish a pattern of getting up and going to sleep at the *same time* every day. Do not drink any caffeinated beverage after dinner. (Better yet, avoid caffeinated beverages altogether.) *Try not to nap during the day.* Napping often disrupts body rhythms and healthy sleeping patterns.

Sleep aids include a drink of low-fat milk before going to bed. Exercise (for example, your daily walk) will also enable you to sleep better. Make sure the temperature in your bedroom is in a comfortable range. Most people sleep best at about 60–65° F.

The use of comfortable ear plugs (for example, Flents ear stopples) and insulated drapes may help a lot if you are bothered by noise. There are, in addition, several devices available that synthesize pleasing natural sounds that help mask unwanted sounds. These are available in electronic stores, some department stores, and some specialty shops. Some find relaxation tapes to be excellent sleep aids. Others are helped by eye shades. Air purifiers do more than anything else to help many get a good night's sleep. (See Chapter 7, Part II, and Resources section.)

Also see (Part II): Taurine, pantethine, lithium, ginseng, piracetam, cysteine/methionine, branched-chain amino acids.

2 *Nicotine/Smoking*

THE HUMAN SIDE: THE CASE OF BENJAMIN

Benjamin had survived it all. He'd been a successful writer in his twenties and early thirties. Then a number of chronic problems set him on a path to addiction. In the past thirty years he has variously been addicted to alcohol, cocaine, heroin, and nicotine. He managed, over the years, to get off the alcohol, cocaine, and heroin—but never the nicotine.

I didn't meet him until he was in his early sixties. He came to me as a patient. When I asked him what was troubling him, he said he had "a fatal illness." Then he paused. Naturally, I was alarmed and asked him which illness he was talking about.

"Cigarettes," he responded.

"You mean you have lung cancer?"

"Not yet," Ben said.

We both laughed, then the conversation turned more serious. It turned out Ben had "tried everything" to quit smoking. He couldn't understand how he could let "this little thing" beat him when he had managed, largely on his own, to escape the grip of heroin, alcohol, and cocaine. He had gone a long way to rebuild his life and his health. His continued dependence on nicotine hung over him like a literal harbinger of doom and a relentless reminder of past mistakes.

He'd been actively fighting his addiction to nicotine for almost ten years, ever since he'd finally freed himself of alcohol.

"I've made a little progress," he said dryly. "I'm down to two packs a day."

It turned out that most of the techniques Ben had tried in his effort to outwit nicotine were of the gimmicky nature: hypnosis, special filters, aversion "therapy," etc. A couple of times he'd exiled himself for protracted periods without a supply of cigarettes—once, on a long hunting trip in the mountains; another time, on a small boat (with two nonsmokers). Then he spent almost a month at sea.

"I was ready to swim the eight hundred miles to shore," he recalls. "The first thing I did when I got back to civilization was buy half a dozen cartons of smokes."

Cold turkey clearly wasn't the answer.

I told Ben I thought I could help him. I had him put in writing his intention to quit smoking and to specify the date on which he would quit. I suggested he pick a date when things would be a bit more relaxed than usual.

He was gung-ho to quit "right now" and get on my program, but I told him that would be a mistake.

"Careful preparation is half the battle," I explained. "People are always quitting on impulse and then, just as often, failing to make it stick."

Part of the preparation included keeping a careful daily diary of cigarette consumption—time of day each cigarette is smoked, feelings and events that precede each cigarette, etc. This helps identify the things that trigger nicotine craving and can be very useful during withdrawal.

You'll learn more about the specifics shortly. Ben used the full nicotine Purification Prescription outlined in this chapter and it worked beautifully for him.

Even before Ben's quit date, I got him started on a mild exercise and relaxation program. I taught him to identify his nicotine triggers and got him to make some important dietary and nutritional changes.

Once he quit, Ben used both nicotine gum and clonidine for a while, the latter a drug that may have remarkable effectiveness in suppressing nicotine-withdrawal symptoms. He also got a special formulation of vitamins, minerals, and amino acids.

Interestingly, Ben felt he benefited most from the breathing exercises I taught him and from the herbs that are part of the prescription.

He said that a freeze-dried preparation of fresh oat plants (not the oats themselves) seemed to be particularly helpful in enabling him to *stay off* cigarettes, not only through the five-week purification period, but later as well. It's been more than a year since Ben successfully quit smoking, and he still gives himself an occasional "booster" course of oats. He says he probably doesn't need them any longer, but he wants "to be safe." (Review the Herbs section of Part II to refamiliarize yourself with some of the remarkable effects that have been reported in scientific studies of oat-plant extracts.)

Last time I heard from Ben, he was planning another sailing trip, again with nonsmoking companions and no cigarettes—and, this time, with no worry about needing any.

THE NATURE OF THE ADDICTION

Perhaps the single most important health message of the 1980s was the report of the surgeon general on nicotine addiction released on May 3, 1988. The report made official what many had already suspected for some time—that nicotine is one of the most addictive substances known to man. In no uncertain terms, the report stated that "the pharmacologic and behavioral processes that determine tobacco addiction are similar to those that determine addiction to drugs such as heroin and cocaine." Many of you may be shocked by the comparison of cigarette smoking with the use of heroin and cocaine, but as a matter of fact, there *are* many similarities. For many years smoking was—and in some circles, still is—considered to be a nonaddictive "habit." This is wishful thinking. Those addicted to nicotine require a comprehensive treatment program, often including the use of certain pharmaceutical agents, stress-reduction techniques, nutritional counseling, exercise, and the use of nutritional supplements and herbs, among other things, in order to break their addiction.

The major forms of nicotine addiction are cigarette smoking and the use of smokeless tobacco. Smokeless tobacco includes snuff, loose-leaf or pouch tobacco, and compressed tobacco, and addiction to these substances results from nicotine absorption through the mucosa (lining) of the mouth. Most of this discussion deals with cigarette smoking, but it can be used by those trying to get off smokeless tobacco as well.

YOU ARE ADDICTED WHEN . . .

You are addicted to nicotine when your body and mind crave it and you become anxious, irritable, or ill when you stop using it for any period of time. Many are addicted without actually knowing it or recognizing it. Those who are addicted typically smoke their first cigarette of the day within thirty minutes after waking; they find that first cigarette to be the most satisfying one of the day, smoke more during the morning than during the rest of the day, and always inhale the cigarette smoke. They usually smoke at least one pack and, sometimes, up to three or four packs a day.

Addiction to nicotine goes something like this. You start smoking cigarettes out of curiosity; wanting to appear more confident, sophisticated, and mature; because of peer pressure; because you want to keep your weight down (especially true for young women); etc. You soon learn to inhale and discover that smoking makes you feel good, more secure.

Specifically, nicotine is a psychomotor stimulant and can make you feel euphoric, more alert, more relaxed, particularly in stressful situations, and you may sense that your memory is better. As you continue to smoke, you will need to smoke ever-increasing amounts to produce the same stimulant, euphoric, relaxant, memory-enhancing effects. This phenomenon is called *tolerance.* Any effort to significantly reduce or stop smoking leads to symptoms of what is called the *nicotine-withdrawal syndrome.* These symptoms include difficulty concentrating, irritability, restlessness, anxiety, headache, drowsiness, lightheadedness, diarrhea and, of course, craving for cigarettes. One way of "treating" this syndrome is by smoking cigarettes.

Addiction to nicotine is sustained by both the "pleasurable" effects of the drug and by the distress that results whenever the drug is withdrawn. Nicotine is a very powerful positive reinforcer, ranking right up there with cocaine and the opiates. It is also a potent negative reinforcer in that even though it doesn't produce a withdrawal syndrome as dramatic as that of, say, alcohol, it nonetheless produces withdrawal symptoms that are remarkably tenacious.

NICOTINE'S EFFECTS IN THE NERVOUS SYSTEM

Nicotine affects both the peripheral and central nervous system. The central nervous system includes the brain and spinal cord. The peripheral nervous system includes the nerves coming out of and going into the spinal cord, those involved in muscle contraction, regulation of the heartbeat, and sensation, among other things. The increase in heart rate and elevation of blood pressure that occur with smoking are related to nicotine's activation of the sympathetic nervous system, a branch of the peripheral nervous system.

The psychoactive effects of nicotine include arousal, particularly with the first few cigarettes of the day; relaxation, particularly in stressful situations; help with concentration; euphoria; reduction of anger; and an antidepressant effect. It appears that these effects are a consequence of nicotine's activation of several of the brain's neurotransmitters and neuropeptides. These substances are chemicals that carry messages from one part of the brain to another. Nicotine leads to the release of the brain neurotransmitters dopamine, acetylcholine, norepinephrine, and serotonin, and the brain neuropeptides vasopressin, growth hormone, and ACTH.

The major effect of nicotine in the brain may be to increase the activity of dopamine in certain areas of the brain where this neurotransmitter is thought to mediate pleasurable sensations. Other addictive drugs, such as cocaine, amphetamines, and opiates, are also believed to have as the major mechanism of their action increased dopamine activity in these same regions.

QUITTING

PREPARATION FOR A QUITTING DATE

It is *not* a good idea to quit smoking the same day that you first have the impulse to do so. Quitting smoking is like planning for a long trip. There are many preparations you have to make before you begin this journey. Give yourself about a week or so to think about your decision and plan out a strategy. Read this chapter carefully and decide which of the options discussed are likely to work best for you. If you find any of the pharmaceuticals described of interest, discuss them with your physician, and of course, you must be under his or her care if you elect to use them. In fact, even if you don't use pharmaceuticals, it is a good idea to discuss your plan to quit with your physician.

As you begin to plan your strategy, do the following:

List the reasons you first started smoking. Typical reasons are: to look more sophisticated; because all my friends smoked; because my girlfriend or boyfriend said that I looked sexier when I smoked; because I wanted to keep my weight down; because it made me look more like a "real man"; etc.

Next, list the reasons why you presently smoke. Typical responses include: it's relaxing; it makes me feel more alert and energetic; it gives me a "lift"; it "mellows" me out; it helps me concentrate, it puts me at ease socially; etc. Put these lists on separate index cards (3 × 5) and always carry them around with you.

On another index card, list the reasons why you want to quit. Responses may include: because smoking is causing a tightness in my chest, cough, and shortness of breath; because I want to stop polluting my lungs as well as those of people I care a lot about; because I don't want to wind up with lung cancer, emphysema, or heart disease; because smoking is causing my skin to wrinkle, etc.

After you have done all of this, set the date on which you plan to quit. Be very realistic. Plan to do this during a relatively stress-free period of your life.

Type or write the following contract on another index card:

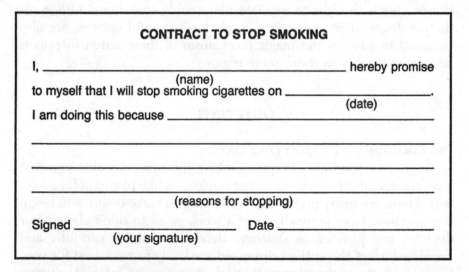

CONTRACT TO STOP SMOKING

I, _____ hereby promise
(name)
to myself that I will stop smoking cigarettes on _____.
(date)
I am doing this because _____

_____

_____
(reasons for stopping)
Signed _____ Date _____
(your signature)

Now that you have settled on a quit date, begin keeping a diary of your smoking. Every time you light up, jot down the date, time, and place in your diary. It is especially important to try to identify any trigger situations that caused you to light up. For example, when talking on the phone, after finishing a meal, when drinking a cup of coffee, after getting out of bed in the morning, after leaving a plane where smoking was not permitted, etc. Mark down all of these trigger situations in your diary. The more conscious you become of these trigger situations, the better the odds for your success in quitting.

Even *before* your quitting date, you should ask yourself, as you light up a cigarette in response to a trigger situation, Do I absolutely need to smoke this cigarette? You may find yourself answering no to this question. You are already beginning to cut down your consumption of cigarettes.

QUITTING AND THE NICOTINE-WITHDRAWAL SYNDROME

Detoxification is the process of ridding the body of contaminants, in this case nicotine, as well as other noxious substances found in cigarette smoke. Abstinence from nicotine in those who have been moderate to heavy cigarette smokers produces the nicotine-withdrawal syndrome. Symptoms of the syndrome include irritability, anxiety, difficulty concentrating, restlessness, light-headedness, headache, muscular aches, drowsiness, insomnia, nausea, diarrhea, and craving for cigarettes. The number and intensity of these symptoms vary greatly among individuals. Those who have been heavy smokers—more than one pack a day for some time—are more likely to experience the most intense withdrawal symptoms, while light smokers—less than one half pack per day—usually experience fewer and less intense symptoms.

Heavy smokers may begin experiencing withdrawal symptoms from thirty minutes to two hours after smoking their last cigarette. Generally, the symptoms are most severe *two to four days after the last cigarette* and then ease up during the following week. A *second* but less intense peak episode of symptoms occurs about *ten days after quitting* and then, from that point on, withdrawal symptoms steadily subside.

It is important for those who are trying to quit to know that *none* of the physical withdrawal symptoms are life-threatening and that most are temporary, lasting no more than one to two weeks. Cigarette cravings last no longer than *three to five minutes,* and their intensity diminishes considerably after abstaining from cigarettes for seven to ten days. Besides craving cigarettes, difficulty concentrating and irritability are the most common complaints during the withdrawal period.

Relaxation and stress-reduction techniques, exercise, a healthy diet and drinking plenty of fluids, nutritional supplements, amino acids, herbs, and pharmaceuticals when appropriate, are critical strategic components of the nicotine Purification Prescription.

Pharmaceuticals

I believe that most smokers can successfully quit *without* the use of pharmacologic agents. However, there are a few pharmaceuticals that have been found to be quite helpful in the treatment of the nicotine-withdrawal syndrome and to decrease cigarette cravings. You should discuss the following agents with your physician, and if he or she believes that one of these may be helpful in your case, then you need to be under your doctor's supervision while using the agent.

NICOTINE GUM

Nicotine polacrilex, also known as Nicorette, is gum containing 2 milligrams of nicotine per piece bound to an ion-exchange resin in a sugarless gum base. When the gum is chewed correctly (see below), nicotine is released and is absorbed through the mucosa of the mouth, where it enters the bloodstream and then travels to the brain. Nicorette gum, *if used properly*, helps ease symptoms of nicotine withdrawal, especially restlessness, irritability, inability to concentrate and, to some degree, cigarette craving.

At first blush, it may appear odd to use nicotine to break a nicotine addiction, and in fact, if the gum succeeds, you stand a good chance of getting hooked on it and will eventually have to wean yourself from it. This is truly a case of fighting fire with fire—but with one major advantage. The Nicorette "fire" is very clean—all that comes out of it is pure nicotine. Nothing is inhaled, and no damage is done to the lungs. In short, Nicorette gum is a much healthier drug delivery system for nicotine than is a cigarette.

Nicorette gum does not, however, completely get rid of cigarette craving. There are a couple of reasons for this. All the satisfying effects that a cigarette smoker obtains occur when the blood level of nicotine is 20 to 30 nanograms per milliliter or higher. The Nicorette gum available in the U.S. produces a blood nicotine level of only about 12 nanograms per milliliter, much lower than the heavy smoker gets from cigarettes. In Europe and Canada, a gum containing *twice as much* nicotine per piece is available, producing blood nicotine levels of about 23 nanograms. Some recent studies indicate that this higher-dose gum is more effective in sustaining abstinence. *Heavy* smokers may therefore want to consider *doubling* their dose of the Nicorette gum available in the U.S.—but should only do this with the consent and supervision of their physicians. The gum available in Europe and Canada contains 4 milligrams of nicotine per piece; the gum available in the U.S. contains 2 milligrams per piece.

A problem with the gum is that while inhaling a cigarette gets nicotine into your blood and brain almost immediately, chewing the gum does this more slowly. So, for the gum to be effective, cigarette craving needs to be *anticipated;* you need to make sure that nicotine from the gum is already in the brain *before* any urge to smoke arises. Two other nicotine delivery systems are currently being developed to deal with this problem. One is a transdermal nicotine patch and the other is a nasal nicotine solution. The nasal nicotine solution most closely mimics the nicotine effect obtained from a cigarette.

Those who want to try nicotine gum should discuss the proper use of the gum and its side effects with their physician. If used properly, the gum can be quite helpful. *Most* people are *not* using it properly. You should have your physician watch you the first time you use the gum—to make sure that you are doing it right. The gum is *not* to be used like ordinary chewing gum. The reason for this is that you want the nicotine to be absorbed into your body through the lining of your mouth. If you chew it like ordinary gum, you will swallow most of the nicotine and much less will get into your blood and brain.

Many people find that chewing ten to fifteen pieces per day of the 2-milligram Nicorette gum helps diminish nicotine withdrawal symptoms and cigarette craving. No more than thirty pieces of the 2-milligram gum per day are advised. The gum is started *immediately* after you quit smoking, and a piece is chewed for *twenty to thirty minutes* whenever you feel an urge to smoke or, better yet, whenever you think an urge to smoke will soon occur. Since it takes a few minutes for the gum to get the nicotine into your brain, it's best to anticipate the urge to smoke, as noted above. Check with the diary that you kept before your quit date. This will help you determine when to anticipate an urge. Alternatively, for the first two to three weeks, you can chew one piece *every hour*.

It is extremely important to chew the gum *gently* and *very slowly* until you taste it *or* feel a tingling in your mouth (usually about fifteen chews). Then stop chewing and let the gum sit between your teeth and cheek, where the nicotine is absorbed through the mucosal lining. When the taste or tingling is almost gone—usually, about one minute—this means that all of the nicotine from the exposed surface of the gum has been absorbed and you should start chewing the gum again *gently* and *very slowly* until you taste it or feel a tingling in your mouth. This time you will only need one or two chews. Again, stop chewing and let the gum sit between your teeth and cheek until the taste or tingling is almost gone. Repeat these processes for a total of about thirty minutes. *Remember. Always chew gently and very slowly. Don't chew the gum if you experience taste or tingling from it.*

Side effects of nicotine gum can include hiccups, nausea, tired jaws, indigestion, and a sore mouth or throat. These adverse effects are usually due to chewing the gum too fast and are usually resolved when the gum is chewed gently and very slowly. You should never chew nicotine gum and smoke concurrently.

Follow your physician's advice on how long to continue use of the gum.

CLONIDINE

Clonidine, also known as Catapress, a blood pressure–lowering agent, has been shown to reduce nicotine-withdrawal symptoms, including cigarette craving. Transdermal (absorbed through the skin) clonidine containing .1 milligrams of clonidine per skin patch is being used with some success in helping some people stop smoking. Discuss this with your physician, who is most likely aware of its use in this context. Although the FDA has not yet approved clonidine for this indication, your physician can prescribe it for this purpose if he or she believes it to be appropriate.

The transdermal clonidine patch (called Catapres-TTS No. 1) is painlessly placed on the skin of the chest or abdomen the day you stop smoking. It is left there twenty-four hours a day for seven days and then replaced each week, for a total of four weeks. You need to be monitored by your physician during this time to make sure that your blood pressure does not get too low (this is usually not a problem). Other potential adverse effects include dry mouth and mild drowsiness. For most, Catapres-TTS No. 1 is well tolerated and clonidine is *not* an addicting drug.

FLUOXETINE (WITH A NOTE ON DOXEPIN)

Fluoxetine (Prozac) is a drug used to treat depression. It is also effective in the treatment of some compulsive behaviors. Craving for cigarettes (or alcohol) leads to compulsive self-administration of these substances. Fluoxetine appears to aid in the reduction and suppression of cigarette as well as alcohol craving in some. As of this writing, the FDA has not approved this substance for these latter indications. A physician, however, can use this FDA-approved drug (approved for the treatment of depression) for these indications if he or she believe it to be appropriate. Of course, it is essential that the physician explain to the patient what is being prescribed and why; what the possible adverse effects are; and so on.

If fluoxetine is going to be used as an aid in your effort to quit smoking, it should be started about *two to three weeks before* your quit date, since it takes a few weeks to become effective in the body. I suggest starting with one tablet (20 milligrams) in the morning for two days. A few get "wired" at this dose, while it makes some others feel tired. Most people tolerate it well. If you have no difficulty with it, increase the dose to one in the morning and one at lunchtime. You may note that fluoxetine already begins to dampen your cigarette craving during the first week of use.

If you do experience the side effects mentioned above with the one tablet in the morning, continue it for another few days to see if there is any reduction of the side effects. This is frequently the case. Some who develop tiredness from the drug may find that they can handle it better if they take one to two tablets in the evening. It helps them sleep better and may still reduce cigarette cravings. Those who continue to feel "wired" from the drug, however, should stop taking it. Some may find that it works great but that they have problems sleeping. For these people, a small dose (10–25 milligrams) of doxepin (Sinequan), just before bedtime can be very helpful. Further, doxepin *itself* has been found to reduce and suppress symptoms of nicotine withdrawal. The combination of fluoxetine during the day and doxepin before retiring could be enormously helpful in your smoking-cessation program.

Fluoxetine and doxepin—if the latter agent is used—should be taken for five weeks to four months after your quit date. During this period, you will be monitored by your physician, who will determine how long you should take these agents.

Foods and Fluids

It will not come as news to you that many, when they stop smoking, begin putting on a few pounds. In fact, this deters quite a few people, in particular women, from quitting. Smokers *do* weigh, on the average, six to ten pounds less than nonsmokers, and when a smoker quits, he or she usually gains some weight during the first year. The weight gain, however, is typically only about three to five pounds, rarely more.

The reasons why smoking causes weight loss are complex and still not fully understood. Smoking is associated both with increased metabolism—that is, energy expenditure—and reduced consumption of food, especially sweets. Hunger is a trigger for many smokers to light up, and smoking a cigarette often suppresses the desire to eat. These effects of smoking appear to be mediated through nicotine. Establishing a good diet and an exercise program will prevent weight gain after the cessation of smoking as well as reduce or suppress cigarette craving.

Hunger is a powerful smoking trigger, so you should try to keep yourself feeling full, *particularly during the first few weeks after you quit smoking*. Eating a healthy breakfast and drinking from 6 to 8 glasses of water a day will go a long way in helping you accomplish this goal. Coffee, caffeinated beverages, and alcoholic beverages are all *strong* smoking triggers. These should definitely be avoided, especially during the first few weeks after you quit. Many who stop smoking begin having cravings for sweets, such as candy, chocolates, ice cream, cake, etc. Sugar and all foods with much sugar in them should be avoided when possible, especially during the crucial first few weeks. Remember, *craving begets craving*.

One good way to keep feeling full *without* gaining weight is to increase your fiber and complex-carbohydrate intake (for tips on how to do this, review Chapter 7 of Part II).

Eat *three* meals a day: breakfast, lunch, and dinner. If you feel yourself getting hungry between meals, drink a glass or two of water or snack on carrot sticks, celery sticks, or other vegetables or fruit. Whole-grain breads or rolls (without butter or margarine) can also be filling and are not calorically dense.

Try to include in your diet such items as garlic, onions, horseradish, chili pepper, ginger, seaweed, tofu, miso, tempeh, and yogurt. For many, these spicy, savory foods significantly decrease cigarette cravings. I've had several patients tell me, for example, that eating *raw* onions helps dampen nicotine craving.

Vitamins and Minerals

Most of the damage—and there is a lot of it—caused by cigarette smoke has to do with the many noxious substances present in the smoke, substances that are generators of toxic free radicals. These substances are much more dangerous to your health than the nicotine itself. They can cause lung disease, heart disease, cancer, premature aging, wrinkling of the skin, and so on. Nicotine is the hook that allows you to be tolerant of these poisons entering your body.

Antioxidants are biological substances that protect against free-radical damage. Smokers have a great need for adequate antioxidant protection, as do those who are quitting. All of the antioxidants found in our bodies are derived from substances in our food, mainly the vitamins and minerals. Vitamin B_{12} levels are decreased in smokers because this vitamin combines with the cyanide in cigarette smoke, helping to detoxify it. Vitamin C is more rapidly eliminated in smokers, resulting in deficiencies. Vitamin E and beta carotene levels are also decreased in smokers.

The following amounts of vitamins and minerals are recommended for both smokers and those who are quitting:

Vitamin	*Recommended Daily Dose*
beta carotene	15–30 milligrams (mg)
vitamin B_1 (thiamine)	1.5–10 mg
vitamin B_2 (riboflavin)	1.7–10 mg
vitamin B_3 (niacin)	20–100 mg
pantothenic acid	10–50 mg
vitamin B_6 (pyridoxine)	2–25 mg
vitamin B_{12} (hydroxycobalamin—preferred form)	6–100 micrograms (mcg)
folic acid	400–800 mcg
biotin	100–300 mcg
vitamin C	100–1000 mg
vitamin D	200–400 mcg
vitamin E	200–400 IU
vitamin K	100–200 mcg

Minerals	*Recommended Daily Dose*
calcium	250–1,500 mg
magnesium	200–400 mg
zinc	15–30 mg
iron	10–15 mg
manganese	2–10 mg
copper	2–3 mg
selenium	50–200 mcg
chromium	100–200 mcg
iodine	50–150 mcg
molybdenum	50–200 mcg

Precancerous changes in lung secretions of smokers were actually *reversed* in those treated with 10 milligrams (10,000 micrograms) of folic acid and 500 micrograms of vitamin B_{12} (as hydroxycobalamin) daily. Smokers (and those who are quitting), who are known to have such changes, should consider this regimen after discussing it with their physicians.

Amino Acids

L-tyrosine can be helpful in reducing several smoking triggers and nicotine-withdrawal symptoms, including tiredness, feeling stressed out, irritability, difficulty concentrating, drowsiness, fatigue, and depressive symptoms. Take from 1,000 to 2,000 milligrams three times a day on an empty stomach (about a half hour before each meal). Those who are taking MAO inhibitor-type antidepressants should *not* take L-tyrosine, since the combination can result in elevated blood pressure in some individuals. Among other things, L-tyrosine is converted to dopamine in the brain. I noted earlier that nicotine appears to produce many of its psychoactive effects by increasing the activity of dopamine in certain regions of the brain.

Herbs

The common oat plant, or *Avena sativa,* has been demonstrated to reduce cigarette cravings. The effects, as noted in Part II, are quite dramatic in some individuals. This substance also has a very mild sedative effect and is well worth trying when quitting smoking. Fresh freeze-dried capsules of the plant are available in some health-food stores (or see Resources section for where these can be obtained). I recommend taking two to three 375-milligram capsules three times a day with meals. Adverse effects are unlikely, and you can take it as long as you need to. You might want to start even before your quit date—and then continue the herb for several weeks. It has been used continuously for months without adverse effects. It's important to get a freeze-dried preparation as the herb otherwise loses its potency.

Other herbs that are useful in nicotine withdrawal and/or abstinence include garlic and onions (see discussion of these earlier in this chapter), red peppers and other hot peppers, ginger, and licorice.

Licorice roots can be obtained in herbal stores and in some health-food stores. Some smokers find it useful to chew on these roots during nicotine withdrawal. Don't chew more than ten small pieces per day and don't continue to use it beyond five weeks. *Don't use licorice if you have high blood pressure, as it contains a substance that can further elevate blood pressure.* If you think you have a tendency to high blood pressure, be sure to consult your physician before using licorice. Chew only small pieces, and if any jaw pain from chewing develops, discontinue. Note that it takes a little chewing before the licorice taste becomes evident. Don't swallow the root after you have chewed it. If any abdominal discomfort or diarrhea (these side effects are rare) develop, discontinue the licorice.

Exercise

Exercise is another pivotal component of your cigarette and nicotine purification program. It is one of the best ways of defusing such smoking triggers as hunger, irritability, and tiredness, and it helps suppress the symptoms of nicotine withdrawal. Exercise itself decreases cigarette craving. If you have any significant heart and/or lung problems, check with your physician before beginning an exercise program and plan one out with him or her. You can start your program immediately. You don't have to wait until you quit smoking. In fact, the program will help you quit.

If you haven't done much exercise, you will want to start off *slowly* and build up *gradually.* Walking is about the best exercise you can do. The goal is to walk about thirty to sixty minutes at least three times a week and, ideally, every day. It is especially important to walk every day during the first few weeks after you stop smoking. Getting into a routine of breathing good air will itself reduce the urge to light up. Try to walk in an area where the air is fresh. Noxious fumes from car exhausts, cigarettes, factories, etc. are themselves smoking triggers. If possible, walk in the morning to get the full benefits of the outdoor light. There is evidence, discussed in Part II, that natural light can help curb addictive behavior.

Review the exercise chapter in Part II to plan your exercise program.

Relaxation and Stress Reduction

Relaxation and stress reduction are crucial in helping to break the vicious cycle of cigarette or nicotine addiction. These techniques will reduce the intensity of smoking triggers, nicotine-withdrawal symptoms, and cigarette craving. Central to all forms of stress reduction is knowing how to breathe correctly. (Review Chapter 9, Part II.) You also need to ensure that the air you breathe is as pure as possible.

This is particularly important to those who are quitting smoking. When you quit smoking, your airways become more sensitive to noxious substances in the air, including, ironically enough, cigarette smoke. The irritant effect can be a smoking trigger. See Chapter 7, Part II and the Resources section of this book to determine how you can best improve the quality of the air you breathe.

Breathing pure air correctly is probably the most important component of your cigarette and nicotine treatment program. Avoid breathing the cigarette smoke of others whenever you can. I cannot overemphasize the importance of this.

If you have problems breathing because of sensitivities or allergies, relaxation and stress reduction are going to be difficult. There are a number of things you can do about it. Of course, cleaning up the air you breathe (in your home and, if possible, your workplace) is by far the most important thing. The use of Nasalcrom, which is a nasal inhaler containing the antiallergy substance cromolyn sodium, is often helpful. This is a prescription drug and is used by taking two whiffs in each nostril four times a day for about two weeks, then twice a day for another week, and finally a maintenance dose of two whiffs in each nostril before retiring. Quite often, people don't sleep well because they have problems breathing at night. This will help.

Now, try some of the breathing exercises described in Chapter 9 of Part II, as well as the relaxation exercises described there. Therapeutic massage and hot baths and showers are also helpful. These activities soften up rigid muscles. Some find mud and mineral baths very useful during nicotine withdrawal.

Support Groups

Feeling lonely is another powerful smoking trigger. For many, a cigarette is an old friend, for some, their best friend. Your physician and/or a buddy or buddies are invaluable as you go through the process of quitting smoking. Some find support groups very helpful. The various support groups are listed and described in the Resources section.

Sleep

Tiredness is one of the most powerful smoking triggers. Many light up and smoke when they feel tired. This is a further reflection of scrambled, out-of-balance neurotransmitters in the brain. The best solution to tiredness is certainly *not* a cigarette but rather a good night's sleep. Establish a pattern of getting up and going to sleep at the *same time* every day. Avoid all caffeinated beverages, especially after dinner.

Sleep aids include a drink of low-fat milk before going to bed. Exercise (for example, your daily walk) and stress-reduction management (see above) will also enable you to sleep better. Make sure that the temperature in your bedroom is 60–65° F, which is the temperature at which most people sleep best.

The use of comfortable ear plugs (for example, Flents ear stopples) and insulated drapes may help a lot if you are bothered by noise. There are, in addition, several devices available that synthesize pleasing natural sounds that help mask unwanted sounds. These are available in electronic stores, some department stores, and some specialty shops. Some find relaxation tapes to be excellent sleep aids. Others are helped by eye shades. The most important blanket to sleep under is a blanket of pure air. Make sure that the air in your bedroom, in particular, is as pure as possible. Consider getting an air purifier. (See Chapter 7, Part II, and Resources section.)

3 Caffeine

THE HUMAN SIDE: THE CASE OF ESTHER

Esther was one of those people who had been drinking coffee for as long as she could remember. The thought of getting up in the morning and *not* immediately having one or two cups of freshly percolated coffee was nearly unthinkable. Esther said she "couldn't live" without her coffee—usually five or more cups a day, sometimes as many as a dozen.

But it appeared she couldn't live with it, either, at least not at all comfortably. Now in her fifties, Esther had discovered that coffee was becoming an increasingly difficult problem for her. Yes, it still gave her a lift, though it seemed to take more and stronger coffee to do that. And now it was letting her down more quickly, resulting in cyclical irritability, insomnia, and nervousness.

Lately, Esther told me, she'd also been suffering from "chest palpitations, muscle twitching," and "cloudy thinking." Her thinking was not so muddled, however, that she had failed to note the association between these symptoms and her coffee intake. She said they seemed to be worse during those periods of heaviest caffeine consumption.

After examining Esther and running some tests (checking out, in particular, her heart palpitations), I confirmed what my patient herself suspected: Excessive caffeine intake was, indeed, at the root of her difficulties. Nearly everybody knows that caffeine (even in small amounts in some susceptible individuals) can cause restlessness and the like; far fewer realize that for many, drinking even two or three cups of coffee a day can lead to serious problems, and drinking *five* or more cups daily for long periods can lead to more serious problems, including increased risk of heart problems, hypertension, and so on.

Once Esther understood all of this, she finally seemed ready to make a real effort to quit drinking coffee. There had, in fact, been a couple of times in the past when, bothered by insomnia, she had tried to quit. Her method had been to quit "cold turkey." What had driven her back to caffeine—and quickly—had been severe headaches that came on within a day of quitting. She found an effective remedy for these headaches in a couple of cups of strong coffee. That worked, whereas the typical painkillers did not.

I told Esther that these headaches are fairly common features of the caffeine-withdrawal syndrome, that they are especially prevalent among those who regularly drink five or more cups of coffee a day and then abruptly quit.

I put Esther on a program in which she weaned herself off coffee *a cup at a time*. And we managed her headaches—very effectively— with the use of feverfew, an herb that has been demonstrated, in scientific studies, to be very useful in migraine and migrainelike headaches, of the sort that characterize withdrawal from heavy caffeine use.

With the use of the amino acid L-tyrosine, Esther's energy and alertness signals are broadcasting strong and clear. Her mind and her thinking have been clarified, in the process, and Esther, two years after treatment, remains caffeine free and feeling sharper and more alert—not to mention better rested—than she has since she was a teenager. Her heart palpitations have disappeared.

THE NATURE OF THE ADDICTION

Most people find it hard to believe that caffeine is an addictive substance. If you drink coffee or other caffeinated beverages—and 80 percent of the U.S. population does so regularly—you may be thinking that it's something you can take or leave anytime you want. And for some, this may be true.

There are a great many, however, who cannot start their day

without a cup or two of coffee and who cannot get *through* the day without at least a few more cups. These people often say they "can't live" without their coffee, specifically the caffeine in their coffee, and they feel sick when they stop drinking it. Dependence on a chemical substance, in this case caffeine, and having withdrawal symptoms upon no longer using it are the hallmarks of addiction.

Caffeinated beverages are widely used throughout the world and have been for hundreds of years. Coffee and tea are the most popular beverages in Western society. Caffeine is found in those drinks, as well as in cocoa, many soft drinks, and several prescription and over-the-counter medications. Caffeine increases the analgesic (painkilling) effect of aspirin and acetaminophen, and many over-the-counter painkillers contain caffeine in combination with these analgesics.

Caffeine itself is sold in drugstores and supermarkets in preparations designed to increase wakefulness. Recently, high-dose (up to 400 mg) caffeine tablets have been heavily advertised in some body fitness and sexually oriented magazines. These ads claim that these products are stimulants, diet aids, and body energizers. Caffeine, in all its forms, is the most widely consumed drug in the developed countries, and possibly in the world.

You will find it useful to know the caffeine content of various beverages and remedies. The following table contains that information:

Caffeine Content of Some Beverages, Foods, and Remedies

Item	Caffeine
Coffee (6-ounce cup)	
Brewed	40–220 milligrams (mg) (average: 100 mg)
Instant	30–145 mg (average: 70 mg)
Decaffeinated	1–6 mg
Tea (6-ounce cup)	
Brewed	20–130 mg
Instant	30–60 mg
Cocoa (6-ounce cup)	2–25 mg
Soft Drinks (12 ounces)	
Mountain Dew	54 mg
Mello Yello	52.5 mg

Tab	46.5 mg
Coca-Cola	45 mg
Dr. Pepper	39.6 mg
Pepsi Cola	38.4 mg

Pain Relievers (1 tablet)

Cafergot	100 mg
Wigraine	100 mg
Excedrin	65 mg
Fiorinal	40 mg
Anacin	32 mg
Darvocet Compound	32 mg

Other

| No-Doz | 100 mg |
| Dristan | 30 mg |

CAFFEINE'S EFFECTS IN THE BRAIN AND BODY

Why do so many people like caffeine? The popularity of caffeine is mainly due to its effects in the brain. Caffeine is a psychoactive stimulant drug. Consumption of the substance often produces increased alertness, decreased fatigue, euphoria, increased vigilance, and elevation of mood. These positive effects are what get most people hooked on the stuff. As few as two, three, or four cups of coffee or other caffeinated beverage a day can make you caffeine-dependent, and may have adverse health effects.

We've been learning a lot recently about the way caffeine acts as a stimulant in the brain, particularly through its interactions with adenosine, a chemical that serves, among other things, as a neurotransmitter in the brain. Adenosine appears to act in the brain by binding to certain nerve cell sites called neuroreceptors and generally quieting down the activity of the brain. Caffeine, which chemically resembles adenosine in certain particulars, competes with adenosine for its neuroreceptor sites. When caffeine binds to these sites, the brain "wakes up" and the person feels more alert and in a better mood. This effect can last for several hours.

Not all the effects of caffeine are pleasant. It can produce sleeplessness, irritability, anxiety, and depression. These symptoms usually occur in those who are chronic, heavy drinkers of coffee or other caffeinated beverages—five or more cups a day for some time—but *can* occur in those who drink only two to four cups a day and even in light coffee drinkers (one or fewer cups a day) if they are very sensitive to the effects of caffeine.

The chronic consumption of more than 250 milligrams of caffeine a day (equivalent to two and a half cups of coffee) *can* lead to what is called *caffeinism* or *caffeine intoxication*. Symptoms of caffeinism include restlessness, nervousness, excitement, insomnia, flushed face, diuresis (excessive urination), heartburn, muscle twitching, rambling flow of thought and speech, heart palpitations, periods of inexhaustibility, and inability to sit still.

There are other adverse effects of chronic caffeine use. Some men who are heavy caffeine users appear to have a twofold greater risk of having heart attacks. This is most likely due to altered lipid metabolism. It has also been shown that some heavy coffee drinkers (five or more cups a day) have significantly higher cholesterol levels than those who do not drink coffee, and that when the coffee drinkers quit drinking coffee, their cholesterol levels fall significantly.

Note that when subjects were asked in one recent study to drink five cups a day of *percolated* or *boiled* coffee, their cholesterol levels rose. Cholesterol levels did *not* rise, however, in those who drank five cups daily of *filtered* coffee.

Caffeine can produce palpitations due to abnormal heart beats, fast heart rates (tachycardia) and can cause intermittent elevation of blood pressure.

Caffeine most definitely affects sleep. Those who consume a caffeinated beverage thirty to sixty minutes before bedtime typically have difficulty falling asleep. Caffeine also leads to decreased total sleep time and an increase in spontaneous awakenings during sleep. In short, if you take caffeine before bedtime, you are likely to have a poor night's sleep.

Those who are dependent on caffeine *do* experience symptoms of caffeine withdrawal when they try to quit drinking coffee and/or other caffeinated beverages. Symptoms of caffeine withdrawal can include irritability, nervousness, restlessness, lethargy, inability to work effectively, headache, yawning, nausea, runny nose, decreased energy, depression, constipation, and caffeine craving. The headache of caffeine withdrawal is typically a generalized throbbing one. It occurs eight to eighteen hours after the last intake of caffeine and peaks three to six hours after its onset.

WHO SHOULD CONSIDER QUITTING OR CUTTING DOWN THEIR INTAKE OF CAFFEINE?

For most people, having one cup of coffee in the morning and no more during the day is highly unlikely to have any harmful effects on their health. In fact, there may be some beneficial effects, such as increased alertness, which can last most of the day, since caffeine remains in the blood for many hours. However, if *any* of the following describes you, then seriously consider quitting or cutting down on your intake of caffeine:

1. If coffee or any other caffeinated beverage makes you anxious, tense, edgy, and/or depressed. A few, who are very sensitive to caffeine, may experience these symptoms with just *one* cup of a caffeinated beverage—coffee, tea, or a soft drink—a day. Some individuals may have these symptoms and not realize that they are caused by caffeine. (They can be caused by other things as well, but quitting coffee should be tried to see if the problems clear up.)

2. If you suffer from premenstrual syndrome (PMS). Caffeine can aggravate the symptoms of PMS.

3. If you suffer from anxiety, panic disorder, or hyperventilation syndrome. Caffeine can aggravate the symptoms of these problems.

4. If you are pregnant or are having difficulty becoming pregnant. There have been some links between heavy caffeine intake in pregnant women and premature birth, miscarriage, stillbirth, and birth defects. Recent studies link heavy intake of caffeinated beverages to female fertility problems.

5. If you have high blood pressure that's difficult to control even with medication (labile hypertension).

6. If you suffer from palpitations such as those caused by premature ventricular contractions of the heart.

7. If you suffer from heartburn, gastroesophageal reflux disease or gastritis, or have a history of peptic-ulcer disease.

8. If you consume 250 milligrams (mg) or more of caffeine a day. See table in this section to determine your probable caffeine intake. More than two cups of coffee a day is not recommended for anyone.

9. If you have problems sleeping.

10. If you "can't live" without your caffeine.

TREATMENT

The first thing to do is to calculate your daily caffeine intake using the table found in this chapter. The average cup of coffee contains about 100 milligrams of caffeine; the average caffeinated soft drink, about 50 milligrams. If you drink five cups of coffee a day, your caffeine intake is 500 milligrams.

I do *not* recommend abrupt withdrawal. It is best to gradually reduce your caffeine intake by about 100 milligrams or one cup of coffee a day. By doing it this way, you will find that your withdrawal symptoms will be much less intense and your chance for success much greater. If you have been drinking, let's say, ten cups of coffee a day (1,000 milligrams of caffeine), then on day one of the program you will be drinking nine cups; on day two, eight cups; on day three, seven cups; and so on. By the tenth day you are caffeine free. The coffee you do drink should be either *filtered* or *instant*. I suggest staying away from boiled or percolated coffee. Never drink coffee after 4 P.M. Decaffeinated coffee is permitted, as is tea or soda without caffeine.

You have made the decision to quit or cut down on your caffeine intake because you want to improve your physical, emotional, and mental health. There are several other things you will want to do as well, things that will also help you get off or cut down on caffeine and prevent you from getting rehooked on this chemical. Relaxation and stress-reduction techniques are central components of your program, as is exercise. Review Chapter 9, Part II.

A healthy diet, as described in Chapter 7, Part II, will also help you resist *all* addictive substances. Some who quit or cut down on caffeine develop constipation. The high-fiber diet described in Chapter 7, Part II, will prevent this.

Here are some other elements for caffeine purification.

Amino Acids

L-tyrosine can be helpful in dealing with many of the symptoms of caffeine withdrawal, including caffeine cravings. It is particularly useful in getting many people through stress situations. I recommend taking 1,000 to 2,000 milligrams three times a day on an empty stomach or about thirty minutes before each meal. Don't take L-tyrosine if you are using an MAO-inhibitor type of antidepressant. Otherwise, this amino acid is largely free of adverse side effects and interactions.

Herbs

One of the worst symptoms of caffeine withdrawal is a migraine-like headache. Not everyone gets these, but many do, and the pain can be quite intense. Feverfew is an herb that has been found to be very useful in the treatment of migraine and migrainelike headaches. Fresh freeze-dried forms of feverfew are now available in some health-food stores. If you do get a caffeine withdrawal headache, try taking two to three capsules of fresh freeze-dried feverfew. If you decide to take an aspirin or an acetaminophen-type analgesic, make sure that it is *caffeine free.*

4 Cocaine and Amphetamines

THE HUMAN SIDE: THE CASE OF MR. O

Mr. O, still in his twenties, was moving up fast in his highly competitive corporation, a corporation that was at least as competitive internally as it was in the marketplace.

"Any failure could mean the ax," Mr. O said. "There was always somebody breathing down my neck, ready to take my place." Success in this company meant "lots of money, a bigger office, a sexier secretary, lots of travel, first-class, while on the road."

At the time, Mr. O found all of this quite intoxicating, except that he could never quite believe it was all happening—or that he was up to it. He felt like a fraud most of the time, he said, and expected to be unmasked at any moment. He felt he was underqualified for his job and that he was "faking it" most of the time. "Inside I was a wreck, outside it was all a front."

Mr. O increased his alcohol intake for a while and it helped, intermittently, get him through some tense times. But the down side was that it tired him out, which put him at a disadvantage with his competitors within the corporation.

Some of those competitors were using cocaine and seemed to be doing very well. Mr. O decided to give it a try. It was an instant hit.

"It was like everything I'd always wanted to be, I suddenly *was*. Other people noticed too. I'd never been a slouch before, but now I was a real dynamo. When I made a pitch for a new policy or concept or sale, even *I* believed everything I was saying. That was a real change."

With his newfound confidence, Mr. O was soon not only the hit of the boardroom but also the bedroom. Everything was going his way.

"I tapered off a few times," he said. "I was worried about the long-term effects." The *short-term* effects of reducing his intake of cocaine, however, worried him even more.

"I hated those feelings—the same old insecurities would always come back, only worse now."

As time went on, Mr. O said he "couldn't even think straight" without cocaine. After a couple of years of use, he was freebasing cocaine at home, snorting it in his car and in public restrooms and in his office—wherever, whenever he could. Sometimes he'd binge and crash. His winning personality and good looks were rapidly being supplanted by a haggard, gaunt visage, a hair-trigger temper, boastful harangues, and deep depressions.

Only *more* cocaine seemed to work—temporarily—to lift him out of those depressions. But by now, he could barely sleep—at least, without help. He experimented with a series of sedatives to help bring him down at night—tranquilizers, sleeping pills, marijuana, alcohol, lots of alcohol.

Mr. O began calling in sick more and more often. Finally, the inevitable happened and *he* was called in and fired—by a man he'd snorted cocaine with on a number of occasions. The man said, "Some can handle it. *You* can't."

Mr. O didn't argue. He was too busy thinking about getting back home—"to do more coke. I was actually relieved I wouldn't have to work anymore."

But when his salary was cut off and his latest girlfriend, who supported him—and his addiction—for a time, had left him, Mr. O was on his own.

"I couldn't believe it. I felt as if I were entirely alone and entirely worthless. I'd thought about it a lot in that last year, but this time I really did it—or tried."

What Mr. O tried was suicide. His attempt failed and he wound up in an emergency room, where I was called in to examine him. I suggested he combine counseling with the program you will learn about in this chapter. I told him there was an excellent chance he could not only rid himself of his addiction but could also build up his self-esteem and help prevent addictive behavior in the future.

"There are healthy ways of building confidence," I added, "bio-chemical ways that are *not* addictive, ways that promote health, not dependence and further disorder."

That was more than a year ago. Mr. O has been cocaine free during that entire period. He has regained his health—and, in fact, is healthier than ever because he no longer feels like a fraud. One of the elements of the cocaine Purification Prescription has even reversed the memory problems Mr. O's addiction resulted in, a long-term problem that afflicts many who abuse this drug.

Today, Mr. O is as successful as he ever was—more so, because now his success is in a company that he truly respects and one in which he is truly respected.

THE NATURE OF THE ADDICTION

Cocaine

The heroine of the Cole Porter musical *Anything Goes* insists she gets no kick from cocaine. The fact is that lots of people have been getting more than just a kick from cocaine during the past few years. Cocaine use has become one of the major problems of our times, even though until about 1980 most of the experts did *not* consider this drug to be an addictive substance.

Cocaine is an alkaloid derived from the leaves of the coca plant, *Erythroxylon coca*. This plant is mainly found in the mountain lands of Peru and Bolivia. Cocaine extracted from these leaves is refined in Colombia. Cocaine, in the form of the coca leaf, has been used for hundreds of years by South American Indians and mestizos (mixture of Indian and Hispanic). Most of these people live or have lived in mountainous regions, where there is less available oxygen. They chew the coca leaf to combat the effects of living at high altitudes, in particular fatigue. It is also used to treat depression and counter hunger. In fact, many of these individuals, who are very poor, use the coca leaf as a substitute for food. This results in severe malnutrition.

In the late 1800s, cocaine was used in the U.S. to treat opium and alcohol addiction. This was reported in a medical paper that was read by Sigmund Freud, the father of psychoanalysis. The paper got Freud interested in the drug and he began using it himself, by injecting it under his skin, to treat episodes of depression. Freud found the results so exciting that he called cocaine a "magical" drug and began recommending its use to others, including the woman he would soon marry. Freud also recommended it for the treatment of what was then called neurasthenia (similar to what we call chronic fatigue syndrome today).

Neither Freud nor his wife became addicted to cocaine, but some of his friends and others that he recommended it to did. For this reason, he and his wife stopped using it and no longer recommended it to others for fatigue or depression. Freud also discovered that cocaine is a remarkable local anesthetic as well as a vasoconstrictor (an agent that can reduce bleeding). It is still used to this day for these purposes, especially in nasal surgery.

At the turn of the century, several over-the-counter preparations containing cocaine were sold as tonics in U.S. pharmacies and elsewhere. One of these tonics was concocted by a Georgia pharmacist in 1886 as a general stimulant and remedy for headaches. It was called Coca-Cola. Cocaine remained an ingredient of Coca-Cola until 1906, when it was replaced by another stimulant, caffeine. At the time, some religious leaders turned public and medical sentiment against cocaine, for moral reasons. An extract of the coca leaf is still used in Coca-Cola, though all the cocaine is first removed from the leaf.

Cocaine was no longer available over the counter, but it continued to remain available under the counter. It became the drug of the affluent, the famous, and the powerful, among others. It also became very expensive—the "champagne of drugs," as many called it. The form used for many years was cocaine hydrochloride (the acid form), and it was typically sniffed or snorted. There was an epidemic of cocaine use in these circles in the 1920s, especially in the U.S. and Europe. It then subsided, except in Germany, where it remained popular throughout the 1930s. Germany was the world's biggest importer of cocaine at that time. Such notables as Hermann Göring, head of the Nazi Luftwaffe, was addicted to the drug. He used it to lose eighty-five pounds.

In the early 1950s and late 1960s, the amphetamines were the most widely used psychostimulants. But word began getting out at the end of the 1960s that amphetamines were *very* dangerous. "Speed kills," became common knowledge, and use of the drug quickly declined. This created a psychostimulant vacuum, and since human nature abhors a vacuum, it quickly became filled with (once again) cocaine.

The 1970s gave birth to the largest epidemic of cocaine abuse ever—an epidemic that continues to this day. Once again society, including the scientific sector, had forgotten history. After the amphetamine epidemic, cocaine looked benign to many. It would be several years before we would finally recognize, as previous generations had done, just how vicious a drug cocaine is.

FORMS OF COCAINE

The South American peasants, as noted, get their cocaine by chewing coca leaves. They use it like chewing tobacco. The cocaine is released from the leaves when they add a little lime (obtained from seashells) to the chew. The cocaine is then absorbed into the body through the mucosal lining of the mouth. Effects are felt within about thirty minutes, peak between thirty to sixty minutes, and last from four to six hours. This is the least addictive form of cocaine.

Most people, however, use the white powder form of cocaine (cocaine hydrochloride) by sniffing or snorting it through their nose. The effects of this form of cocaine are more dramatic. There is a "rush" within ten minutes, effects peak between fifteen to forty minutes and last about one hour. Snorting is considerably more addictive than chewing.

A far more potent form of cocaine is called freebase cocaine. This form is obtained by converting the acidic form of cocaine, cocaine hydrochloride, to its basic form, which is then usually smoked. Smoking freebase cocaine is the fastest way of getting the full effects of the drug. The rush comes on within *seconds*, the effects peak in less than a minute but last only fifteen to thirty minutes. This form is highly addictive. It is also dangerous to prepare freebase cocaine, since volatile, inflammable solvents are used in the process. Many had never heard of freebase cocaine until the comedian Richard Pryor almost burned himself to death while preparing it.

Cocaine remained the champagne of drugs, that is, a drug that only the affluent could afford, until the early 1980s. At that time, a relatively inexpensive form of freebase cocaine emerged on the scene, called *crack*, so named because of the sound the rocklike substance makes as it burns. Crack has created countless new addicts, many of them very young. And with the advent of crack has come a formidable new wave of crime, much of it well organized and richly financed. Crack is far and away the most addictive form of cocaine. You can become addicted to it in a few weeks. There's no doubt that crack kills—and with far greater ferocity than the amphetamines.

The *least* used form of cocaine is intravenous cocaine. When cocaine hydrochloride is taken intravenously, the rush comes on in about one minute, the effects peak between one to two minutes and last from twenty to thirty minutes. The addictive potential of intravenous cocaine is high, although not as high as with smoked cocaine.

EFFECTS OF COCAINE AND THE ADDICTIVE PROCESS

In the beginning, casual use of *snorted* cocaine produces heightened alertness, a sense of well-being, reduced anxiety and social inhibitions, heightened energy, self-esteem, sexuality, and euphoria.

Some, particularly those who *genuinely* have high self-esteem to begin with, can continue this casual use and never get addicted. That is, they really *can* say no to cocaine without suffering adverse effects from abstaining. For others it's not so easy. The drug fills in a lot of "gaps," boosts confidence, etc., and the impulse is, of course, to keep those good feelings flowing—by taking more cocaine. And over time, it takes more and more to do the job.

Cocaine and the amphetamines, as psychomotor stimulants, appear to activate those parts of the brain involved in exploration and investigation. To put it another way, these are parts of the brain that are involved in search behavior—for basics, such as food and sex. Survival of the individual, as well as the species, obviously depends on these parts of the brain functioning in a healthy manner. Cocaine tricks the brain into believing that it has accomplished its survival missions by activating these brain centers and artificially rewarding them. This is why cocaine suppresses your appetite, and although it may initially enhance sex drive, its continued use eventually makes you lose interest in sex.

The rewarding effects of cocaine appear to be mediated primarily by the brain neurotransmitter dopamine. Cocaine use also leads to increased activity of the neurotransmitters serotonin and norepinephrine. But with continued and compulsive use of cocaine, the activity of dopamine, serotonin, and norepinephrine *decreases*. Now, instead of feeling wonderful, you start feeling rotten in spite of using more and more of the drug. Even if you do feel fleetingly good, those around you are likely to find you unbearable.

The pleasurable feelings that you had when you first started using the drug have now given way to irritability, paranoia, confusion, impulsiveness, hyperactivity, insomnia, a racing heartbeat, palpitations, tremulousness, lack of desire to eat or to drink fluids, weight loss, anger, sometimes hallucinations and, of course, a tremendous craving for cocaine. If you don't get the stuff, you are headed for a crash, which is the first phase of the *abstinence syndrome.*

THE COCAINE-ABSTINENCE SYNDROME

The cessation of cocaine use in someone who has become addicted to it produces the cocaine-abstinence syndrome, which often develops in three stages: *the crash, withdrawal symptoms,* and *extinction.*

The crash typically occurs following a cocaine binge. Symptoms of the crash include extreme exhaustion, depression, anxiety, agitation, and insomnia. Within one to four hours after the initial crash, there is a tremendous hunger for sleep. This usually leads to the use of sedatives, such as the benzodiazepines (Valium, Xanax, etc.), opiates (such as heroin), marijuana, and alcohol. Incidentally, the combination of cocaine and heroin (known as a speedball) is what killed the actor John Belushi.

During the crash phase, which typically lasts three or four days, periods of excessive sleep alternate with periods of excessive hunger, reflecting the chaos that is taking place in the brain. In the long run, however, cocaine suppresses appetite.

After the crash, comes the next stage: *withdrawal.* Withdrawal symptoms may occur in *some* right after they stop using cocaine—*without* any intervening crash. Cocaine-withdrawal symptoms include: intense fatigue, lethargy, depression, slowness in thinking, inability to experience pleasure, limited interest in life events and social activities, anxiety, suicidal thoughts, prolonged disturbed sleep, paranoia, and cocaine craving. Withdrawal symptoms increase in intensity from twelve to ninety-six hours after they begin, and the fatigue and depression can last from six to eighteen weeks before being resolved (unless treated).

The third phase of the cocaine-abstinence syndrome is the *extinction* of pleasurable memories associated with taking cocaine. Typically, most of the *bad* memories related to cocaine use are forgotten, but not the good ones. Extinction of the latter takes longer. Cocaine memories and cravings are evoked by a variety of circumstances, moods, people, places, other drugs and substances that look like cocaine, pipes, spoons, syringes, etc. Cocaine is like an old girlfriend or boyfriend. Passing by a certain street, eating a certain food, smelling a certain perfume or aftershave lotion can easily trigger fond memories of her or him. If these conditioned "cues" fail to be followed by the cocaine reward, their strength will diminish and they will eventually become "extinct." The treatment program described later in this chapter *speeds up* the extinction process.

MEDICAL COMPLICATIONS OF COCAINE

Excessive use of cocaine can lead to angina (heart pain) and heart attacks (this is what killed basketball player Len Bias), malnutrition and significant weight loss, seizures, strokes, cardiac arrhythmias, renal failure, liver failure, elevated blood pressure and heart rate, severe depression, manic-depressive illness, paranoid psychosis, memory problems (may remain years after cocaine is stopped), and birth defects and other complications in women who consume even small amounts of cocaine during pregnancy.

Perforation of the nasal septum (cartilage between the nostrils that supports the nose) is not uncommon in those who are chronic cocaine snorters. Even more common is a chronically congested and runny nose. Local ulceration can occur in those who apply cocaine to the underside of their tongue or gums, palate, inside their eyelids, vagina, penis, or anal region. Some men apply cocaine to the tip of their penis as a local anesthetic to prevent premature ejaculation.

Cocaine has been used by both men and women to decrease the pain of anal intercourse. This was not an uncommon practice among gay males, especially in the 1970s. Cocaine can cause anal ulceration, allowing all sorts of infectious organisms to pass through the anorectal wall into the body; thus the drug, used in this way, might be an overlooked cofactor in AIDS, particularly since it is also immune suppressive.

Amphetamines are known to be neurotoxic. That is, they cause destruction of nerve cells in the brain. The mechanism appears to be free-radical-induced oxidation of dopamine. The oxidized dopamine itself appears to destroy nerve cells by a free-radical mechanism. Recently, evidence has emerged that a similar process occurs with cocaine use. The neurotoxicity of cocaine could account for many of its damaging effects, particularly the long-term memory problems that are encountered in cocaine users even many years after its cessation. This finding could lead to useful new treatment approaches, some of which will be discussed in this chapter.

Amphetamines

Amphetamine use was very popular in the early 1950s and again in the late 1960s. At that time, many physicians readily prescribed amphetamines for the treatment of obesity; narcolepsy (pathological inability to stay awake); hyperactive, minimally brain damaged children; for sustaining activities such as studying or driving; and for decreasing fatigue and minor depression.

Amphetamines, like cocaine, are psychomotor stimulants. Their effects include increased alertness, physical activity, wakefulness, a sense of well-being, decreased feelings of fatigue, reduction of appetite, and enhanced performance in a wide variety of tasks. There are a few different amphetamines, including dextroamphetamine (Dexedrine), methamphetamine (Methadrine), and amphetamine sulfate (Benzedrine). Amphetamines are also street drugs, going by such names as uppers, pep pills, speed, crystal, and crank.

Amphetamine abuse in the late 1960s, particularly that of methamphetamine, demonstrated that these drugs can be extremely dangerous. Intravenous use of methamphetamine, as well as use of large oral amounts of the drug, was found to be addictive, to cause paranoid psychosis, to cause violent behavior, and to lead to the use of other addictive drugs such as intravenous heroin. "Speed Kills" became a slogan on buttons and bumper stickers in the Haight-Ashbury district of San Francisco in the late 1960s. The reference was to the high frequency of death and the violence associated with methamphetamine usage.

An important meeting took place in January 1970, at the Salk Institute in La Jolla, California. The topic was drug abuse, and the attendants included major research scientists, physicians, legal people, legislators, media people, and a few Nobel Prize winners. A major conclusion of that conference was that amphetamines should be considered dangerous and addictive and that their use should be severely restricted.

The message got out, and since that time the use of amphetamines, both by physicians and in the street, has been considerably reduced. Amphetamines are still prescribed for the treatment of narcolepsy and hyperactive, minimally brain damaged children but, even in these conditions, on a much more limited basis than before.

Amphetamines and cocaine are similar in many particulars. They both exert their action in the brain by increasing the activity of the neurotransmitters dopamine, norepinephrine, and serotonin. Their euphoric effects appear to be due to the increase in activity of dopamine in the brain's reward and pleasure centers. Heavy, chronic use of the amphetamines leads to decreased activity of these same neurotransmitters. They are both addictive, cocaine generally more so than the amphetamines, and the withdrawal symptoms are similar.

The primary difference between the amphetamines and cocaine is the duration of action. Amphetamines remain in the bloodstream much longer than cocaine. Cocaine binges, characterized by frequent readministration of the drug, usually last about twelve hours. Amphetamine binges often last more than twenty-four hours, with the user readministering the drug every several hours.

TREATMENT

Abstinence from cocaine and amphetamines produces no medically dangerous withdrawal symptoms. Therefore, detoxification of these drugs and rehabilitation can for the most part be undertaken on an *outpatient* basis. Of course, you should be monitored by a physician skilled in cocaine or amphetamine detoxification, and it is mandatory that you have medical supervision if you use any of the prescription drugs described in this section.

Inpatient detoxification is advisable if you are addicted to other drugs, such as opiates and/or alcohol as well as cocaine and/or amphetamines; if there is a question of your becoming suicidal during detoxification; if you have no support system (wife or husband, family, friends) to assist you during this time; if you feel you need to be in an inpatient setting for success; or if you have a significant medical problem. Discuss this with your physician.

Outpatient treatment includes education sessions, peer support groups, individual therapy, family therapy, and all of the therapeutic components described below. Review this section with your physician before starting.

Amino Acids

The goal of the amino-acid prescription is to nourish the brain with nutrient precursors of some of the neurotransmitters and restore normal neurotransmitter production and balance. They decrease cocaine or amphetamine craving and help with depression, fatigue, anxiety, and disturbed sleep. Begin taking amino acids on day one.

L-tyrosine is the nutrient precursor of dopamine and norepinephrine. Take 1,000 to 2,000 milligrams of L-tyrosine three times daily
on an empty stomach or from twenty to thirty minutes before each
meal. L-tyrosine usually comes in 500-milligram capsules or tablets
(capsules recommended). The only adverse effect of L-tyrosine would
be overstimulation. This is unlikely at these doses. However, if it
does occur, decrease the dose by half.

Pharmaceuticals

Pharmaceuticals relieve crash symptoms; they prevent cocaine
and amphetamine craving, and relieve long-term depression.

Amantadine, or Symmetrel, is a dopamine releaser. Amantadine
is given at 100 milligrams three times a day, starting the first day, for
a total of three weeks. The adverse side effects may be slight nausea,
confusion, and light-headedness. These symptoms are usually mild. If
they are too bothersome—unlikely—consider discontinuing the drug.
Amantadine has proven quite useful in quieting many of the symptoms of withdrawal.

If on the third or fourth day after detoxification you experience
symptoms of cocaine craving, cocaine dreams, agitation, depression,
or actual cocaine use, then I suggest you take *bromocriptine* (Par-
lodel). Some who receive this drug, especially *during* the first three
days of detoxification (*not* recommended), have symptoms of dizziness, nausea, and feel like they will pass out. These symptoms are not
nearly as severe if the drug is started *after* the first three days of
detoxification. However, if you *do* experience these symptoms, report them to your physician as soon as you can.

There are several protocols for the administration of bromocriptine. The following one is recommended: Start with 2.5 milligrams
twice a day for three days; then taper down to 1.25 milligrams three
times a day for three days; then 1.25 milligrams twice a day for three
days; then 0.625 milligram three times a day for three days; then
0.625 milligrams twice a day for three days; then 0.625 milligrams
twice a day for two days, then stop the medication.

Desipramine is started on the first day at a low dose and then
increased. It can be effective in preventing long-term depression.
Begin by taking 25 milligrams before bedtime. If you feel speedy,
anxious, jittery, or in any way odd after taking this drug, report this
to your physician, who may decide to try another antidepressant,
such as trazodone (see below). Feeling speedy and jittery are internal

stimuli that may remind you of a previous drug experience and trigger craving for cocaine or amphetamine.

If you don't have these symptoms on desipramine, I recommend continuing that dose (25 milligrams) before bedtime for four days; then increasing it to 50 milligrams before bedtime for four days; then to 75 milligrams before bedtime for four days; then 100 milligrams before bedtime. Again, if you have any of the above symptoms, report them to your physician. Desipramine is usually given from 100–200 milligrams a day and takes from two to three weeks until it works. Your physician, who is closely following you, will determine the optimal dose for you and how long you should be on this medication. Other side effects can include dry mouth, blurred vision, mild dizziness, and sedation.

If you can't tolerate desipramine, I suggest trying *trazodone*, which may have fewer side effects. Again, start with 25 milligrams before bedtime. Note any side effects and report them to your physician. If you tolerate this dose, continue the same dose (25 milligrams) for four days; then increase to 50 milligrams before bedtime for four days; then 75 milligrams before bedtime for four days; then 100 milligrams before bedtime for four days. Like desipramine, it takes about two to three weeks for trazadone to work, and the optimal dose is usually between 100 to 200 milligrams a day.

Some cocaine or amphetamine addicts have an underlying component of manic-depressive illness. For those, a trial of *lithium*—maintaining a therapeutic level and monitoring for any side effects—may be helpful. It is essential that this diagnosis be made by an experienced physician.

Vitamins and Minerals

Cocaine abuse is frequently accompanied by malnutrition in general and by deficiencies in many of the vitamins and minerals, particularly vitamins B_1, B_6, and C. I recommend the following amounts of vitamins and minerals to be taken in supplementary form daily.

Vitamins	Recommended Daily Dose
beta carotene	15–30 milligrams (mg)
vitamin B_1 (thiamine)	50–100 mg
vitamin B_2 (riboflavin)	1.7–10 mg

vitamin B_3 (niacin)	20–100 mg
pantothenic acid	10–50 mg
vitamin B_6 (pyridoxine)	10–20 mg
vitamin B_{12}	6–100 micrograms (mcg)
folic acid	200–400 mcg
biotin	100–300 mcg
vitamin C	250–1,000 mg
vitamin D	200–400 IU
vitamin E	30–400 IU
vitamin K	100–200 mcg

Minerals	*Recommended Daily Dose*
calcium	250–1,000 mg
magnesium	200–400 mg
zinc	15–30 mg
iron	10–15 mg
manganese	2–10 mg
copper	2–3 mg
selenium	50–200 mcg
chromium	100–200 mcg
iodine	50–150 mcg
molybdenum	50–200 mcg

Food and Fluids

Because cocaine abuse is frequently accompanied by malnutrition, it is essential that you begin practicing healthy dietary habits in order to heal any damage caused by the drugs. Review Chapter 7 of Part II.

Exercise

You should start in on an exercise program at the very beginning of your detoxification program. Exercise is essential to reduce the intensity of cocaine- or amphetamine-withdrawal symptoms, to reduce and suppress drug craving and to prevent relapse. Review Chapter 9 of Part II.

Relaxation and Stress Reduction

I cannot overemphasize the importance of relaxation and stress-reduction management. These techniques are vital for the reduction of external stresses and building up of self-esteem. Review Chapter 9 of Part II.

Herbs

Valerian is a mild sedative prepared from the roots of the plant *Valeriana officinalis*. It can be helpful in reducing the intensity of some of the cocaine- or amphetamine-withdrawal symptoms. Fresh freeze-dried valerian is available in 325-milligram capsules at many health-food stores (see Resources section). Alternatively, a tea can be prepared from the root of the plant. During the first three weeks of drug withdrawal, I recommend taking two capsules of fresh freeze-dried valerian three times a day or drinking 1 cup of tea prepared from the root of the plant every two to three hours while awake. It will also help you sleep better.

Support Groups

Your physician and his or her assistants, as well as family and friends, will be invaluable as you go through detoxification and rehabilitation. There are a number of support groups that can also be very helpful to you. These include Narcotics Anonymous and Cocaine Anonymous. See the Resources section for further information on other support groups.

Other

Many who have been heavy cocaine or amphetamine users complain of problems with their memory even years after they have stopped using the drugs. The drugs themselves can cause damage to nerve cells in the brain. Phosphatidylcholine is often helpful with memory problems. (See Lipids chapter, Part II.) One-gram capsules containing 90 percent phosphatidylcholine are available (see Resources section). Three capsules taken three times daily may significantly improve your memory.

I am presently involved in some research with a substance that appears to *reverse* some of the brain damage caused by drugs such as cocaine and also appears to be very helpful in the treatment of many addictions. This substance is called liposomal superoxide dismutase, or LIPSOD. I expect it to be a major component in drug detoxification programs in the future.

5 *Opioids*

THE HUMAN SIDE: THE CASE OF DR. S

Dr. S, an M.D., had recovered from surgery that successfully removed a cancer of the colon. He experienced considerable pain afterward from adhesions within the colon that resulted from the surgery itself. At first he was treated with Tylenol and codeine. When he complained that this still didn't do the painkilling job, his physician gave him a more powerful drug, called Vicodin. Both Vicodin and codeine are opioids, a family of drugs that also include such substances as morphine and heroin.

Dr. S began using up his Vicodin faster than his prescriptions specified. He was always calling for refills, complaining he was still in pain. Somewhat reluctantly, his physician granted his request for a still more potent opioid analgesic, called Percocet.

"That was more like it," Dr. S later told me. "I really started feeling great on the Percocet." Again, he was soon taking far more than he was supposed to, not so much to avoid pain now as to derive a pleasurable high from the drug.

It was while on Percocet that he began faking prescriptions and getting extra supplies of the drug in that fashion. After a while, Percocet began to fail him, and he moved "up" to Dilaudid, the most powerful of all the oral opioids. Finally, he progressed to intravenous injections of Dilaudid. Intravenous Dilaudid is actually a more potent analgesic than either heroin or morphine.

Dr. S said that after an injection, he sometimes felt a pleasure akin to sexual orgasm, followed by an intense euphoria that would persist for a few hours. Soon Dr. S was injecting himself daily. With continued use, however, even these daily injections couldn't reproduce the pleasurable effects the first few injections had created. The craving for more of the drug continued to intensify. Soon, he was injecting himself twice a day.

By now, Dr. S had some unwitting accomplices in his efforts to get the drug. Through various ruses, he persuaded some of his M.D. colleagues to write Dilaudid prescriptions for imaginary patients, then picked up the prescriptions himself, using assorted fake names. He was quite creative and tireless in these manipulations, but they took up an increasing amount of his time, and his practice began to suffer.

It was hurting anyway, because patients had begun to notice—and be wary of—his peculiar mood swings. Sometimes he was happy and energetic to the point of mania; other times, almost surly or depressed and unresponsive. There were several times when he nodded off at his desk while talking with a patient.

Some physicians, who by now suspected a drug problem, confronted him. He exploded in anger and denied everything. Meanwhile, his wife, no longer able to put up with his unpredictable behavior, left him, and his grown children and their families, after also unsuccessfully trying to get him to seek treatment, began avoiding him.

It wasn't until a colleague turned him in for issuing fraudulent prescriptions that Dr. S admitted everything. His career as battered as his health, he finally sought treatment. He had failed two efforts to get off opioids when he consulted me. Now he was addicted to methadone, which he had been given in his previous treatment program.

I put him on my opioid Purification Program, a program that often avoids the use of methadone and on which he was able to achieve successful withdrawal in a few weeks. Dr. S remains drug free eight months later and reports no craving for opioids or any other addictive drug. He has retired from medical practice but has been reunited with his wife and family.

THE NATURE OF THE ADDICTION

Opium is a plant product derived from the opium poppy (*Papaver somniferum*). In one form or another, it has been used by humans for centuries. The Chinese said the drug conferred a state of peace and tranquility and a feeling that all was well with the world. Since Mao Tse-tung, however, did *not* believe that all was well with the world, one of the first things he did when he became China's chairman was to forbid its use.

Derivatives of opium are, to this day, medicine's most powerful painkillers. Sir William Osler, the father of modern medicine, once referred to morphine, one of those derivatives, as "God's own medicine." Opioids, derivatives of opium or substances with similar properties, are called narcotic analgesics because one of their effects is to cause sedation or drowsiness. Opioids are also frequently used as cough suppressants and occasionally to control diarrhea.

Opioids are commonly abused drugs, and about 50 percent of those who do abuse them become addicted to them. Heroin, a highly potent opioid, is not used as an analgesic in medicine but is a street drug. It is mainly used intravenously, and because of the habit of sharing needles, many heroin addicts have contracted such diseases as hepatitis, malaria, and AIDS. Intravenous heroin users are one of the highest-risk groups for AIDS. Fortunately, the incidence of heroin use has not significantly increased during the past several years.

Opioid drugs include opium itself, morphine sulfate (also known as MS), heroin, hydromorphone (Dilaudid), oxycodone and acetaminophen (Percocet), oxycodone and aspirin (Percodan), hydrocodone and acetaminophen (Vicodin), codeine, levorphanol (Levo-Dromoran), methadone (Dolophine), and merperidine (Demerol). All of these substances are addictive. Nonopioid substances that produce an opiate-type addiction are propoxyphene (Darvon) and pentazocine (Talwin and others). All of the above, except heroin, are prescription drugs.

Codeine is typically prescribed in combination with acetaminophen and, occasionally, with aspirin. For example, Tylenol 3 contains 325 milligrams of acetaminophen and 30 milligrams, or ½ grain, of codeine per tablet; Tylenol 4 contains 325 milligrams of acetaminophen and 65 milligrams, or 1 grain, of codeine per tablet. An acetaminophen-and-codeine combination is available over the counter in Canada and Europe. This product contains 325 milligrams of acetaminophen and 10 milligrams of codeine per tablet. Its addictive potential is low when used as directed. There are also codeine-and-aspirin combinations, for example, Empirin combined with codeine. Cough medicines that contain opioids include Robitussin DAC (codeine), Tussi-Organidin (codeine), and Tussionex (hydrocodone).

If taken *orally*, the painkilling potency (per given weight of drug) from greatest to least is as follows: levorphanol (Levo-Dromoran), hydromorphone (Dilaudid), methadone (Dolophine), oxycodone (Percocet, Percodan), hydrocodone (Vicodin, Tussionex), and codeine. This order *also* ranks the *addictive* potential of these drugs, with codeine having the lowest addictive potential.

If taken *intravenously* or *intramuscularly*, the painkilling potency (per given weight) is, from greatest to least: hydromorphone, levorphanol, heroin, morphine, methadone, oxycodone, merperidine, and codeine. Methadone is a longer-acting drug; heroin, hydromorphone, morphine, and oxycodone are shorter-acting. Adding an antihistamine—for examine, Vistaril—to these drugs can boost their potency.

EFFECTS OF OPIOIDS AND THE ADDICTIVE PROCESS

The initial "high" that you get from an opioid consists of a feeling of euphoria and a dissolving of all bodily and mental pain. It has an antidepressant effect for many. Those who rapidly inject themselves with heroin talk about a warm flush that they experience in their skin and a sensation in the pelvic region similar in quality and intensity to sexual orgasm. These heroin-induced sensations last for about a minute at most and are followed by a milder, pleasurable feeling that can last for two hours or longer. The opioids are both psychostimulant drugs—such as cocaine and amphetamines—and sedatives. After the euphoria comes a feeling of drowsiness.

Those who like the pleasurable effects produced by the drug may continue its use. With continued use, more and more of the drug is required to get the same initial pleasurable effects. This is the phenomenon known as *tolerance*. You can become addicted to an opioid drug in *less than two weeks* if you use it daily in ever-increasing amounts. If you stop, you will then experience unpleasant withdrawal symptoms, which can be vanquished by taking still more of the drug. The avoidance of these withdrawal symptoms, coupled with pleasant opioid memories, are the cement of addiction.

When you are addicted to an opioid, some of the effects produced by it are no longer so pleasant. Constant opioid craving and compulsive administration of the drug are taxing on all systems of the body and brain. The euphoria produced by the drug is not nearly as good as the first time you took it; the drowsiness is more intense, and you may find yourself constantly nodding off; your skin is itchy; you become constipated; you feel anxious; you lose interest in sex; you feel cold, among other things. But you continue to pursue the memory of those wonderful first "highs."

Both the stimulant and the sedative actions of the opioids are mediated by the brain's neurotransmitters and neuropeptides. The stimulant action of the opioids appear to be mediated by the neurotransmitter dopamine. The opioids increase the activity of dopamine in certain regions of the brain that have to do with pleasure and reward. These are the same regions where the psychostimulants cocaine and amphetamines have their effects. Repeated heavy use of opioids seems to have the opposite long-term effect, *decreasing* dopamine activity, so that more and more opioid is needed to produce the pleasure—and the pleasure is never the same as it was initially.

The brain makes its own opioids. Neuropeptides (molecules made from amino acids) called endorphins (for endogenous morphine), enkephalins, and dynorphins are all naturally produced in our brain and modulate perceptions of pain, mood and, most likely, cravings. These substances work by binding to regions on nerve cells in the brain called receptors. They do this in a key-and-lock manner.

Opioid drugs bind to endorphin receptors. This is how they have their pain-reducing effects, and possibly their sedative and mood-altering effects as well. With continued use of the opioids, however, these receptors become less sensitive to them. That is, the cylinders of the locks become a little harder to turn by the opioid keys, and more and more of the drug is needed to "force" the locks open. This phenomenon is called *downregulation* of the endorphin receptor. A consequence of this downregulation is to throw the normal relationship between endorphins and their receptors completely out of balance. This creates a mental type of diabetes, if you will, where the opioid drugs become the insulin. Opioid addiction, among other things, is a disease of the endorphin receptor.

OPIOIDS' EFFECTS ON THE IMMUNE SYSTEM

Opioids are immunosuppressive. Those addicted to these drugs are more susceptible to infections and have lower resistance to cancer. Cellular immunity, the type that is severely abnormal in AIDS, appears particularly vulnerable. Some immune cells have receptors for the opiatelike neuropeptides that our bodies produce, similar to the receptors in the brain, as was discussed above. It is likely that chronic opioid use causes disturbances in those receptors and hence in the immune cells.

ABSTINENCE AND WITHDRAWAL

Withdrawal from the opioids is rarely life-threatening. It can, however, be quite unpleasant. Symptoms can include a flulike state, with muscle aches, runny nose, sweating, fever, nausea, vomiting, diarrhea, severe leg and back cramps, insomnia, stomach cramps, yawning, anxiety, and gooseflesh. The first symptoms begin about eight to twelve hours after the last dose. These are the flulike symptoms. The other symptoms listed above usually occur from two to three days after the last dose, slowly subside, and then disappear in seven to fourteen days. This is without any treatment. Treatment will reduce or suppress opioid-withdrawal symptoms.

Methadone, which is a longer-acting opioid, gives a similar withdrawal picture, except the time course is different. With methadone, the first symptoms begin one to two days after the last dose, peak at about the third day, and last about two to three weeks.

In all cases, opioid craving begins with the first withdrawal symptoms. The intensity of the symptoms will depend on the length of time you have been addicted, the quantities consumed, and the routes of administration. A long-time, heavy intravenous heroin user is likely to experience much more severe withdrawal symptoms, for example, than a long-time user of oral codeine. The object of treatment is to reduce or suppress these symptoms in order to get you off the drug successfully and for good.

TREATMENT

Abstinence from opioids is rarely life-threatening. Some of the symptoms may be unpleasant, but there are ways of reducing and suppressing them—described below. Detoxification can generally be achieved on an outpatient basis. If your opioid-dependence history has been brief or if your dependency has been on one of the less potent opioids (such as codeine), you have a good chance of becoming drug free by following the components of the following program *without* using pharmaceuticals. Those with a history of heavy, chronic use of opioids, particularly the more potent ones, will probably require the use of pharmaceuticals during detoxification. Review the program with your physician before starting.

Amino Acids

Amino acids are used to restore normal neurotransmitter production and balance, to decrease opioid craving, and help reduce or suppress opioid-withdrawal symptoms.

Start taking the amino acids on the first day of abstinence.

L-tyrosine is the precursor of the neurotransmitters dopamine and norepinephrine. Take 1,000 to 2,000 milligrams of L-tyrosine three times a day on an empty stomach or twenty to thirty minutes before meals. L-tyrosine comes in 500-milligram capsules and tablets. I recommend the capsules. Continue taking the amino acid for five weeks or for as long as needed.

D-phenylalanine is an amino acid that helps increase the level of some of the *natural* opioids made in the brain. It works by inhibiting their enzymatic breakdown. Maintaining high levels of the brain's own opioids will help mend the disturbed brain opioid-receptor interactions that addiction to these drugs has created. D-phenylalanine in the form of *DL-phenylalanine* is available in many health-food stores (or see Resources section). Take 1,000 milligrams of DL-phenylalanine three times a day on an empty stomach or twenty to thirty minutes before meals. You can take this amino acid at the same time as you take L-tyrosine. DL-phenylalanine comes in 375- or 500-milligram capsules or tablets. Take the capsules. If you can obtain the 500-milligram form, it is more convenient to use. Take for three weeks or as long as needed.

L-aspartic acid has been found to reduce or suppress opioid-abstinence symptoms. Take 1,000 to 2,000 milligrams four times a day on an empty stomach for two weeks. If you are withdrawing from methadone, take for three weeks.

Vitamin and Minerals

Vitamin	Recommended Daily Dose
beta carotene	15–30 milligrams (mg)
vitamin B_1 (thiamine)	1.5–10 mg
vitamin B_2 (riboflavin)	1.7–10 mg

vitamin B₃ (niacin)	20–100 mg
pantothenic acid	10–50 mg
vitamin B₆ (pyridoxine)	10–25 mg
vitamin B₁₂	6–30 micrograms (mcg)
folic acid	200–400 mcg
biotin	100–300 mcg
vitamin C	60–1000 mg
vitamin D	200–400 IU
vitamin E	30–400 IU
vitamin K	100–200 mcg

Mineral	Recommended Daily Dose
calcium	250–1,000 mg
magnesium	200–400 mg
zinc	15–30 mg
iron	10–15 mg
manganese	2–10 mg
copper	2–3 mg
selenium	50–200 mcg
chromium	50–200 mcg
iodine	50–150 mcg
molybdenum	50–200 mcg

Pharmaceuticals

METHADONE

Methadone, an opioid with a long duration of action, has been successfully used in the treatment of opiate abstinence in those who are *heavy* chronic users of a *high-potency* opioid, such as intravenous heroin. Methadone can *only* be administered by a physician who is affiliated with a *licensed* methadone program. Methadone suppresses withdrawal symptoms. There are a number of ways of using methadone. Treatment can begin by replacing the opioid you have been taking with an amount of methadone of equivalent potency. This is called *methadone replacement therapy*. Methadone is then weaned down so that in two weeks you are off this drug. If you follow the other components of my program, using methadone in this manner is more likely to be successful.

Alternatively, methadone treatment begins with replacement therapy and then proceeds to *maintenance therapy*. The methadone dose is slowly reduced to an amount that still suppresses withdrawal symptoms and is then maintained for a variable period of time at this lower dose. This is called *methadone maintenance*. Methadone maintenance must also be supervised by a physician affiliated with a licensed institution. When you are ready, methadone itself is gradually withdrawn.

CLONIDINE

The blood pressure–lowering agent clonidine is effective in suppressing opioid-withdrawal symptoms. Its use must be very carefully supervised by your physician since it is used in this context at a high dose and causes hypotension (low blood pressure), dry mouth, dizziness, and drowsiness. These adverse effects usually wear off during the first few days. Clonidine is given in this context at from 1 to 2 milligrams daily in three divided doses for four to six days and then it is weaned down so that you are off of the drug by seven to ten days. These doses are *much* higher than those used for the treatment of high blood pressure.

For those dependent on methadone, clonidine is usually given at the same starting dose for about ten days and then weaned down so that you are off of the drug by fourteen days. The initial dose of clonidine is adjusted to the dose necessary to suppress withdrawal symptoms. I don't recommend a dose higher than 2.9 milligrams a day. *Remember, your blood pressure requires very close monitoring while on clonidine, at these doses.*

NALTREXONE

Naltrexone is a drug that blocks the opiate receptors in the brain so that if you take an opioid, the drug will not produce any pleasurable, potentially addictive effects. Naltrexone is usually started about a week after the beginning of opioid abstinence, when most of the withdrawal symptoms have disappeared. The usual maintenance dose is 50 milligrams a day.

Herbs

VALERIAN

Valerian is a very mild sedative prepared from the roots of the plant *Valeriana officinalis*. It can be helpful in reducing the intensity of some of the opioid-withdrawal symptoms, especially anxiety, irritability, and restlessness. Fresh freeze-dried valerian is available in 325-milligram capsules in some health-food stores (or see Resources section). Alternatively, a tea can be prepared from the root of the plant. During the first two weeks of opioid abstinence (first three weeks for methadone), I recommend taking two capsules of fresh freeze-dried valerian three times a day and also at bedtime, if necessary, or drinking 1 cup of tea prepared from the root of the plant every two to three hours.

OATS

The common oat plant (*Avena sativa*) appears to reduce opioid craving (see Chapter 5, Part II). It also has a very mild sedative effect and is well worth trying right at the very beginning of opioid abstinence. Fresh freeze-dried capsules of the plant are available in some health-food stores (see Resources section). I recommend taking two to three 375-milligram capsules three times a day with meals. Take it for two weeks (three weeks if you are getting off methadone) or for as long as needed. Adverse effects are highly unlikely.

Lipids

PHOSPHATIDYLCHOLINE

Phosphatidylcholine may be helpful in reducing or suppressing the symptoms of opioid withdrawal (see Chapter 3, Part II). One-gram capsules containing 90 percent phosphatidylcholine are available (see Resources section). I recommend taking three capsules three times daily with meals for the first two weeks of opioid abstinence (three weeks for methadone) and afterward as needed.

Also, review material on the lipid complex AL-721 in Chapter 3, Part II.

Food and Fluids

Those addicted to opioids generally have poor dietary habits. Review Chapter 7, Part II. Make sure that you drink at least 6 to 8 glasses of water daily.

Exercise

An exercise program should begin at the very start of your detoxification program. Among other things, exercise releases *natural* opioids in your brain. This will reduce or suppress opioid craving. Review Chapter 9, Part II.

Relaxation and Stress Reduction

Relaxation and stress-reduction techniques also liberate natural opioids in your brain. These techniques are vital for the reduction of external stresses and will help suppress withdrawal symptoms and craving. Therapeutic massage is very good for withdrawal-related muscle cramps as well as to reduce your stress level generally. Review Chapter 9, Part II.

Support Groups

Your family, friends, and your physician and his or her assistants will be invaluable as you go through detoxification. There are a number of support groups that can also be very helpful to you, such as Narcotics Anonymous (see Resources section).

Other

Diarrhea and abdominal cramping are some of the most annoying withdrawal symptoms. Imodium will help alleviate them. Take two tablets initially (2 milligrams) and then one after each diarrheal movement, up to eight a day. Imodium is a prescription item at this strength. At lower strengths, it is available over the counter.

6 Benzodiazepines/Barbiturates

THE HUMAN SIDE: THE CASE OF MS. V

Ms. V began having panic attacks in her mid-thirties. She soon had a history of being rushed to emergency rooms with symptoms that made her—and others—believe she was having heart attacks or other cardiac crises. These attacks were characterized by racing pulse, heart palpitations, alternating flushes and pallors and, sometimes, profuse sweating.

Eventually, Ms. V was properly diagnosed as having a panic disorder. People who suffer from these disorders are very sensitive to biochemical changes, even some very subtle changes, in their bodies. These sensitivities are often misperceived as being life-threatening, and a panic attack ensues. Often, sufferers are not aware of any sensitivity. Instead, they merely experience a sudden feeling of impending crisis or doom; often, they feel that they cannot breathe.

The physician who diagnosed the panic disorder, in the case of Ms. V, prescribed the tricyclic antidepressant imipramine. This drug has been helpful in some cases like this, but in some others it has actually made matters worse. This was the case with Ms. V. She was highly sensitive to the drug, and the changes it produced in her body and brain set off new panic attacks.

Next, Ms. V was given the anti-anxiety agent Xanax, currently one

of the most popular prescription drugs and a member of the benzodiazepine family of pharmaceuticals, which includes Valium and Librium. The dose of Xanax was gradually increased, and at 6 milligrams
per day (in three divided doses of 2 milligrams each), Ms. V was
finally panic free.

There were costs, however, for the drug made Ms. V feel tired
and sluggish a good deal of the time. She'd always had a weight
problem. After a couple of years on Xanax, it was a major problem.
Because the drug made her so tired, she'd given up all effort at
exercise and was becoming seriously obese.

Ms. V had smoked for more than a decade. To try to pep herself
up—and lose some weight—she began smoking more. She also began
drinking more coffee. But she didn't feel more energetic.

Ms. V was aware that Xanax (and the other benzodiazepines) can
produce lethargy and fatigue, and she tried a few times to taper off
the drug. Each time she tried, however, she experienced one of her
dreaded panic attacks. She felt caught between, as she put it, "a
frightening rock and a fat, tired place."

Finally, Ms. V decided she had to get off the drug. She was
warned by her physician that this wouldn't be easy, that even people
who take this class of drugs for prolonged periods for anxiety, not to
mention panic disorders, often suffer significant withdrawal symptoms which, while rarely life-threatening, can be quite unpleasant.
These often include anxiety, insomnia, tremors, sweating, nausea,
depression, and more.

Ms. V would have to face all of that *plus* a recurrence of panic
attacks. The withdrawal symptoms, in fact, could be counted on to
make those attacks even worse and more frequent than usual. Ms. V
decided the only way she could possibly handle this would be to
check into a drug detoxification center, where she would have constant help and monitoring.

The detoxification plan she opted for called for nearly a month's
inpatient treatment at a cost of more than twelve thousand dollars.

Some of these programs are better than others. "This one," Ms. V
said, "was bad. Real bad." In fact, Ms. V added, "The next few weeks
turned into the worst experience of my life." The program for which
she was paying twelve thousand dollars consisted of a gradual taper-
ing of the Xanax "and a lot of group meetings and counseling sessions," none of which seemed to address her particular needs. No
attention was paid to her smoking and caffeine habits or to her various

chemical sensitivities. Nutrition was almost entirely ignored, and exercise was optional.

"By the end of the month, I'd gone through more panic attacks than I can remember, and within days of getting out of there, I was right back up to where I'd been"—back to 6 milligrams of Xanax a day.

It was a few months after this that Ms. V was referred to me. When I first saw her, she was deeply depressed and heavily overweight. One of the first things I noticed was how rapid and shallow her breathing was—she was another of those I call the futile breathers. There is an epidemic of this kind of breathing. It is one of the usually overlooked hallmarks of the various anxiety and panic disorders. Even though these people are taking a lot of breaths, they are getting a minimal amount of oxygen.

I told Ms. V, after she related her detoxification experience to me, that I had quite a different program in mind for her—one that would cost her very little, would proceed on an outpatient basis, and would not only overcome her drug dependence but would also greatly lessen the severity and frequency of her panic attacks. You'll learn about all of the particulars of that program shortly.

Most useful were the breathing exercises, which helped Ms. V normalize a number of biochemical imbalances. She quickly learned how to use these exercises to abort panic attacks. With their continued use, she was able to prevent most panic recurrences. (See Chapter 9, Part II, to review the breathing exercises.)

I also got Ms. V on a good nutritional plan that included cleaning up her various environmental sensitivities (Chapter 7, Part II). This included a reduction in caffeine intake.

Within five weeks, Ms. V was free of her dependence on Xanax and well on the road to vanquishing her panic disorders. When we subsequently extinguished her craving for nicotine as well, the last vestiges of the panic disorder disappeared entirely and has not resurfaced in a year and a half.

THE NATURE OF THE DEPENDENCE/ADDICTION

Benzodiazepines

Benzodiazepines are widely prescribed drugs. They are used for the treatment of anxiety, depression, panic disorders, insomnia, muscle spasms, seizures, control of blood pressure in those with difficult to control hypertension, and in the treatment of the alcohol-withdrawal syndrome (see Chapter 1, Part III).

Benzodiazepines are frequently abused. For example, they are often used to come down from psychostimulants (cocaine and amphetamines) or to self-treat "crash" symptoms that occur during early abstinence from these drugs. They are also used to increase the intensity and/or duration of the intoxication of many other addictive drugs, such as alcohol, as well as for their own calming and disinhibiting effects.

There are many benzodiazepines. Those most commonly used in the treatment of anxiety are diazepam (Valium), alprazolam (Xanax), lorazepam (Ativan), chlordiazepoxide (Librium), clorazepate (Tranxene), and oxazepam (Serax). Commonly used benzodiazepines for the treatment of insomnia include flurazepam (Dalmane), temazepam (Restoril), and triazolam (Halcion). Xanax is very popular in the treatment of panic disorders and agitated depression disorders. It is currently as popular as Valium was in the past. Xanax is unlikely to cause depression, whereas many of the other benzodiazepines may. The various benzodiazepines have different durations of action. Valium and Librium are long-acting, while Halcion is short-acting.

There is considerable concern about the addictive potential of the benzodiazepines. Some may, in fact, become addicted to these drugs, but it's more likely that one will become *dependent* on them. Let's sort out the difference between addiction and dependence. Addiction is characterized by escalating drug intake in order to obtain the desired effect, usually euphoria, and the occurrence of a withdrawal syndrome. Persistent craving for ever more drug is uncommon in the case of benzodiazepines, but there is a withdrawal syndrome related to these drugs when they are used for prolonged periods. Because of withdrawal symptoms, many have difficulty discontinuing use of the drugs. Such individuals are drug dependent.

Benzodiazepine dependence can develop if you take high doses of the drug daily for a few months or if you take lower doses for a longer period of time. For example, 80 to 120 milligrams of Valium daily can lead to dependence in from forty to fifty days. Some may become dependent on these drugs in much less time. This is particularly true for older people. Others who are at higher risk of becoming addicted to benzodiazepines include those with histories of other drug abuse, in particular abuse of alcohol and opioids.

Some actually do become addicted to benzodiazepines, craving escalating doses. Many more, however, are dependent than are addicted. Real benzodiazepine *addiction* is usually a sign of addiction to other drugs as well, especially alcohol and opioids.

BENZODIAZEPINES' EFFECTS IN THE BRAIN

The effects of benzodiazepines are mediated by increasing the activity of the brain neurotransmitter gamma aminobutyric acid (GABA). GABA works by binding to certain nerve-cell receptors in the brain, leading to decreased firing of those nerve cells. That is, GABA is an inhibitory neurotransmitter that decreases electrical activity in certain brain regions. It is a natural sedative.

Benzodiazepines bind to sites on the nerve cell that are different from the GABA receptor site. When this occurs, the activity of GABA increases. You can think of the whole process as follows: GABA is a key, the GABA receptor is the cylinder of a lock, and the benzodiazepine is the grease. When the cylinder of the lock (GABA receptor) is greased by the benzodiazepine, it is easier for the key (GABA) to turn the lock. In biochemical terms, the benzodiazepine "allosterically" activates the interaction between GABA and its receptor.

Long-term benzodiazepine intake probably has a deleterious effect on the relationship between GABA and its receptor. There is evidence that long-term treatment by these drugs decreases the sensitivity of nerve cells to the inhibitory effects of GABA and produces abnormal changes in the benzodiazepine receptor sites, the GABA receptors, and the interaction between GABA and its receptor. It's as if the lock and key have gotten rusty. One can think of this as a neurotransmitter-receptor disease. This disease is unmasked when the drug is withdrawn and most probably accounts for the withdrawal syndrome. In fact, a disorder of the neurotransmitter-receptor to begin with may make one vulnerable to the addictive effects of benzodiazepines.

THE WITHDRAWAL SYNDROME

If you are addicted to and/or dependent on a benzodiazepine and abruptly discontinue its use, you will most likely experience symptoms of the benzodiazepine-withdrawal syndrome. Depending on the dose and the duration of your drug use, the symptoms can range from mild to intense and can last from two to three weeks. They are rarely life-threatening. The symptoms include anxiety, insomnia, jitteriness, irritability, fatigue, headache, muscle aches and twitches, shakiness, tremor, sweating, dizziness, difficulty concentrating, nausea, loss of appetite, depression, increased sensitivity to noise, light, and odors, abnormal taste sensation and, rarely, seizures. Some of the symptoms, such as anxiety and insomnia, may not be true withdrawal symptoms but a recurrence of those symptoms for which you were treated in the first place.

One of the most intense withdrawal symptoms is a severe hyperinsomnia that occurs after using high-dose Halcion—a short-acting benzodiazepine—daily for more than a few weeks. This postdrug insomnia is much more severe than the insomnia for which the drug was originally used. The insomnia that may occur after discontinuing a longer-acting benzodiazepine is much less severe in intensity. We'll get to treatment shortly.

Barbiturates

Barbiturates are sedative-hypnotics that at one time—before the advent of the benzodiazepines—were frequently prescribed by physicians for the treatment of insomnia and anxiety. They are rarely prescribed for these reasons today. Barbiturates *are* used, however, in some headache medications and for the treatment of seizures and brain injuries. Barbiturates are sometimes abused and have *high* addictive potential.

There are several barbiturates. These include amobarbital (Amytal), butabarbital, pentobarbital (Nembutal, also known as yellow jackets or yellows), secobarbital (Seconal, or reds or red devils), thiopental (Pentothal, or truth serum), and phenobarbital. The drugs have different durations of action. Phenobarbital, which is commonly used in the treatment of seizures, is a long-acting barbiturate, thiopental is an ultra-short-acting one, and the others listed above are short- to intermediate-acting.

The short-acting barbiturates, such as Seconal and Nembutal, have the greatest addictive potential and are the ones most commonly abused. Acute effects of these drugs include euphoria and release from tension, and sexual and aggressive disinhibitions. Those who want more of these effects continue to take the drug; escalate its use because of becoming tolerant to the initial effects; and in one to two months, become hooked on it. If they then discontinue the drug, they develop severe withdrawal symptoms, the nature of which we will discuss shortly.

In many ways, the effects of barbiturates and alcohol are similar. Barbiturate intoxication resembles alcohol intoxication. Symptoms include slurred speech, a general sluggishness, memory problems, difficulty in thinking, poor emotional control (tearfulness one moment, for example, laughter the next), irritability, faulty judgment, difficulty paying attention, sexual and aggressive disinhibition, unsteady gait and, occasionally, paranoid ideas and thoughts of suicide. An overdose of barbiturates can kill you. Some commit suicide in this manner. Even lower doses of a barbiturate, when combined with alcohol, can result in cessation of breathing.

Barbiturates work by depressing the activity of all excitable tissue. The brain is exquisitely sensitive to them. They also depress the function of the heart muscle and skeletal muscles and affect a wide range of biological functions. Barbiturates bind to components in cell membranes, such as phosphatidylcholine, and continued use causes distortions in these vital structures. Barbiturates essentially put the brain to sleep by depressing the "conversations" of nerve cells, conversations that depend on fluid cell membranes. Prolonged heavy barbiturate use rigidifies the membranes and "freezes" them, in effect, and if you defrost them too quickly, by suddenly discontinuing the drug, the results can be disastrous.

Abrupt withdrawal of barbiturates after prolonged heavy use can be life-threatening. Here again, we have similarities between barbiturates and alcohol. Abrupt withdrawal of large doses of alcohol used for prolonged periods of time can also be life-threatening. Abrupt withdrawal of any other addictive drug is generally *not* life-threatening.

Severe withdrawal symptoms may include delirium, generalized seizures, paranoid psychosis, hyperthermia (with temperatures as high as 108° F), and death. Less severe withdrawal symptoms include elevated heart and respiration rates, tremulousness, severe anxiety and dread, muscular weakness and aching, insomnia, sweating, nausea and vomiting, and a blood-pressure drop upon standing associated with dizziness. Obviously, detoxification of barbiturates should never be done by abruptly stopping the drug. Withdrawal from barbiturates usually takes from two to three weeks.

TREATMENT

Benzodiazepines—Dosing Down

Benzodiazepine detoxification can be done on an outpatient basis. Benzodiazepines should *not* be withdrawn abruptly. Their dose should slowly be tapered down. You can either taper the drug on which you are dependent by about 10 percent a day or, if you are on a *short-acting* benzodiazepine—such as Halcion, Ativan, or Serax—you can switch to an equally potent amount of a *longer-acting* benzodiazepine—such as Valium or Librium—and taper that drug down by about 10 percent a day. Switching to the long-term benzodiazepine will, generally, make withdrawal easier. Discuss this, as well as the other suggestions described in this section, with your physician; you should be under his or her supervision while you are undergoing detoxification. If you are addicted to other drugs, such as alcohol, opioids, and/or cocaine, an *inpatient* detoxification program would be advisable.

Barbiturates—Dosing Down

Barbiturate detoxification is best done on an *inpatient* basis, in order to prevent any potentially life-threatening withdrawal symptoms. Basically, your physician needs to determine the amount of barbiturate you have been taking. If you are not sure, there is a test he or she can use to determine this, called the pentobarbital tolerance test. Once the dose has been determined, it is converted into an equivalent dose of phenobarbital. Phenobarbital is the drug of choice for barbiturate withdrawal for these reasons: It is a long-acting barbiturate; it is safer than the shorter-acting ones; and it maintains a fairly constant blood level throughout the day. Phenobarbital is weaned down over about a two-week period.

Amino Acids

L-TYROSINE
L-tyrosine can be helpful for the withdrawal-related symptoms of depression, fatigue, and difficulty in concentrating. Try 1,000 to 2,000 milligrams (in capsule form) three times a day on an empty stomach or twenty to thirty minutes before meals. You can take this throughout the withdrawal period (about two to three weeks) and then afterward as necessary.

Pharmaceuticals

Insomnia is a frequent symptom occurring during withdrawal. Pharmaceuticals that can be helpful are the following:

Diphenhydramine (Benadryl, Sominex, and others) is an over-the-counter antihistamine that is also a sedative. The recommended dose is 25–50 milligrams before bedtime as necessary.

Doxepin (Sinequan and others) is an antidepressant that, at low doses, is a good sleep aid and can also help with withdrawal-related muscle aches. The recommended dose is 25 milligrams at bedtime, as necessary; this is a prescription item.

Buspirone (BuSpar) is a newer anti-anxiety agent that has a very low potential for dependence or addiction. It can be very useful in treating benzodiazepine or barbiturate-withdrawal-related anxiety. The hitch is that it takes a few weeks before it has an effect and therefore needs to be started two to four weeks *prior* to withdrawal of the benzodiazepine or barbiturate. The usual dose is 5 to 10 milligrams three times daily. It does *not* produce withdrawal symptoms, sedation, or psychomotor impairment.

Herbs

Valerian is a very mild sedative prepared from the roots of the plant *Valeriana officinalis*. It can be helpful in reducing the intensity of withdrawal-related anxiety, jitteriness, and insomnia. During the first two to three weeks of withdrawal, try two capsules of fresh freeze-dried valerian three times a day and at bedtime. The capsules contain 325 milligrams of valerian and are available in some health-food stores (or see Resources section). Alternatively, a tea can be prepared from the root of the plant, and you can take a cup or two of this tea every two to three hours.

Vitamins and Minerals

I recommend taking the following supplements to replenish any deficiency caused by benzodiazepine and barbiturate abuse. *Folic acid* is particularly important.

Vitamin	Recommended Daily Dose
beta carotene	15–30 milligrams (mg)
vitamin B_1 (thiamine)	1.5–10 mg
vitamin B_2 (riboflavin)	1.7–10 mg
vitamin B_3 (niacin)	20–50 mg
pantothenic acid	10–50 mg

vitamin B$_6$ (pyridoxine)	10–25 mg
vitamin B$_{12}$	6–30 micrograms (mcg)
folic acid	800–1,000 mcg
biotin	100–300 mcg
vitamin C	60–1,000 mg
vitamin D	200–400 IU
vitamin E	30–400 IU
vitamin K	100–200 mcg

Mineral	Recommended Daily Dose
calcium	250–1,000 mg
magnesium	200–400 mg
zinc	15–30 mg
iron	10–15 mg
manganese	2–10 mg
copper	2–3 mg
selenium	50–200 mcg
chromium	50–200 mcg
iodine	50–150 mcg
molybdenum	50–200 mcg

Food and Fluids

Review Chapter 7, Part II for guidelines. Make sure that you drink at least 6 to 8 glasses of water daily. A good diet is necessary to mend your brain and cellular membranes.

Exercise

An exercise program should begin at the very start of your purification process or—better yet—before. Exercise will help reduce or suppress anxiety and help you sleep better. Review Chapter 9, Part II for guidelines.

Relaxation and Stress Reduction

Relaxation and stress-reduction techniques are important for a successful outcome of your purification program. Progressive relaxation and anxiety management will help you deal with anxiety and stress *without* the use of drugs. Therapeutic massage will also help relieve withdrawal-related muscle cramps as well as reduce your stress level generally.

Proper breathing, as emphasized in the case history that begins this chapter, is of vital importance in all of the Purification Prescriptions, but it is particularly crucial in situations characterized by anxiety.

For exercises, including the vital breathing exercises, related to relaxation and stress management, see Chapter 9, Part II.

7 Cholesterol/Fats/Stagnant Blood/Excess Weight

CHOLESTEROL/FATS

Most people today grab their food on the run, eat lots of fatty foods, and have high levels of cholesterol and blood that does not flow as freely through arteries and veins as it should. The fact is, our heart and blood vessels were not "built" to withstand the kind of dietary insults we have visited upon them in the last hundred years. Our ability to process and rid the body of cholesterol by means of the low-density lipoprotein (LDL) receptors in our cells has not kept pace with our escalating consumption of dietary fat and cholesterol. Such a diet, combined with decreased physical activity and lives filled with emotional stress, has overwhelmed the relatively sparse LDL receptors. The consequence of all this has been an epidemic of atherosclerosis, heart attacks, and strokes, among other ills.

Our high-fat, high-cholesterol diet has been called the SAD diet (for standard American diet) by Sonja and William Connor, two pioneering dietary researchers whose *New American Diet* (Fireside, 1989) is an excellent guide—complete with 350 recipes—to a healthy diet. The SAD diet is doing something even more insidious than clogging our arteries. It is adversely affecting the health of *all* our cells. Specifically, it produces cell membranes that are less fluid, more rigid, and less permeable to the inflow of the oxygen needed to keep us youthful, healthy, and energetic. We need to start thinking in terms of atherosclerotic cells, as well as atherosclerotic arteries, in terms of cellular heart attacks, as well as "coronaries."

The following program will help lower your serum cholesterol level, increase the amount of high-density lipoprotein (or HDL cholesterol, which is the "good" cholesterol), and also help keep your cell membranes in a fluid state. It should also make you feel more energetic and less tired. In five weeks or less, you can lower your cholesterol levels by *at least* 20 percent. In some cases, my patients have achieved 50 percent reductions in that time period.

Diet

GOAL 1
To cut fat intake to 20–25 percent of total caloric intake, with special emphasis on cutting down on saturated fats. Reduce daily cholesterol intake to no more than 100 milligrams.

To accomplish this: Limit your intake of animal food to no more than 6 ounces of fish, 5 ounces of poultry (*without* the skin), or 4 ounces of red meat daily. Clams, oysters, and scallops have a low fat and cholesterol content, so they also fall into the 6-ounce category. Lobsters, crabs, and shrimp, however, must be limited to 4 ounces daily—just like red meat.

Start getting into the habit of selecting only the leanest meats, and use them to garnish dishes increasingly composed of vegetables rather than as main courses in and of themselves. Get into Oriental, Mediterranean, and Mexican cuisines.

Substitute fish for red meat. Fish is rich in the omega-3 polyunsaturated fatty acids. These are "good" fats, which help reduce serum triglyceride and LDL-cholesterol ("bad" cholesterol) levels and help increase the fluidity of cell membranes.

Chicken and turkey are better choices than red meats, too. Both, when skinned, contain lesser amounts of cholesterol and saturated fat. Game meat, such as venison, is a lean meat.

If you eat cheese, eat the low-fat variety. Most cheese, including cheddar, Swiss, American, Velveeta, cream cheese, and most commercial cheese spreads are among the very highest-fat cheeses and their intake should be as low as possible. If you eat these cheeses, limit your intake to no more than 4 ounces a day—and for every 1 ounce of cheese you eat, you should skip 1 ounce of meat for that day, if you are to arrive at the 20 percent goal. Low-fat cheeses include Reduced Calories Laughing Cow, Lite-line cheeses, and part-skim ricotta.

Substitute a soft margarine for butter. Substitute 2 percent–fat milk for whole milk, then move to 1 percent and, finally, if possible, to skim milk. Substitute low-fat frozen yogurt, sherbets, and ices for ice cream. Low- and no-fat ice creams are now available. Substitute mock sour cream for the real stuff. Low-fat yogurt with garlic seasoning is another excellent sour cream replacement.

Drop regular mayonnaise and Miracle Whip from your diet. Both are 65 percent pure fat. Substitute low-fat varieties. Better yet, switch entirely to monounsaturated vegetable oils, such as olive oil, and polyunsaturated oils, such as corn, safflower, cottonseed, and soybean. Try to *avoid* coconut and palm oils (saturates) and *hydrogenated* oils (check labels). In any case, use even the "good" fats in moderation.

Egg yolks, as we all know by now, are rich in cholesterol. Use egg substitutes, such as Egg Beaters, Scramblers, and Avoset, which contain little or no cholesterol, instead. It is not necessary to eliminate egg whites, which are rich in protein, from your diet.

GOAL 2
To increase intake of carbohydrates to 65 percent of total caloric intake, with emphasis on complex, unrefined carbohydrates.

To accomplish this: Eat at least two servings of whole-grain or potato dishes at each meal (for example, cereal and whole-wheat toast at breakfast; a burrito and corn chips at lunch; baked potato and whole-grain rolls at dinner).

Eat 1 cup of cooked legumes (peas, beans of different types) several times a week, as main courses, side dishes, or in salads. Eat 2 to 4 cups of other vegetables daily (fresh, in salads, cooked as side dishes, or in dishes in which meats are used as garnishes).

Eat three to four pieces of fresh fruit daily.

GOAL 3
Protein intake should be from 12 to 15 percent of your caloric intake, with decreased reliance on animal protein and increased reliance on vegetable protein.

If you follow the other suggestions listed in this chapter, you will accomplish this goal. Also, increase your consumption of soybean products, which are good vegetarian sources of protein. Soybean foods include soybean sprouts, cooked soybeans, roasted soy nuts, soy milk (the liquid left after soybeans have been crushed in hot water), miso (a fermented soybean paste often used to prepare a soup), tempeh (a fermented soybean cake), and tofu.

GOAL 4

To increase intake of fiber to about 50 to 60 grams daily. Soluble fiber helps reduce cholesterol.

The typical American consumes 10 to 12 grams daily. It's not difficult to get 50 grams or more. To accomplish this, you would, for example: Eat a third of a cup of cooked beans, a bowl of whole-grain cereal (rolled oats are a particularly good choice), a sandwich made of whole-wheat bread, a serving of rice, a medium-sized apple and a small banana, a small serving of peas, or one or two servings of cooked vegetables.

Other good sources of soluble fiber include edible seaweeds (review Chapter 4, Part II) and the edible Mexican cactus called nopal. The nopal is now available in many grocery stores.

It is possible to lower cholesterol levels by up to 20 percent through an increase in soluble-fiber intake alone. You can achieve this in a few weeks by eating 1 cup of oat bran and 3 to 4 ounces of lima, navy, pinto, or soy beans daily, along with two to three oat bran muffins daily. A heaping teaspoon of psyllium mixed in water and taken two to three times daily will further reduce your cholesterol. Psyllium, derived from an Indian plant, is available in health-food stores.

Have your cholesterol, LDL cholesterol, and high-density lipoprotein (or HDL cholesterol, "good" cholesterol), measured before increasing your soluble dietary-fiber intake and then again in about four to five weeks. You and your physician will be pleasantly surprised.

Other cholesterol reducers: Garlic and onions can lower your total cholesterol as well as increase your HDL cholesterol. Just *one* white or yellow onion daily can raise HDL cholesterol *by up to 30 percent* in a few weeks in those with *low* HDL-cholesterol! Make garlic and onions a generous part of your daily vegetable fare.

Vitamins, Minerals, and Other Supplements

There are several *general* reasons for taking a good vitamin and mineral supplement. There are also *specific*, very potent cholesterol-lowering vitamins and other supplements I'll get to shortly.

Increasing your vegetable and fiber intake, as advised above, increases your need for adequate intake of minerals and some vitamins, such as beta carotene and riboflavin. Fiber, phytates, and oxalates bind to minerals and some vitamins, making them unusable in the body. So you need more vitamins and minerals to overcome this problem.

Free-radical damage is involved in the process of atherosclerosis, as well as in the rigidification of cellular membranes and other pathological processes. Vitamins and minerals form substances in the body that protect against this damage.

Magnesium, among other things, is involved in the regulation of blood-vessel tone. Magnesium deficiency can cause muscle spasm in arteries, including those that feed the heart, decreasing blood flow through those arteries. The magnesium intake of many people is deficient.

For these and many other reasons, I recommend the following vitamin and mineral regimen:

Vitamin	Recommended Daily Dose
beta carotene	15–30 milligrams (mg)
vitamin B₁ (thiamine)	1.5–10 mg
vitamin B₂ (riboflavin)	1.7–10 mg
vitamin B₃ (niacin)	20–100 mg
pantothenic acid	10–50 mg
vitamin B₆ (pyridoxine)	2–25 mg
vitamin B₁₂	6–30 micrograms (mcg)
folic acid	200–400 mcg
biotin	100–300 mcg
vitamin C	60–1,000 mg
vitamin D	200–400 IU
vitamin E	30–400 IU
vitamin K	100–200 mcg

Mineral	Recommended Daily Dose
calcium	250–1,000 mg
magnesium	200–400 mg
zinc	15–30 mg
iron	10–15 mg
manganese	2–10 mg
copper	2–3 mg
selenium	50–200 mcg
chromium*	200 mcg
iodine	50–150 mcg
molybdenum	50–200 mcg

* chromium in the form of chromium picolinate

Now let's look at some specific cholesterol-lowering agents.

NICOTINIC ACID

Nicotinic acid can lower cholesterol by up to 25 percent in a few weeks. It can also lower serum triglycerides (fats) and raise desirable HDL-cholesterol levels. Nicotinic acid is a B vitamin. However, at the doses required to lower cholesterol, it must be considered a pharmaceutical agent and those who do use high-dose nicotinic acid must be supervised by a physician. It *is* one of the best cholesterol-lowering agents there is.

Many, however, cannot tolerate the side effects of nicotinic acid. These include the "niacin flush" (burning, itching, reddening sensation, usually in the face, neck, arms, and upper chest, which may persist for half an hour or longer and is caused by nicotinic acid's ability to dilate blood vessels) and, in some, heart palpitations. Nicotinic acid at high doses *can,* in addition, cause abnormal blood liver tests, decreased glucose tolerance, elevated uric-acid levels and, rarely, liver disease. Recently, a long-acting form of nicotinic acid has come on the marketplace that appears to have fewer and less intense side effects.

Doses from 1,000 to 5,000 milligrams per day may be necessary in order to achieve the desired cholesterol-lowering effect. If you are interested in trying nicotinic acid and dietary methods of lowering cholesterol have failed for you, discuss the vitamin with your physician and have your cholesterol, triglyceride, and HDL-cholesterol levels checked, as well as your fasting glucose, uric acid, and liver functions at the outset. Use one of the newer long-acting forms of nicotinic acid.

Start with a dose of 250 milligrams *with food.* You may experience mild symptoms of the niacin flush. If you do, take only 250 milligrams twice a day, with meals, for about three days. You will probably note that the symptoms have subsided. If they have, increase the dose to 500 milligrams twice a day, with meals, for another three days, then 500 milligrams three times a day with meals. The above is meant to be a guideline. The important thing is *not* to increase the amount until you can tolerate the dose you are on.

Have your cholesterol, triglyceride, and HDL-cholesterol level checked again after four to five weeks on nicotinic acid. These values should have improved considerably. If your *initial* cholesterol level, after trying to get it down by dietary attempts, is *greater than 250,* you will probably need to go to a higher dose of nicotinic acid—1,000 milligrams three times a day with meals—in order to get your cholesterol level down to an acceptable value. Build up to that dose slowly, as discussed above.

Nicotinic acid can be a vital part of your cholesterol-lowering program. Always remember, however, that nicotinic acid used in the doses discussed here is a *drug*—even though you can get it without a prescription—and its use at these doses should *not* be attempted without supervision by your physician. Those with a history of pepticulcer disease, cardiac arrhythmias, liver disease, diabetes, and gout need to be especially careful about taking this substance.

CHROMIUM PICOLINATE

Chromium, in the form of chromium picolinate (now available in health-food stores), may lower serum cholesterol and raise HDL cholesterol by up to 5 percent or more in a few weeks at doses of 200 micrograms daily.

PANTETHINE

Pantethine, an activated form of the vitamin pantothenic acid, may lower cholesterol by up to 15 percent and triglycerides by up to 30 percent in a few weeks. Pantethine is available in 300-milligram capsules. The suggested dose is 600–1,200 milligrams daily. It's best to split this up into two to four doses, taking one 300-milligram capsule at a time. No significant adverse side effects have been noted at these doses. Pantethine can be found in many vitamin stores. It appears to be most effective in those with very high cholesterol levels to begin with.

FISH OILS

Fish-oil supplements are very popular. These contain the omega-3 polyunsaturated acids eicosapentaenoic acid (EPA) and dodocahexaenoic acid (DHA). EPA and DHA both appear to have LDL-cholesterol-lowering effects in those with elevated serum triglycerides.

Those who do not eat fish (the best way of getting your omega-3s), who have not been able to successfully lower their cholesterol with dietary maneuvers, and who have both elevated cholesterol and triglyceride levels may want to try a fish-oil supplement. Try 2–4 grams daily in divided doses. Make sure that the fish-oil supplements you use are free of vitamins A and D (to avoid potentially toxic effects) and that they contain vitamin E to prevent the oil from becoming rancid. Side effects may include burping accompanied by a fish taste (which can be minimized by taking the capsules with meals and by always keeping them refrigerated), bloating, abdominal cramping and, at a higher dose, slight weight gain.

Higher doses can also cause prolonged bleeding time, comparable to the effect of two aspirins. Those taking anticoagulants should not take fish oils without their physicians' knowledge and approval.

Exercise

Regular exercise is a vital component of your cholesterol-lowering program. It can help you control your weight as well as increase your helpful HDL-cholesterol level. Refer to Chapter 9, Part II for details.

Relaxation and Stress Reduction

Relaxation and stress-reduction techniques, such as deep breathing, meditation, and therapeutic massage, have been demonstrated to help lower cholesterol levels as well as to generally improve all aspects of one's physical, mental, and emotional health. See Chapter 9, Part II, for details.

STAGNANT BLOOD

Cholesterol is not the only factor that pollutes our blood vessels. Cellular elements in our bloodstream called platelets, important in the prevention of hemorrhaging and for wound repair, among other things, can also gum things up and thus contribute to atherosclerosis. It is vital that we keep our blood platelets from easily sticking to each other as they course through our bloodstream. Abnormal platelet stickiness leads to the production of abnormal blood clots, which in turn decrease the flow of blood to vital organs, such as the heart and the brain. This often results in heart attacks and strokes.

Our standard American diet, with its high amounts of saturated fats and cholesterol, promotes sticky platelets. They stick because, among other things, their membranes are rigid, not fluid and slippery. We can influence the fluidity of cellular membranes by what we eat, as previously noted. Polyunsaturated and monounsaturated fats promote greater fluidity and less stickiness. The omega-3 polyunsaturated fatty acids found in fish significantly increase membrane fluidity. This is probably the reason why fish are themselves so graceful and fluid.

The diet I recommend for cholesterol lowering is the same diet I recommend for maintaining fluidity of platelet membranes. Fish, onions, garlic, ginger, and hot, spicy foods in particular keep blood from stagnating or coagulating too readily. Hot chili peppers also keep the blood flowing, as has been demonstrated in several scientific studies. Just adding a few peppers to one dish a day can help.

Some vitamins and minerals are also important for the maintenance of platelet membrane fluidity. The vitamin and mineral supplement that I recommended in the previous section serves here as well. Those who do not eat fish may want to consider taking a fish-oil supplement. For those in whom there are no contraindications, a 325-milligram aspirin daily decreases platelet stickiness and will prevent abnormal clot formation. Discuss the advisability of taking an aspirin (or even less) a day with your physician. Finally, you should know that smoking increases platelet stickiness. Review Chapter 2, Part III for information on how to stop.

EXCESS WEIGHT

Obesity and eating disorders are highly complex issues. They involve biologic (genetic, biochemical, physiological), psychological, social, and cultural factors. A weight-loss or eating-disorder program that does not concern itself with all of these factors is unlikely to be successful.

Many have genetic or biochemical propensities to obesity. These propensities flourish in the context of a diet rich in fats, such as the standard American diet, for example. The fat content of our bodies is directly related to the fat content of our diets. There is no more important factor in weight reduction than the modification of your fat intake.

If you reduce your fat intake to 20 percent of total calories, increase the intake of your complex carbohydrates and dietary fiber, restrict your caloric intake—even modestly—and use the other recommendations that are listed below, you will not only lose weight but, far more important, you will *keep the weight off permanently.* As you already probably know all too well, being overweight makes you more easily tired and puts you at risk for many serious diseases.

BINGE EATING

Many who are overweight are *binge* eaters. Also, those with eating disorders, such as bulimia nervosa (binging and purging) and anorexia-bulimia, engage in binge eating. Compulsive overeating is similar in many ways to compulsive drug use. And, as is the case with compulsive drug use, some of the brain's neurotransmitters and neuroreceptors appear to be in an abnormal state. In particular, there is evidence of decreased activity of serotonin in binge eaters. Serotonin activity in certain areas of the brain is associated with satiety (feeling full); low serotonin activity in these regions leaves you feeling hungry no matter how much you eat, while high serotonin activity in these same regions makes you feel full.

Sugar-rich foods are often craved during binge eating. These foods lead to more L-tryptophan from the diet going to the brain. L-tryptophan gets converted to serotonin in that organ. Binge eating thus appears to be an attempt to correct serotonin deficiency in the brain. It can be viewed as an attempt at self-healing.

Increased serotonin also improves mood. Binge eating occurs in many who experience seasonal depression, the so-called seasonal affective disorder (SAD), and in some sufferers of premenstrual syndrome. Again, binging can be viewed as a self-healing maneuver, in this case an attempt to ameliorate depressive symptoms. The problem is that when SAD (seasonal affective disorder) turns to SAD (standard American diet) for relief, weight gain or, more specifically, fat gain is the inevitable consequence.

The following recommendations are for those who are overweight and/or are binge eaters.

Diet

The dietary guidelines are similar to those given for cholesterol control earlier in this chapter. Review and follow them. A caloric deficit of 500 calories a day will produce a weight loss of about one pound per week. Caloric deficit means that your caloric intake is less than the amount of calories your body expends, in this case 500 calories a day. Restricting the caloric intake of the above diet to 800–1,200 calories daily should be sufficient to produce a weight loss of about one or two pounds weekly. This may not be as dramatic as the weight loss achieved by very low-calorie diets. However, you will be much healthier if you do it slowly, *and* the weight will stay off for good. It *won't* on the lower-calorie diets.

Remember that water is a good way to fill yourself up and prevent dehydration. Drink at least 6 to 8 glasses of pure water a day. Also, hot chili pepper foods can help burn off some calories.

Vitamins and Minerals

Follow the recommendations for vitamins and minerals provided earlier in this chapter. Those with bulimia nervosa and anorexia-bulimia may have deficiencies in several vitamins and minerals. They especially should take a well-balanced and complete vitamin-and-mineral supplement, as should *all* those on weight-reducing diets.

Dietary Fiber

Dietary fiber has a filling effect. By increasing your intake of complex carbohydrates, you will at the same time be increasing your intake of dietary fiber. Another thing you can do to help fill you up without filling you out is to blend a teaspoon or two of psyllium fiber with water and drink this about fifteen to twenty minutes before each meal. Psyllium fiber is widely available in health-food stores.

Exercise

Regular exercise will speed up your metabolic rate, which means that you will expend more calories a day. This is vital to controlling your weight. See Chapter 9, Part II for details.

Light

Exposure to full-spectrum lighting can be helpful to control food cravings, particularly for sweets. It is also helpful in reducing depressive symptoms of premenstrual syndrome and seasonal affective disorder. The best way to get full-spectrum lighting—and get your exercise at the same time—is to take an hour-long walk in the morning. This assumes that the weather is good and the sun is shining.

Artificial full-spectrum lighting is available. The most widely used kind is the Vita-Lite, which is available as separate light bulbs or in units (see Resources section). An hour or two of exposure to these lights in the early morning can reduce or suppress cravings for sweets and can improve your mood as well. For more information, review Chapter 8, Part II.

Amino Acids

L-TYROSINE

L-tyrosine is converted to the neurotransmitters norepinephrine and dopamine in the brain. Norepinephrine activity in certain regions of the brain appears reduced in those with bulimia nervosa. It may be reduced, as well, in others with binge-eating problems. L-tyrosine may have antidepressant and psychoenergizing effects, too. It may even increase one's metabolic rate. Try 1,000–2,000 milligrams of L-tyrosine (capsule form) on an empty stomach or about twenty to thirty minutes before meals three times a day. You can continue to take L-tyrosine for five weeks or longer.

Relaxation and Stress Reduction

Relaxation and stress-reduction techniques, such as deep breathing, regular exercise, meditation, and therapeutic massage, can be very helpful in any weight-reduction program, especially to decrease food cravings and increase your self-esteem. See Chapter 9, Part II for details.

Pharmaceuticals

Pharmaceutical agents *for weight reduction* should only be used if all of the above recommendations have not been successful. Pharmaceuticals may be appropriate at the outset, however, for those with *eating disorders*, such as bulimia nervosa and anorexia-bulimia. I do *not* recommend the use of amphetamines *at any time*. The following are some of the more effective substances. Their use *must* be supervised by a physician.

FLUOXETINE (PROZAC)

Prozac is an antidepressant that increases activity of serotonin in certain regions of the brain. It has also been found effective in decreasing cravings for certain abused drugs *and* for food in some. It may be particularly effective in those with sweet cravings. One tablet

(20 milligrams) twice a day (at breakfast and lunch) is a dose that may work to decrease cravings for sweets and reduce and suppress binge eating. It usually takes a few weeks before the drug becomes effective.

Adverse effects can include nausea, nervousness, and insomnia. Rarely, people become tired on the drug. The side effects are generally not severe, and most tolerate the drug well. Your physician will decide the length of your Prozac program.

FENFLURAMINE (PONDIMIN)

Fenfluramine is another drug that increases the activity of serotonin in certain regions of the brain, although by a different mechanism than does Prozac. Individuals with seasonal depression have been successfully treated with this drug. It reduces the symptoms of depression, suppresses excessive intake of simple-carbohydrate-rich foods (chocolates, cake, candy, pastries, etc.), and diminishes fatigue.

Fenfluramine also reduces *snack* intake among those who crave simple carbohydrates (foods containing sugar), although not in those who do *not* crave simple carbohydrates. Fenfluramine has this effect if given two to three times a day before meals. Side effects can include dry mouth, diarrhea, and itching. Drowsiness is occasionally experienced by those who take the drug. Your physician will decide how long the drug should be continued. In general, it should not be used for more than four to six weeks, because it can lose its effectiveness upon prolonged use.

PHENTERMINE (IONAMIN)

Phentermine is a long-acting stimulant drug. It is *not* an amphetamine but has amphetaminelike properties. Its abuse potential is low. It has been shown to decrease food craving and help in weight reduction. Side effects include nervousness and insomnia. Its effectiveness appears to diminish after several weeks.

Some have found a combination of fenfluramine and phentermine to be more effective in decreasing food cravings and producing weight loss than either one alone.

Behavior Modification

Behavior modification is an important component in weight-reduction programs. Keeping a food journal and writing down the kinds and amounts of food eaten, the places where they are eaten, and any emotions or feelings (craving, anger, depression) you may have at the time can help you identify eating triggers. Psychotherapy, and family and other support groups, are frequently helpful. Don't forget exercise and relaxation and stress-reduction techniques (see above).

8 Chemotherapy/Radiotherapy Detoxification

Chemotherapy and radiotherapy can produce long-term remissions in patients with some types of cancer. The acute and long-term adverse effects of these therapies, however, are well known. The acute side effects, most typically nausea and vomiting, can be treated with variable success. The long-term effects are another matter. These include damage to the heart, lungs, nervous system, immune system, kidneys, bladder, and intestine, among other things.

Most of the long-term adverse effects of chemotherapy and radiotherapy appear to be due to free-radical damage. Free radicals are highly reactive molecular forms, mainly of oxygen, that can cause considerable damage to cells and tissues when they react with biological structures. Nearly all the presently used chemotherapeutic agents, as well as radiotherapy, generate free radicals. In fact, this is how they kill cancer cells. However, these free radicals can also injure noncancer cells.

For many years it was thought that anything that benefits normal, noncancer cells also helps cancer cells—that is, nourish or boost the normal cells and you will be feeding the cancer. Conversely, starve the normal cells and you will starve the cancer. These beliefs are faulty. Cancer cells and normal cells differ in a number of respects. Cancer cells can survive better with less oxygen, and they are more sensitive to the toxic effects of free radicals.

Cancer cells appear to be in a redox state different from noncancer cells. *Redox* refers to the aerobic status of cells. It now appears that *anti*oxidants can be used to protect normal cells from radiation and chemotherapy *without* reducing the therapeutic benefits of those treatments. Most of the biological antioxidants are derived from vitamins and minerals.

CHEMOTHERAPY

The following is a list of some long-term side effects of commonly used chemotherapeutic agents and a discussion of some specific substances that may prevent them.

1. Doxorubicin (Adriamycin)—Adriamycin in high doses can cause significant cardiotoxicity, including heart failure. The antioxidants alpha-tocopherol (vitamin E), selenium, and coenzyme Q_{10} may protect against this toxicity.

2. Bleomycin (Blenoxane), busulfan (Myleran), carmustine (BCNU), chlorambucil (Leukeran), cyclophosphamide (Cytoxan), lomustine (CCNU), melphalan (Alkeran), and mitomycin (Mutamycin)—these can cause fibrosis of the lungs. This is due to free-radical damage of the lungs. Antioxidants such as vitamin E, selenium, beta carotene, and vitamin C may protect against this toxicity. Mitomycin, BCNU, and CCNU can also cause kidney toxicity while Cytoxan can cause bladder toxicity. Antioxidants may protect against these effects.

   A common problem in those receiving bone-marrow transplants is venoclusive disease, or VOD. VOD is due to fibrosis of the veins and is related to the use of Cytoxan, which is used in this context to prevent bone-marrow rejection. Free radicals most likely mediate this disorder, and antioxidants may help protect against it.

3. Vincristine (Oncovin)—this drug can cause peripheral neuropathy—a disease of the peripheral nervous system manifested by loss of sensation, loss of some reflexes, reduced motor strength, and paresthesias (abnormal sensations, such as feeling "pins and needles"). The amino acid glutamic acid may protect against this nerve toxicity.

4. Cisplatin—this substance commonly leads to magnesium, cal-

cium, and potassium deficiencies. This can be prevented or treated with these minerals.

5. Cortisonelike steroids—these are commonly used in cancer therapy. Among other things, these substances cause loss of calcium, magnesium, and potassium. This also can be prevented or treated with these minerals.

Consult your doctor before using any of the substances discussed in this chapter.

Vitamins, Minerals and Other Supplements

1. The following vitamin and mineral prescription is recommended for all those receiving chemotherapy. *It is most effective if started well in advance of chemotherapy,* but it can be helpful later on as well. Consult with your physician about this regimen.

Vitamin	Recommended Daily Dose
vitamin A	2500–5000 IU
beta carotene	15–30 milligrams (mg)
vitamin B_1 (thiamine)	1.5–10 mg
vitamin B_2 (riboflavin)	1.7–10 mg
vitamin B_3 (niacin)	20–100 mg
pantothenic acid	10–50 mg
vitamin B_6 (pyridoxine)	2–25 mg
vitamin B_{12}	6–100 micrograms (mcg)
folic acid	200–400 mcg
biotin	100–300 mcg
vitamin C	100–1000 mg
vitamin D	200–400 IU
vitamin E[†]	200–400 IU
vitamin K	100–200 mcg

Mineral	Recommended Daily Dose
calcium*	250–1500 mg
magnesium**	200–400 mg
zinc	15–30 mg
iron	10–15 mg
manganese	2–10 mg
copper	2–3 mg

selenium†	100–200 mcg
chromium	50–200 mcg
iodine	50–150 mcg
molybdenum	50–200 mcg

* Those with hypercalcemia (elevated levels of calcium in their blood) should *not* take extra calcium.
† Those receiving Adriamycin should take the higher dose.
** Those receiving cisplatin should take the higher dose.

Those taking methotrexate may want to avoid folic acid supplements while they are using the drug, but not afterward. However, ther is *no* evidence that this is necessary to do and there *is* evidence that folic acid supplementation may protect against the side effects of methotrexate.

Those with renal failure and elevated blood magnesium levels should not take magnesium supplements.

2. L-Glutamic acid—for those receiving vincristine, 1,500–2,000 milligrams daily of L-glutamic acid in divided doses is recommended. Start with a low dose, 50–100 milligrams. Some with MSG (monosodium glutamate) sensitivity may be sensitive to glutamic acid. The magnesium and vitamin B_6 in the vitamin and mineral supplement help protect against this problem. If you have no adverse reaction to the low dose (and such reactions are rare), go to the full dose.

3. Coenzyme Q_{10}—those receiving Adriamycin can take from 30–100 milligrams daily of coenzyme Q_{10}, in divided doses, during treatment.

Diet

Review Chapters 4, 5, and 7 of Part II. Include in your diet edible seaweed, cruciferous vegetables, dark-green leafy vegetables, fruits, and shiitake mushrooms. Those who have lost their appetite from cancer therapies may try eating foods they never ate before. This sometimes helps. Recently, high doses of a progesteronelike substance, megestrol acetate (Megace), has been shown to stimulate appetite in those with loss of appetite and weight loss. Discuss this option with your physician.

Exercise/Relaxation and Stress Reduction

Exercise, relaxation, and stress-reduction techniques can help improve your immune system. Review Chapter 9, Part II.

Herbs

Some herbs appear to protect powerfully against the side effects of chemotherapy and radiotherapy, as well as boost immune-system activity. These herbs include ginseng, *Astragalus membranaceus,* and *Ligustrum lucidum.* See Chapter 5, Part II.

An astragalus tonic can be made by boiling 9–16 grams of the root of the herb. This should be drunk daily for a week.

A ligustrum tonic can be made by boiling 6–15 grams of the fruit of the herb. Drink this daily for a week.

Wheat-grass and barley-grass juice can also be protective. These are available in fresh form in some health-food stores. Powdered forms are available in almost all such stores. Several scientific studies have demonstrated the protective effects of these and other green vegetables, especially those in the cruciferous family. See also Chapter 7, Part II.

RADIOTHERAPY

Radiotherapy destroys cancer cells by free-radical mechanisms. These same free radicals are responsible for the late effects of radiation, those that occur several months *after* the treatment. These late effects include fibrosis (hardening) of the heart, lung, intestine, brain, etc. Where the fibrosis occurs depends on where the radiation was applied. Antioxidants may protect normal cells against these adverse effects without reducing the therapeutic effects of radiation.

The recommendations for vitamins and minerals, exercise, relaxation and stress management, and herbs are the same as for chemotherapy.

9 *Environmental Toxins/Allergens/Other Noxious Substances*

PASSIVE POLLUTION

Have you noticed that more and more people are complaining of fatigue, suffering from more allergies, and having more frequent and longer-lasting colds and other infections than usual these days? Perhaps you are one of these sufferers. If so, many of you have been told that nothing is wrong with you, that you are under a lot of stress and need to relax, that you are depressed and/or that it's "all in your head."

The fact is, however, many of us are being passively polluted by a multitude of noxious substances, substances that are sapping our physical and mental energies. These include inhalant allergens (pollens, dust, animal dander, molds); air pollutants (carbon monoxide, sulfur oxides, hydrocarbons, nitrogen oxides, particulate matter, cigarette smoke, ozone, formaldehyde, glues, paints, adhesives, deodorizers, perfumes, cleaning substances, etc.); food allergens; food additives (monosodium glutamate, sulfiting agents, etc.); pesticides, herbicides, fungicides; heavy metals; aluminum; ionizing radiation (X rays, gamma rays, radon, and other radioactive substances); ultraviolet radiation; water pollutants; and acid rain.

To many, the pollution problem seems overwhelming. But even

as governments and other groups struggle to deal with global pollution, there is much that we as individuals can do to remove pollutants from our own immediate environments and to protect ourselves against their adverse health effects. This chapter tells you how to do this.

FOOD ALLERGIES AND SENSITIVITIES

Many people experience adverse reactions after eating certain foods. These reactions can occur immediately upon eating the food or can be delayed, often occurring hours, or in some cases even days, after the food is eaten. Symptoms of these reactions can include abdominal cramping and gas, diarrhea, nasal congestion and discharge (runny nose), sneezing, shortness of breath, tightness in the chest, wheezing, heart palpitations, hives, headaches, and fatigue.

These symptoms are similar to those of inhalant allergies, such as hayfever. Because of this, many have assumed that all such reactions to foods are *allergic* reactions. Many of these, however, are *not*, in fact, allergic phenomena. Allergic responses involve immunological mechanisms. Many adverse reactions to foods do *not* involve such mechanisms. For this reason, standard allergy testing is usually of little value in this context.

I prefer to use the term *food sensitivity* for *any* abnormal response to an ingested food. Food *allergy* should only be used if the food sensitivity is known to have an immunological component. You may wonder why this distinction is so important. I make the distinction so that you won't waste a lot of money and time going through an extensive "food allergy work-up." The true food allergies are not very common, and those who have them generally know they have them (due to violent reactions) and avoid the foods that provoke them. Food sensitivities, on the other hand, are more difficult to detect.

The leading food sensitizers are milk and milk products (butter, buttermilk, cheese, cream, ice cream, and yogurt), shellfish (crab, crayfish, lobster, prawns, and shrimp), wheat and wheat products, chocolate, eggs, nuts, peanuts, and tomatoes. Other offenders include citrus fruits (orange, lemon, lime, grapefruit, tangerine, and kumquat) and citrus-fruit juices, soy and soy products, all seasonings (except salt in moderation), all fried foods, caffeinated beverages, diet drinks, all canned or frozen foods, most food additives (especially artificial colors and preservatives), alcoholic beverages, and yeast products.

The best way of treating food sensitivities is to *avoid* the food or foods causing problems. The method for determining the culprit foods is called dietary elimination or the elimination diet. Here are the basic rules.

Avoid entirely for one week all of the items listed in the above paragraph. Select foods from the following:

Vegetables: artichokes, asparagus, beans (yellow, wax), beets, broccoli, brussels sprouts, cabbage, cauliflower, celery, cucumber, eggplant, green beans, lettuce, potatoes (white or sweet), string beans, squash, yams. Note that those sensitive to tomatoes may also be sensitive to other members of the nightshade family, which includes (besides tomatoes) eggplant, white potatoes, bell pepper, and cayenne pepper. Avoid those.

Fruits: apples (baked), bananas, melons of all kinds, cooked peaches and pears (not canned), mangos, papayas, apricots, fresh dates, and fresh figs. *Stay away from dried fruits of all kinds.*

Grains: rice and rice cereals, oats and oatmeal.

Meats: veal, lamb, venison, poultry (chicken, turkey, cornish hen, game birds—but don't eat the skin).

Oils: olive oil, safflower oil.

Fluids: tea (herbal teas without caffeine); water ("pure" water only—see, Water Pollutants, below; be sure to drink 6 to 8 glasses of water daily); fruit juices (unsweetened and without additives only—including apple, papaya, pear, peach, and apricot; *no* citrus juices).

Sugar, honey, and salt: use sparingly; do not use any other sweeteners or seasonings.

Stay on this diet for one week. Then start adding other foods that you like, *one by one.* Add one, wait two or three days, and then if you still aren't having any adverse reactions, go on to another one, and so on, waiting two or three days in between each new food addition. In about four to five weeks, you should have identified most or all of the foods to which you are sensitive. Make sure that you thoroughly wash in pure water all the vegetables and fruits you eat. Take your time. Keep a food diary and record the foods that give you any problems.

In addition, I recommend that you take a hypoallergenic nutritional supplement containing the following amounts of vitamins and minerals:

Vitamin	*Recommended Daily Dose*
beta carotene	15–30 milligrams (mg)
vitamin B₁ (thiamine)	1.5–10 mg
vitamin B₂ (riboflavin)	1.7–10 mg
vitamin B₃ (niacin)	20–100 mg
pantothenic acid	10–50 mg
vitamin B₆ (pyridoxine)	2–25 mg
vitamin B₁₂	6–30 micrograms (mcg)
folic acid	200–400 mcg
biotin	100–300 mcg
vitamin C	60–1000 mg
vitamin D	200–400 IU
vitamin E	30–400 IU
vitamin K	100–200 mcg

Mineral	*Recommended Daily Dose*
calcium	250–1000 mg
magnesium	200–400 mg
zinc	15–30 mg
iron	10–15 mg
manganese	2–10 mg
copper	2–3 mg
selenium	50–200 mcg
chromium	50–200 mcg
iodine	50–150 mcg
molybdenum	50–200 mcg

Cromolyn, or sodium cromoglycate, is a flavonoidlike substance that has antiallergy properties. It has been used for some time in the treatment of allergic asthma and it has also been used effectively (mainly in Europe) to prevent symptoms of food allergy or sensitivity. If food withdrawal (elimination diet) is not successful in the treatment of your food sensitivity, cromolyn use should be considered. It is a prescription drug and must be used under a physician's supervision. Although it is FDA approved, it is not yet approved for the treatment of food sensitivity in this country. Your physician, however, can use it for this if he or she believes it to be appropriate. Side effects are mild even at high doses.

Cromolyn is used *orally* for the treatment of food sensitivity. The form that can be used orally in the U.S. is Gastrocrom, which is used for the treatment of the rare disorder mastocytosis. For treatment of food sensitivity, the contents of one to two capsules are dissolved in ½ cup of warm water and taken one-half hour before meals. Those who develop only symptoms of *nasal* congestion and sneezing after eating certain foods may instead consider using cromolyn in the form of a nasal spray called Nasalcrom. Discuss this with your physician.

FOOD ADDITIVES

Many substances are added to foods in order to impart or enhance flavor, as preservatives and antioxidants and as coloring and texturing agents. Various of these additives can make some people quite ill. These include monosodium glutamate (MSG), sulfiting agents, nitrites, and tartrazine.

MONOSODIUM GLUTAMATE (MSG)

MSG is a widely used additive for enhancing the flavor of foods. MSG is the sodium salt of glutamic acid, an amino acid. It is often found in Chinese-restaurant foods, bouillon cubes, canned and packaged soups, processed foods of all kinds, frozen entrees, salad dressings, prepared sauces, and appetizers, among others. MSG is available as a condiment, sold as MSG, Accent, or Ajinomoto Powder. The average intake of MSG is less than 1 gram per day. Many Chinese dishes, however, contain large amounts of the substance. You could be getting from 5 to 10 grams of MSG in the average Chinese meal, up to 3 grams from a serving of wonton soup alone.

Those who are sensitive or allergic to MSG often suffer from the so-called Chinese restaurant syndrome, or CRS. Symptoms of the classic CRS include palpitations, dizziness, general weakness, and numbness at the back of the neck, which gradually radiates to both arms and into the back. Other symptoms are tightness and pressure in the upper chest, shortness of breath, wheezing, headache, abdominal cramps, and diarrhea. Up to 30 percent of those eating Chinese food report *some* adverse reactions.

You are almost certainly sensitive to MSG if you develop symptoms such as those discussed above within twenty to thirty minutes after you start eating a Chinese meal or any meal that is heavily seasoned with MSG or if you have an asthmatic attack (shortness of breath, chest pressure, wheezing) that occurs from one to fourteen hours after eating a Chinese meal or any meal heavily seasoned with MSG.

The best way to treat MSG sensitivity is to *avoid* the substance. Some Chinese restaurants do not use MSG. Others will not use it if you request no MSG. Check the labels of the foods you eat.

Vitamin B_6 (pyridoxine), 50 milligrams daily, may *prevent* MSG sensitivity symptoms. Those who are MSG sensitive and who eat out a lot should consider taking B_6. Doses much higher than 50 milligrams daily taken for prolonged periods of time are *not* recommended because of potential adverse side effects.

SULFITING AGENTS

Sulfiting agents are additives that are used in foods, alcoholic beverages (wine, beer), and medications as preservatives and antioxidants. Commonly used sulfiting agents are sulfur dioxide, sodium sulfite, sodium bisulfite, sodium metabisulfite, potassium sulfite, potassium bisulfite, and potassium metabisulfite. Sulfiting agents can cause serious problems in those sensitive to them. A number of deaths have been attributed to these substances in recent years.

Many foods and beverages contain sulfiting agents, especially dried fruits (excluding dark raisins and prunes), *nonfrozen* lemon and lime juice, salad-bar lettuce, beer, wine, champagne, shrimp, sauerkraut and sauerkraut juice, prepared potatoes (frozen, canned, dried), grape juice, wine vinegar, prepared avocado dip or spread (guacamole), prepared cole slaw, and prepared gravies and sauces. It is more likely that you will be exposed to these additives if you eat out in restaurants, since many foods served in these establishments, especially salads, are treated with them to maintain fresh appearance.

Symptoms of sulfite sensitivity include hives, difficulty swallowing, chest tightness, shortness of breath, sneezing and, in a few cases, death. Most commonly, sulfiting agents cause asthmatic attacks in those sensitive to these agents. Reactions can be particularly severe in those with histories of severe asthma.

You are probably sensitive to sulfiting agents if you have adverse reactions shortly after eating dried fruits, shrimp, a restaurant salad, any of the other foods mentioned above that are high in sulfites or after drinking wine, champagne, or certain beers; if you have an asthmatic attack after eating in a restaurant, particularly after eating a salad; if you have adverse reactions to certain foods in restaurants but do not have them to the same foods when they are eaten at home; if you have an asthmatic attack after using a certain medication.

The best way to treat sulfite sensitivity is to *avoid* foods, beverages, and medications that contain sulfiting agents. In particular, avoid salad bars at restaurants. Read labels, and ask your physician if any of your medications contain these additives.

Vitamin B_{12}, in doses of 1,000–5,000 micrograms orally, or 2,000–

4,000 micrograms sublingually (under the tongue), has been shown to help *prevent* adverse symptoms in those who are sulfite sensitive. It's prudent for those who *are* sensitive to these substances and who eat out a lot to take 2,000–4,000 micrograms of vitamin B_{12} sublingually on a once-a-day basis.

The trace element molybdenum is necessary for the activity of the enzyme sulfite oxidase. This enzyme metabolizes sulfites. A daily intake of 50–200 micrograms of molybdenum is recommended for those who are sulfite sensitive. Both molybdenum (a mineral) and sublingual B_{12} lozenges are available in health-food stores.

NITRITES AND NITRATES

Sodium nitrite and sodium nitrate are used in foods as preservatives (to prevent the growth of bacteria that cause botulism) as well as to fix the color and improve the tastes of certain foods. Nitrites and nitrates form nitrosamines, which can cause stomach cancer. Though these additives are somewhat restricted, they are still used in many foods. Foods that usually contain nitrites or nitrates include cured meats, bacon, bologna, frankfurters, deviled ham, meat spreads, potted meats, spiced ham, vienna sausages, smoke-cured tunafish products, and smoke-cured shad and salmon.

Sensitivity to nitrites and nitrates manifests itself as a headache following consumption of foods containing these additives. The headache is known as the hot-dog headache, and the best way to treat it is to *avoid* foods containing nitrites or nitrates.

Vitamin C and vitamin E can effectively prevent the conversion of these additives to carcinogenic nitrosamines. It is prudent for those who eat foods rich in the additives to take 100–1,000 milligrams of vitamin C and 200–400 IUs of vitamin E daily. In fact, since many are exposed to nitrates in drinking water, it is prudent for nearly *everybody* to take these supplements.

TARTRAZINE

Tartrazine is a coal-tar derivative that is widely used as a food-coloring agent; it is also known as Yellow Number 5. It is found in frankfurters, salad dressings, catsup, canned vegetables, imitation flavorings and extracts, soft drinks, colored candy, and desserts, among other foods.

Some people are very sensitive to this food dye. Symptoms of sensitivity include hives and asthmatic attacks. Most people who are sensitive to tartrazine are sensitive to aspirin as well. Some who are sensitive to aspirin are sensitive to tartrazine. You are possibly sensitive to tartrazine if you develop asthmatic symptoms after ingesting artificially colored foods; if you have a history of aspirin sensitivity; and/or if you have chronic hives of unknown origin. Avoidance of foods containing tartrazine, if you have any of the above problems, may help you feel much better.

WATER POLLUTANTS

Many toxic substances pollute our drinking water. These toxins include lead and other heavy metals, aluminum, pesticides, herbicides, organic substances (such as carcinogenic trihalomethanes derived from chlorine), industrial byproducts, and potentially infectious organisms that are not killed by the typical disinfectants. By now, most people are aware that the water they drink is less than pure. But exactly how impure it is, and what can be done about it? The first step is to have your water tested. Call your local health department or look in your Yellow Pages under "Environmental" or "Water Testing." As a minimum, have your water tested for lead.

A number of home water-filtration units are available, ranging in price from inexpensive to a few hundred dollars. See Resources section under Water Purification Systems for a review of these systems. Some of the best are the least expensive.

If you do use tap water, let the water run for about a minute if it has not been run for a while, and in all cases, for about ten seconds to flush out any contaminants that can collect in the water from the plumbing (e.g., lead). Always use cold water for cooking since hot water absorbs more of these contaminants.

Be aware that you may also be absorbing toxins through your skin when showering or taking a bath. Let the water run awhile before using it for showering or bathing to flush out contaminants from the plumbing. Better yet, use a filter on your shower or tub as well.

Remember: *Pure* water is essential for all of the Purification Prescriptions. It is very important that you drink 6 to 8 glasses a day of the purest water you can obtain.

AIR POLLUTION

There is *no* nutrient that is as important to us as oxygen. We can live without food for a few weeks and without fluid for about seven days. But we *cannot* live without oxygen for more than about four minutes. We require around a pound of oxygen a day to burn our food-fuels to produce energy. Pure oxygen is a colorless, odorless gas and makes up 21 percent of the air we breathe. The air most of us breathe (both indoors and outdoors), however, is anything but pure. It is flavored, colored, and textured by a multitude of contaminants, many of which are quite poisonous.

Five major pollutants account for nearly 98 percent of all outdoor air pollution. These are carbon monoxide (52 percent), sulfur oxides (18 percent), hydrocarbons (12 percent), particulate matter (10 percent), and nitrogen oxides (6 percent). Transportation (primarily the automobile) accounts for 60 percent of the pollutants, industry for 18 percent, electric-power generation for 13 percent, space heating for 16 percent, and refuse disposal for 3 percent.

Ozone is one of the major culprits. It is a form of oxygen that is harmful for us to breathe and is produced in a reaction involving emissions from automobile exhausts. Many cities, such as Los Angeles, San Diego, St. Louis, and Denver, now frequently have unacceptably high ozone levels.

Although oxygen is absolutely essential for life, there are forms of oxygen that can destroy and kill. These forms are called free radicals. Free radicals are thought to be involved in all of the degenerative diseases associated with aging (cancer, atherosclerosis, Alzheimer's disease, arthritis, etc.), as well as aging itself. Air pollutants such as the nitrogen and sulfur oxides and ozone increase the free-radical loads of our bodies. Those who are exposed to these pollutants should ensure that their diets are rich in antioxidants and other substances that can protect against the toxic consequences of air pollutants (review Chapter 7, Part II), and they should also take a vitamin and mineral supplement rich in antioxidants, such as the one recommended earlier in this chapter.

Indoor air is not exempt from pollution. Sources of indoor air pollution include formaldehyde (used in plywood, particleboard, fiberboard, permanent-press clothing, carpet backings), benzene (used in many cleaning solvents), synthetic fibers and fabrics, plastics, insulation materials, glues and other adhesives, solvents, paints, stains, new cleaning substances, deodorizers, various aerosols, faulty air conditioners, humidifiers and dehumidifiers, gas stoves, heaters, fireplaces (the ones that use energy-saving inserts), wood-burning stoves (especially those without catalytic converters), kerosene-burning heaters, and radon.

Many people who are exposed to these indoor air pollutants come down with a number of health problems, such as watery or itchy eyes, stuffy noses, sore throats, frequent colds, recurrent headaches, difficulty in breathing, memory problems, and chronic fatigue. This condition is known as the sick-building syndrome. Almost all of these problems could be substantially reduced with better ventilation. Sick buildings are typically ones that have been constructed to keep *in* the heat during the cold seasons and keep *out* the heat during the warm seasons. They are buildings that are tightly sealed and don't "breathe."

If you have health problems and suspect that they are due to toxic substances such as formaldehyde, carbon monoxide, or radon in the air you are breathing in your home or place of work, look in the Resources section of this book to learn who can assist you. The best protection against indoor pollution, as noted above, is good ventilation. The simplest way to ventilate your office or home is to open your windows—even a crack will help. If there are no windows, then a local exhaust system can be installed that vents through a collecting device to the outside.

If you are considering an air-purification system, check the Resources section of this book for a review of the various kinds. If you use an air conditioner, thoroughly clean it *at least once every month*. Follow manufacturers' instructions on the cleaning process. Many people use humidifiers to help them breathe better. The best type to use is the *steam* vaporizer. If you have an ultrasonic humidifier, do not use it with plain tap water. You may inhale aluminum, lead, organic gases, and other toxins that are in the water. Instead, use *demineralized* water. You can prepare your own demineralized water by running tap water through a demineralization filter (see Resources section) or you can use *distilled* water. Store-purchased "de-ionized" water often contains significant amounts of minerals and other impurities. Make sure you clean your humidifier frequently, according to manufacturers' instructions.

Some *house plants* are great purifiers. They can filter indoor air pollutants, such as formaldehyde, carbon monoxide, and benzene. Elephant ear, heart-leaf philodendrons, and the aloe vera plant are good for formaldehyde; the green spider plant is good for carbon monoxide; Gerbera daisies and chrysanthemums filter out benzene; and golden pothos is good for formaldehyde, carbon monoxide, and benzene. Make sure you place about an inch of the type of gravel that you use for an aquarium *over* the top of the soil in which the plants are potted, in order to prevent the growth of molds.

INHALANT ALLERGIES

Carbon monoxide, nitrogen and sulfur oxides, ozone, formaldehyde, and benzene all are very democratic with respect to whom they poison. That is, they spare *no one*. Inhalant allergens, on the other hand, can cause adverse reactions, occasionally quite severe, in some, but have no effect in others. The most common inhalant allergens are dusts, molds, animal dander, cat saliva, and pollens from grasses, trees, and weeds.

Allergic rhinitis (drippy nose and nasal congestion) is the most common type of inhalant allergy. Some suffer from allergic rhinitis during certain seasons, others, all year round. Seasonal allergic rhinitis is more commonly known as hay fever. Hay fever is typically caused by airborne pollens. Hay fever that occurs in the spring is due to tree pollens. Summer hay fever is due to grass and weed pollens, and hay fever occurring in the fall is due to weed pollens. Allergic rhinitis that occurs throughout the year is also known as perennial allergic rhinitis. Symptoms of allergic rhinitis include sneezing, stuffy nose, runny nose, sometimes itchy eyes and, not infrequently, fatigue. Inhalant allergens can also cause spasm of the breathing tubes (bronchospasm) leading to shortness of breath, wheezing, chest tightness, and asthmatic attacks.

In contrast to testing for food allergies, testing for inhalant allergies is worthwhile. If you have persistent or recurrent symptoms of stuffy, runny nose and sneezing, you should see your physician and discuss with him or her the advisability of allergy testing.

Once you have been diagnosed as having a specific allergy, your best defense is *avoidance* of the allergens involved. Seriously consider getting an air-purification system (see Resources section) for your home, particularly for your bedroom. If you have carpets at home, make sure they are clean. Better yet, get rid of them—especially those in the bedroom. Medicines used in the treatment of allergic rhinitis include antihistamines (astemizole [Hismanal], chlorpheniramine, brompheniramine, terfenadine, [Seldane]), decongestants (pseudoephedrine), cromolyn (Nasalcrom), and topical steroid nasal sprays (beclomethasone and flunisolide). Hismanal and Seldane are nonsedating antihistamines. A multivitamin and multimineral supplement is recommended (see regimen detailed earlier in this chapter).

LEAD/CADMIUM/ALUMINUM

LEAD

Lead's history as a highly toxic substance dates back centuries. Lead is still very much with us, and millions of people in the U.S. are still exposed to toxic amounts of it. Sources of lead exposure include leaded gasoline, old plumbing, newer plumbing containing lead solder, certain Mexican and some other imported ceramics, batteries, and paint pigments. Lead can enter our bodies from air, water, and food. Although acute lead toxicity is not as common as it once was, chronic low-dose exposure continues to be a real problem, manifesting itself in more subtle but still dangerous ways. It is likely that lead is contributing to depression, memory problems, fatigue, and other health problems in many people.

Some nutrients are known to protect against lead toxicity. These include calcium, magnesium, copper, and iron. Also, vitamins B_6 (pyridoxine), B_{12}, C, and E and the trace mineral selenium may protect against lead toxicity. A vitamin and mineral supplement is recommended for those at risk for lead exposure. (See vitamin and mineral recommendations earlier in this chapter.)

Milk protects against lead toxicity because of calcium. Fats *increase* the absorption of lead into the body. A low-fat diet is therefore protective. *Alginates*, which are found in *brown* seaweed (hijiki, kombu, wakame, and arame), and polysaccharides found in *red* seaweed (nori, agar, dulse) decrease the absorption of lead. Liberal intake of edible seaweed is recommended.

CADMIUM

Cadmium has long been recognized as a toxic substance. Cadmium can enter our bodies from air, food, or water. Food is the most likely source. This heavy metal can cause damage to the liver and kidneys. It may also be responsible for some cases of high blood pressure, particularly in combination with lead. Substances that protect against cadmium toxicity include alginates, selenium, zinc, copper, iron, calcium, and vitamin C.

ALUMINUM

Heavy metals such as lead and cadmium are commonly thought to be very toxic, and they are. Aluminum is a light metal, the very real toxicity of which we are just beginning to appreciate. Aluminum is the cause of brain and bone disease in patients with chronic kidney failure who have been on long-term dialysis. High concentrations of aluminum have been found in the brains of patients with Alzheimer's disease and are thought to be a contributing factor in this disorder. Aluminum exposure is associated with a number of health problems, including memory difficulties, learning disorders, and other neurological problems.

Aluminum is found in many antacids, antiperspirants, and baking powder, among other things. It is the most abundant metal in the earth's crust. Acid rain is dissolving the metal, allowing it to enter into our water and food supplies for the first time in the history of our planet. The toxic effects of aluminum appear to be mediated mainly by antagonizing magnesium. These toxic effects are magnified in animals fed diets low in magnesium. Magnesium should thus protect against aluminum toxicity. Magnesium deficiency is quite common. A daily intake of 400 milligrams of magnesium is wise for those who are at risk for aluminum exposure. Avoidance of aluminum-containing substances and the use of purified water are recommended for everyone.

RADIATION

Radiation commonly refers to high-energy radiation, such as X rays or gamma rays that are capable of penetrating tissue and causing molecular disruption. In a stricter sense, this type of radiation is called ionizing radiation. Radiation of lower energy is nonionizing radiation and includes radio, TV, microwaves, and radar emissions.

Radioactivity refers to ionizing radiation emitted by isotopes of certain elements. Einstein's famous equation, $E = mc^2$ refers to the transformation of the mass of these isotopes to ionizing radiation. This is the principle behind the atomic bomb. Ionizing radiation may kill immediately or very quickly, as it did in Hiroshima, Nagasaki, and Chernobyl—or its effects can linger on in the body for many years, to cause cancer eventually, for example.

All of the toxic effects of ionizing radiation are mediated through free radical mechanisms. Consequently, biological antioxidants can confer protection against these toxic effects. Radioactive pollutants produced following the meltdown of a nuclear reactor—let's say, Chernobyl—include isotopes of iodine, cesium, barium, and strontium. Alginates, found in brown seaweed, protect against the toxicity of strontium, barium, and possibly cesium as well. Nonradioactive iodine protects against the toxic effects of its radioactive isotope.

Those at risk for radiation toxicity (those exposed to large doses of X rays or radionuclides used for diagnostic and therapeutic purposes) should consider taking a vitamin and mineral supplement rich in biological antioxidant precursors, such as the combination recommended earlier in this chapter. Two to three ounces of edible *brown seaweed* weekly may confer significant protection against toxicity of radioactive strontium, barium, radium, and cesium. A hundred milligrams of iodide daily for seven to fourteen days helps protect against toxicity due to acute radioactive iodine exposure. It should be started right at the beginning of such exposure in order for it to be most effective.

Edible seaweed is a remarkable purifying and healing food. We should all include a liberal amount of it in our diets. As we have seen, it is protective against some of the most vicious poisons on our planet: radioactive strontium, radium, barium, and cesium, as well as the heavy metals cadmium and lead. You will discover many tasty seaweed recipes in Juel Anderson's *Sea Green Primer* (see Resources section). It is also a great cholesterol-lowering food. Some of its components inhibit the growth of viruses as well, including HIV, the AIDS-related virus. There are not too many foods that we can say all this about. No wonder fish love it. For more on edible seaweed, see Chapter 4, Part II.

10 *Pure for Life*

THE END *AND* THE BEGINNING

We have journeyed far together and have arrived at the end—but only the end of this book. Finishing this book means beginning, starting a life free of the polluting and addicting substances that rob us of energy, predispose us to illness, disorder our minds, dull our spirits, and diminish our days.

You know what to do; you know how to begin. So get started, not tomorrow or next week, but *right now.* You're five short weeks—or less—from experiencing a wonderful state of mind—mind uncontaminated by harmful drugs, allergens, environmental toxins, and disordered brain chemistry.

In just five weeks, you can purge your body and brain of drugs and other pollutants, even those that have plagued you for years. And in that same brief period of time, you can set in motion a preventive program that will help protect you from any further or future contamination or addiction. If you follow the foregoing prescriptions, you can do more than just get clean in five weeks; you can make this a lifelong habit of health.

"ISN'T THERE JUST SOME PILL I COULD TAKE?"

Most people are relieved when I tell them that even the most contaminated and disordered cells of our brains and bodies can often be cleaned up and put back into proper working order in just a few weeks. But occasionally I get a patient who, after hearing me outline one of my five-week prescriptions, still says, as Julia did, "Isn't there just some pill I could take?"

In this quick-fix society of ours, even five weeks of effort is, for many, a seemingly insurmountable obstacle. What I've found often works in these cases is a one-step-at-a-time approach. In Julia's case, for example, I was dealing with a patient whose multiple drug addictions had so severely damaged and depressed her brain chemistry that her responses were almost universally negative.

Julia had come to see me "in desperation," as she put it. She said I was her last chance. Yet she couldn't get started on the treatment program I outlined for her. She'd look at the list of things to do and just shake her head wearily. To my promise that if she would follow the prescription, she would feel better than she had in years, she responded: "I don't have the energy to feel well" and "I'm too sick to feel well." Rather than abandon (or throttle) the poor woman, I told her I would be by to pick her up the following morning. Julia looked slightly startled—a good sign. My patient wasn't quite dead yet. When I refused to tell her *why* I would be by, she looked even more alive.

Early the next day I did, in fact, pound on Julia's door. To my surprise, she answered promptly. I'd clearly piqued her curiosity. She tried to retreat, however, when she saw me in my exercise outfit. Ten minutes of threats and cajolery later, we were out the door, Julia clad in her most comfortable clothing. We drove to the beach and joined some other people for a forty-minute walk.

Julia lagged far behind the group but picked up the pace a little after the first twenty minutes. I walked with her, first listening to her nonstop complaints, then enjoying her silence and, finally, her smiles and tears, as she began to draw in, with something akin to wonder, the natural beauty all around us.

"My God," she whispered, looking out over the water. "I forgot there's a real world out here."

Julia quickly became a regular at the beach. Rain or shine, she was there, walking, later jogging. And soon, if she felt down later in the day, she'd take a "booster stroll" to pick up her spirits. Next, I moved her into dietary and micronutrient therapy. One step at a time, she was soon in the full embrace of the Purification Prescription I had designed for her.

A year has passed since I knocked on Julia's door that morning. At that time, she had been addicted to alcohol and cocaine for years. Her marriage had dissolved and her career as a caterer—once one of the most successful in Southern California—was in a shambles. Today, Julia exudes confidence, energy, health, and success. She has restored her career—and, in fact, has significantly expanded her business—and is dating a man she says is "Mr. Right—or as close to it as you can get."

It is best, of course, to implement the prescriptions as directed in the preceding chapters. If this doesn't work for you, however, pick out the element or component that seems easiest and start with that. You're very likely to find that the other elements will quickly fall into place.

THE REWARDS OF GETTING CLEAN

I won't deny that the purification process doesn't entail some hard work and, yes, some pain. And without motivation—without the desire to get clean and stay that way—*no* purification program will work. The prescriptions I've provided help bolster confidence and willpower at their biochemical roots, but you'll still have to work at it—some more than others.

Is it worth it? Most of you know the answer to that. You wouldn't have read this book otherwise. The high costs of a polluted body or an impure mind have been detailed earlier in this book (review Chapter 2, Part I).

Whenever anyone asks me if it's worth it, I immediately think of Ron. When I first saw him four years ago, he had just been expelled from medical school, in his final year. The son of a noted surgeon, Ron had excelled in his studies and appeared destined for a brilliant career in medicine—up until cocaine began dictating destiny.

Ron told me he had begun using cocaine a couple of years earlier. "At first it was a novelty," he recalls. "Finally it became a necessity— or so I thought." He liked the extra energy it gave him—something all medical students need more of, it often seems. Of course, he soon needed more and more of the drug to achieve the same level of energy and attendant "good feelings." Within a year, by his reckoning, "I was afraid to be without it. I needed it every day."

Ron had always enjoyed a good relationship with his parents, brothers, and sisters. He had always had supportive friends and professors who were enthusiastic about his potential. He wasn't a cocaine addict "waiting to happen." The pressures of medical school, coupled with lack of sleep and less than optimal nutrition (medical students are notorious for their poor eating habits), no doubt played roles in his susceptibility, but there was no black hole in his life waiting to be filled with drugs. As I pointed out in Part I, given the nature of the world we live in today, we are *all* at risk for addictive behavior.

Here was a young life as promising as they come in distinct danger of being snuffed out. Here was a once athletic, handsome, sunny, and brilliant young man presenting himself to me twenty-five pounds underweight, haggard, jaundiced, suicidal, and looking twenty years older than he should have.

Like so many of my drug-dependent patients, Ron had lost sight of what he had once been. He defined himself now almost entirely in terms of a drug and his need for it. Like Julia, he had lost sight of the rest of the world. As part of Ron's treatment, I had him visualize himself as he had once been—healthy, happy, confident, and drug free. I have yet to encounter anyone who hasn't experienced at least some real joy and satisfaction in life. Focusing on that joy and satisfaction, however fleeting or distant it might be, can help anchor an individual long enough to introduce other healing components.

At first, for Ron, this meditative exercise was forced and mechanical. Even then, however, it had a relative calming, centering effect, and gradually, it began to reanimate my patient. Through memory and visualization, Ron began to recapture pieces of his old self.

Today Ron is a highly successful physician dedicated to the treatment of a very difficult set of disorders. I know personally of at least a hundred lives that have been saved and enriched by Ron's work. It is hard to believe that he is the same shattered individual I treated just four years ago. How tragic, not only for Ron and his family but also for medicine and society at large, if his life had ended then.

Does Ron think it was worth it?

"I can't believe you'd even ask that," he says now.

"Ah, yes," I answer, "but four years ago . . ."

"What's so amazing," Ron interjects, "is how close healing is, how close to all of us, if we could just see it, just a perception away."

Ron's absolutely right. I continue to marvel at how quickly and eagerly many "hopeless" addicts find hope and embrace anew health, wholeness, and life when given even small biochemical corrections, the sort that proper diet, optimal light, micronutrients, exercise, and the other purifying elements we've been discussing can fuel.

The difference between healthy behavior and addictive behavior can, as we all know, be the difference between life and death—and yet, those differences can be bridged in the microscopic space of mere molecules.

The way is clear. The bridge is before you. Cross it.

Resources

AIR QUALITY

1. Write to the American Society of Heating, Refrigerating, and Air-conditioning Engineers, Inc. (ASHRAE) to obtain the invaluable pamphlet *Ventilation for Acceptable Indoor Air Quality*. Contains much useful information.

   1791 Tullie Circle N.E.
   Atlanta, GA 30329

2. Refer to your Yellow Pages under "Air Pollution Control." Call and obtain literature on the various home units that are available (see text in next section). Try to become as educated as possible before purchasing.

3. National Environmental Health Association (NEHA) is an organization dedicated to the protection of environmental health. An excellent source of information on environmental issues.

   720 South Colorado Blvd., South Tower, 970
   Denver, CO 80222, (303) 756–9090

DRUG ABUSE

Treatment Centers

Sunshine, L., and Wright, J. W. *The 100 Best Treatment Centers For Alcoholism and Drug Abuse.* New York: Avon Books, 1988.

Not listed in the above book is Brunswick House in Amityville, Long

Island, New York. Brunswick House is the largest private alcoholism-treatment facility in New York State. Its medical director, Joseph D. Beasley, is one of the pioneers in the treatment of chemical dependency.

National Clearinghouse for Alcohol and Drug Information. P.O. Box 2345, Rockville, MD 20852, (301) 468-2600. Write or call for an up-to-date listing of the alcohol and drug authorities for all states and territories.

Where to Get Help

ALCOHOL
National Council on Alcoholism
(800) 622-2255

COCAINE
Psychiatric Institutes of America
(800)-COCAINE

NICOTINE
American Cancer Society
(800) 227-2345

Support Groups

(All the groups listed below follow the Twelve Step format except those identified as *not* doing so).

1) Alcoholics Anonymous, or AA. The granddaddy of all drug abuse support groups. Every community in the U.S. has at least one AA group.

   AA Headquarters
   Box 459
   Grand Central Station
   New York, NY 10163
   (212) 686-1100

   or

   Cocaine Anonymous
   6125 Washington Boulevard, Suite 202
   Los Angeles, CA 90230
   (213) 559-5833

2) Cocaine Anonymous (CA)
Check your phone book

3) Narcotics Anonymous (NA)
Check your phone book

   or

Narcotics Anonymous
PO Box 9999
Van Nuys, CA 91409
(818) 780-3951

4) Women for Sobriety
(does not follow Twelve Step format)
Box 618
Quakertown, PA 18951
(215) 536-8026

5) Al-Anon and Alateen
For families of alcoholics:

Al-Anon Family Group Headquarters, Inc.
PO Box 862
Midtown Station
New York, NY 10018-0862
(212) 302-7240

6) For adult children of alcoholics:

Al-Anon (see above)

   and

Adult Children of Alcoholics
PO Box 3216
2522 W. Sepulveda Boulevard, Suite 200
Torrance, CA 90505
(213) 534-1815

   and

National Association of Children of Alcoholics (referral scource
for non–Twelve Step formats)
31582 Coast Highway
South Laguna, CA 92677
(714) 499-3889

7) Smokers Anonymous World Services
2118 Greenwich Street
San Francisco, CA 94123
(415) 922-8575

Book for Smokers

Highest recommendation.

Ferguson, T. *The No-Nag, No-Guilt, Do-It-Your-Own Way Guide to Quitting Smoking.* New York: Ballantine Books, 1989.

EXERCISE

Book

Cooper, R. K. *Health and Fitness Excellence.* Boston: Houghton Mifflin Company, 1989.

Walking

Walking is now thought to be the best exercise. There are thousands of walking clubs and associations that provide information on walking trails throughout the world. For information, send a self-addressed stamped envelope to:

Walking Clubs
P.O. Box 509
Gracie Station
New York, NY 10028

Equipment

Cross-country skiing is considered one of the best aerobic exercises. The NordicTrack duplicates this exercise. Many believe the Nordic-Track is the best piece of exercise equipment that you can get. Call (800) 328-5888 or (612) 448-6987 (in Minnesota) for a free brochure. The address is NordicTrack, 141 Jonathan Boulevard, North Chaska, MN 55318.

HERBS

There is little to no quality control on most of the herbal products currently available. Happily, there are a few herbal companies that are attempting to establish more stringent practices in the production of herbal products. One of these companies is the Eclectic Institute, located at 11231 S.E. Market Street, Portland, OR 97216, (800) 332-HERB or (503) 256-4330 (in Oregon). Many of the herbs are prepared by freeze-drying freshly harvested plants. They are available in some health-food stores.

The *Herbal Gram* is a quarterly newsletter that presents a balanced view on the subject of herbs. It is published by the American Botanical Council and the Herb Research Foundation. A subscription is $18 for one year and can be obtained from Herbal Gram, P.O. Box 201660, Austin, TX 78720.

HOME POLLUTION

For general home pollution problems, contact the Consumer Product Safety Commission at (800) 638-2772 or your state health department or regional office of the Environmental Protection Agency (EPA). Look under "Environmental" or "Laboratories" in the Yellow Pages for local independent laboratories that can explain testing procedures for particular pollutants that may be found in the home. The American Council of Independent Laboratories, 1725 K Street, N.W., Washington, DC 20006, (202) 887-5872, may also be able to recommend a testing laboratory in your area. The home is assessed for presence of any harmful air contaminants as well as for ventilation efficiency or flow rate of fresh air per occupant. An acceptable rate of fresh air supply per person is 24 to 25 cfm (cubic feet per minute).

Asbestos

The phone number of the asbestos division of the EPA is (800) 835-7600. For information on asbestos in consumer products or in homes, call (800) 638-2772. This is the number for the U.S. Consumer Product Safety Commission (CPSC). For names of labs qualified to test and analyze asbestos samples: (800) 334-8571, ext. 6741 (EPA). For technical assistance: (800) 424-9065 (EPA).

The EPA publishes the *Asbestos Fact Book*. For a free copy, write to United States Environmental Protection Agency, Office of Public Affairs (A-107), Washington, DC 20460.

For a copy of *Asbestos in the Home*, published by the CPSC and the EPA, write to Superintendent of Documents, U.S. Government Printing Office, Washington, DC 20402, (202) 783-3238. This publication was designed to help consumers understand the potential dangers of asbestos in the home and what to do about them.

Formaldehyde

For a copy of *Formaldehyde: Everything You Wanted to Know but Were Afraid to Ask*, send a self-addressed envelope to Consumer Federation of America, 1424 16th Street, N.W., Washington, DC 20036.

The Consumer Product Safety Commission, (800) 638-2772, has a list of formaldehyde-testing kits and where they can be purchased. Assay Technology, Palo Alto, CA 94303, sells a formaldehyde home monitoring kit, phone (800) 833-1258; in California: (415) 424-9947.

Lead

To obtain an excellent pamphlet on lead, entitled *Preventing Lead Poisoning in Young Children*, write to U.S. Department of Health and Human Services, Public Health Service, Centers for Disease Control, Center for Environmental Health, Chronic Disease Division, Atlanta, GA 30333.

Radon

1. Get a list of the public and private Environmental Protection Agency (EPA)-approved organizations doing radon testing by contacting your local state health office or local branch of the EPA, or write: Radon/Radon Progeny Cumulative Proficiency Report, EPA Press Office, Washington, DC 20460. The cost of testing is $10–$50, depending on the type of monitor used. EPA hotline is (800) 334-8571.

2. Other information booklets from the above agencies: *Radon Reduction Methods* and *A Citizen's Guide to Radon*.

3. Call the hotlines several states have set up to answer questions about radon: Illinois (800) 672-3389; Maryland (301) 225-6981; New Jersey (800) 648-0394; New York (800) 342-3722; Pennsylvania (800) 237-2366; and Virginia (800) 468-0138.

4. Radon-testing kits are available from the FREE Market, Dept. RTK, 1001 Connecticut Avenue, N.W., Suite 638, Washington, DC 20036; phone (202) 466-6350; from Air Check, P.O. Box 100, Penrose, NC 28766; phone (800) CK-RADON; from Terradex Corporation, 3 Science Road, Glenwood, IL 60425-1579; (312) 755-7911.

5. A device called a Dranjer is designed to keep radon from wafting in through basement drains, a common entry point. Dranjers are sold by some hardware chains and cost about $20. The Dranjer Corporation is located at 1441 Pembina Highway, Winnipeg, Man., Canada R3T 2C4.

6. EPA pamphlets: *A Citizen's Guide to Radon: What It Is and What to Do About It; Radon Reduction Methods: A Homeowner's Guide;* and *Interim Indoor Radon and Radon Decay Product Measurement Protocols.*

LIGHTING

Standard incandescent bulbs and standard cool-white fluorescent bulbs do not provide full-spectrum lighting, the kind that appears to be most beneficial to health.

Chromalux is an incandescent bulb, made by the Luminarian Corporation of Finland, that is superior to the standard one. It is available through specialty lighting stores and distributors. It is a long-life bulb and retails for about $7.50. The Chromalux comes in 60-, 100- and 150-watt sizes. Duro-Test also makes a superior incandescent bulb called Neo-White. The Neo-White is similar to the Chromalux bulb. It comes in 60- and 100-watt sizes and is also available through specialty lighting stores and Duro-Test distributors (see below).

The most widely used full-spectrum fluorescent light is the Vita-Lite made by Duro-Test. The Vita-Lite is available through specialty lighting stores and Duro-Test distributors. A distributor in your area can be located through your local Yellow Pages or the company,

Duro-Test Corporation, 2321 Kennedy Boulevard, North Bergen, NJ 07047.

A fluorescent light unit with a high rate of illumination is the Ultra-Bright Medic Lite 10,000. This unit may be particularly beneficial for those with seasonal affective disorder (SAD). For information on this unit, contact MedicLight at 34 Yacht Club Drive, Lake Hopatcong, NJ 07849; (201) 663-1214.

Full-spectrum light tubes and systems designed by Dr. John Ott, a pioneer in the development of this type of lighting, are available through Baubiologie Hardware. For a free catalog, phone (408) 372-8626, or write to Baubiologie Hardware, 207B 16th Street, Pacific Grove, CA 93950.

NUTRITION

Invaluable Books

1. Carper, Jean. *The Food Pharmacy*. New York: Bantam, 1988.

2. Connor, Sonja L., and Connor, William E. *The New American Diet*. New York: Fireside, 1989.

   An excellent diet book with many substitutions to help make the transition from the standard American diet painless.

3. Ford, Richard, and Anderson, Juel. *Sea Green Primer. A Beginner's Book of Sea Weed Cookery*. Berkeley, California: Creative Arts Book Company, 1983.

   Seaweed is the source of alginates, other unique soluble fibers, and an excellent source of some vitamins and minerals. Lots of valuable information about seaweed. A number of good recipes showing what can be done with these vegetables from the sea.

4. Harris, Bob. *Growing Shiitake Commercially*. Madison, Wisconsin: Science Tech Publishers, 1986.

   The Japanese forest mushroom, or shiitake, is expensive (fresh shiitake costs up to $20 a pound). This manual instructs you on how to grow your own.

5. Harris Lloyd J. *The Book of Garlic*. Berkeley, California: Aris Books, 1980.

   The history, chemistry, and sociology of garlic. Lots of good recipes, too.

6. Hendler, Sheldon Saul. *The Complete Guide to Anti-Aging Nutrients*. New York: Simon and Schuster, 1985; Fireside, 1986.

7. Hendler Sheldon Saul. *The Doctors' Vitamin and Mineral Encyclopedia*. New York: Simon and Schuster, 1990.

8. Lappe, Frances Moore. *Diet for a Small Planet*. New York: Ballantine Books, 1982.

9. Pennington, Jean A. T., and Church, B. S. *Food Values of Portions Commonly Used*. 15th ed. New York: Harper and Row, 1989.

   The complete nutrient content—calories, cholesterol, fat, protein, carbohydrate, fiber, salt, vitamins and minerals—of all the foods you eat. An invaluable reference.

10. Pritikin, Nathan. *The Pritikin Promise*. New York: Simon and Schuster, 1983.

11. Robertson, Laurel; Flinders, Carol; and Ruppenthal, Brian. *The New Laurel's Kitchen: A Handbook for Vegetarian Cookery and Nutrition*. Berkeley, California: Ten Speed Press, 1986.

12. Shurtleff, William, and Aoyagi, Akiko. *The Book of Tofu*. New York: Ballantine Books, 1979. *The Book of Miso*. New York: Ballantine Books, 1981. *The Book of Tempeh*. New York: Harper and Row, 1979.

    In addition to being excellent cookbooks, these books provide fascinating information about the history and biology of these foods. Particularly interesting is *The Book of Miso*.

NUTRITIONAL SUPPLEMENTS

Supplements are obtainable at your local health-food store, drugstore, or supermarket. Good products are available by mail order from:

1. NutriGuard Research
   P.O. Box 865
   Encinitas, CA 92024
   (800) 433-2402, Ext. 10.
   (800) 426-6374 (within California)

2. Bronson Pharmaceuticals
   4526 Rinetti Lane
   La Canada, CA 91011-0628
   (800) 521-3322
   (800) 521-3323 (within California)

Lecithin capsules containing 90 percent phosphatidylcholine, as well as a concentrated phosphatidylcholine liquid, are available from:

Advanced Nutritional Technology, Inc.
P.O Box 3225
Elizabeth, NJ 07207
(800) 624-6543
(201) 354-2740, Ext. 42 (within New Jersey)

RELAXATION

Books

Downing, G. *The Massage Book*. New York: Random House, The Bookworks, 1988.

Hendler, Sheldon Saul. *The Oxygen Breakthrough*. New York: William Morrow, 1989; Pocket Books, 1990.

Lawrence, D. B. *Massage Techniques*. New York: Perigee Books, 1986.

Relaxation Tapes

These can be obtained from your local bookstores, particularly those that deal in New Age materials.

"Deep 10 Relaxation" tape can be obtained from:

Interstate Industries
P.O. Box 130
Nellysford, VA 22958
(804) 361-1500

Marsona Sound Conditioner

Available in some electronics stores. A good device to mask out and reduce the annoyance of unwanted noise. Those with problems sleeping should consider this or a similar unit.

Flotation Tanks

For catalog, call: (800) FLOAT 88; (516) 587-9854 (within New York).

Also:

Enrichment Enterprises, Inc.
77 Cedar Street
Babylon, NY 11702

These units are relatively expensive.

Respiration feedback is a technique for deep relaxation developed by the German psychiatrist H. Launer, who has had much success with its use.

Respiration-feedback units (expensive) can be obtained from:

Human Dynamics
6000 Park of Commerce Blvd.
Boca Raton, FL 33487
(800) 624-3982
(407) 994-4700 (within Florida)

SULFITE TESTING

Sulfite test strips are available without prescription. For information, write to:

Center Laboratories
35 Channel Drive
Port Washington, NY 11050
(800) 645-6335
(516) 767-1800 (within New York)

WATER PURIFICATION

Before you decide on the system you want, if any, comparison-shop and educate yourself on the various devices available. Contact your local water supplier or state health department for a list of state-certified water-testing laboratories that can analyze your tap water for a wide variety of contaminants.

Your regional EPA will send you a list of contaminants that you may want to test for. If you have any questions call the EPA Drinking Water Hotline, (800) 426-4791 or (202) 382-5533 (in Washington, DC).

Systems

1) **Brita:** Contains an activated silverized carbon filter and an ion exchange resin. Removes bacteria, lead, copper, and chlorine compounds. Is inexpensive, does not require installation, and is easy to use. Made in West Germany and distributed by Brita (Canada) Inc., 373 Front Street East, Toronto, Ont. M5A 354, and Brita America, Inc., 321 Commercial Avenue, Palisades Park, NJ 07650. Now being carried by many health-food stores.

2) **Activated charcoal filter:** Many different models are available. These filters are attached directly to the faucet and remove organic substances and gases that pass through them. These filters remove the taste and odor of chlorine and chloramines. They should be changed frequently.

3) **Culligan Aqua-Clear System:** This more expensive system provides three-way filtration: a particulate filter for removal of small particles; an activated charcoal filter, which removes chlorine, chloramines, other substances that affect taste and odor, and lead; and reverse osmosis, which reduces levels of dissolved impurities such as heavy metals (lead, mercury, etc.) and sodium.

   Contact your Culligan dealer for information. The Culligan Aqua-Clear System is installed under your sink.

4) **Seagull IV:** This system, which is also installed under your sink, utilizes a complex filter that is made from powdered carbon bonded together with other materials, and removes chlorine, chloramines, bacteria, asbestos, heavy metals, and radioactive debris. There are distributors throughout the U.S. for the Seagull IV. Information can be obtained through these distributors, or write:

The Glass Bubble
2815 Elm Street
Dallas, TX 75226

For their *To Your Health Catalogue,* phone (800) 233-2606 or (214) 939-9080 (within Texas). The pressed-carbon-block filters, such as those used in the Seagull IV, are becoming increasingly popular. Amway's water-treatment system also uses this type of filter.

Bibliography

PART I

Chapter 2: Polluted Body/Impure Mind

Abbott, R. D., et al. 1986. Risk of Stroke in Male Cigarette Smokers. *New England Journal of Medicine* 315:717–720.

Alder, J., et al. 1988. Crack. *Newsweek* (February 28):64–79.

Anonymous. 1989. Another Deadly Danger of Cocaine. *Emergency Medicine* (March 30):100–102.

Anonymous. 1987. Crack. *The Lancet* II: 1061–1062.

Anonymous. 1988. Estimate of U.S. Radiation Exposure Doubles. *Internal Medicine World Report* (January 15–21):3.

Anonymous. 1986. Indoor Air and Human Health. *The Lancet* I: 1419–1420.

Anonymous. 1985. Lead/It's Everywhere. *Emergency Medicine* (June 15):60–91.

Anonymous. 1987. Passive Smoking. *Internal Medicine World Report* (February):3.

Anonymous. 1985. The Price of a Paunch. *Medical World News* (February 11):74.

Baird, D. D., and Wilcox, A. J. 1985. Cigarette Smoking Associated with Delayed Conception. *Journal of the American Medical Association* 253:2979–2983.

Barnes, D. M. 1988. Drugs: Running the Numbers. *Science* 240:1729–1731.

Barry, J., et al. 1989. Effect of Smoking on the Activity of Ischemic Heart Disease. *Journal of the American Medical Association* 261:398–402.

Benowitz, N. L. 1988. Pharmacological Aspects of Cigarette Smoking and Nicotine Addiction. *New England Journal of Medicine* 319:1318–1330.

Bergman, M. M., and Gleckman, R. A. 1988. Infectious Complications in Alcohol Abusers. *Hospital Practice* (September):145–156.

252   BIBLIOGRAPHY

Birakos, J. N. 1989. The Changing Face of Air Pollution. *The Chemist* (May).

Bray, G. A., and Gray, D. S. 1988. Obesity/Part I—Pathogenesis. *Western Journal of Medicine* 149:429–441.

Brown, R.; Pinkerton, R.; and Tuttle, M. 1987. Respiratory Infections in Smokers. *American Family Physician* 36:133–140.

Burton, B. T., et al. 1985. Health Implications of Obesity: An NIH Consensus Development Conference. *International Journal of Obesity* 9:155–169.

Chasnoff, I. J. 1989. Cocaine and Pregnancy—Implications for the Child. (editorial) *Western Journal of Medicine* 150:456–458.

Chasnoff, I. J., et al. 1989. Temporal Patterns of Cocaine Use in Pregnancy. *Journal of the American Medical Association* 261:1741–1744.

Chesebro, M. J. 1988. Passive Smoking. *American Family Physician* 37:212–218.

Cocores, J. A., and Gold, M. S. 1989. Substance Abuse and Sexual Dysfunction. *Medical Aspects of Human Sexuality* (February):22–31.

Cohen, L. A. 1987. Diet and Cancer. *Scientific American* 257 (November):42–48.

Comfort, A. 1984. Alcohol as a Social Drug and Health Hazard. *The Lancet* I: 443–444.

Council on Scientific Affairs. 1989. Formaldehyde. *Journal of the American Medical Association* 261:1183–1188.

Cregler, L. L. 1988. Cardiovascular Effects of Alcohol. *Primary Cardiology* (August):38–44.

———. 1989. The Heart and Cocaine. *Primary Cardiology* (April):23–24.

Davies, K.J.A., et al. 1982. Free Radicals and Tissue Damage Produced by Exercise. *Biochemical and Biophysical Research Communications* 107:1198–1205.

Davis, J. W., et al. 1989. Passive Smoking Affects Endothelium and Platelets. *Archives of Internal Medicine* 149:386–389.

Desmond, S. 1987. Diet and Cancer—Should We Change What We Eat? *Western Journal of Medicine* 146:73–78.

Diamond, I. 1989. Alcoholic Myopathy and Cardiomyopathy. (editorial) *New England Journal of Medicine* 320:458–459.

Diamond T., et al. 1989. Ethanol Reduces Bone Formation and May Cause Osteoporosis. *American Journal of Medicine* 86:282–288.

Director-General, World Health Organization Report. 1986. Tobacco Use and World Health: A Situation Analysis. *PAHO Bulletin* 20:409–417.

Dixon, S. D. 1989. Effects of Transplacental Exposure to Cocaine and Methamphetamine on the Neonate. *Western Journal of Medicine* 150:436–442.

Dwyer, J. H., et al. 1988. Low-Level Cigarette Smoking and Longitudinal Change in Serum Cholesterol Among Adolescents. The Berlin-Bremen Study. *Journal of the American Medical Association* 259:2857–2862.

Eichner, E. R. 1989. Gastrointestinal Bleeding in Athletes. *The Physician and SportsMedicine* 17(May):128–140.

Embry, C. K., and Jones, J. D. 1988. Chemical Dependency in the Elderly. *Internal Medicine* 9 (July):139–142.

Esajian, J. 1989. Not Killer Smogs but Lung-Cripplers. *Medical Tribune* (January 19):7.

Fanning, O. 1988. Report of the Surgeon General. The Health Consequences of Smoking: Nicotine Addiction. *Internal Medicine World Report* 3 (June 1–14):3.

———. 1989. Report of the Surgeon General. Reducing the Health Consequences of Smoking: 25 Years of Progress. *Internal Medicine World Report* 4 (February 15–28):2–3.

Feinman, B. N. 1989. Neurologic Sequelae of Cocaine. *Hospital Practice* (January 30):97–104.

Fielding, J. E., and Phenow, K. J. 1988. Health Effects of Involuntary Smoking. *New England Journal of Medicine* 319:1452–1460.

Gawin, F. H., and Ellinwood, E. H., Jr. 1988. Cocaine and Other Stimulants. *New England Journal of Medicine* 318:1173–1182.

Gelman, D., et al. 1989. Roots of Addiction. *Newsweek* (February 20):52–57.

Gill, J., et al. 1986. Stroke and Alcohol Consumption. *New England Journal of Medicine* 315:1041–1046.

Hackney, J. D., and Linn, W. S. 1989. Assessing the Risk to Human Health from Common Air Pollutants. *The Chemist* (May):12.

Haglund, K. 1988. Exercise Found to Spur Cardiac Vulnerability to CO. *Medical Tribune* (December 29):8.

Harris, T., et al. 1988. Body Mass Index and Mortality among Nonsmoking Older Persons. *Journal of the American Medical Association* 259:1520–1524.

Hegedüs, L., et al. 1988. Independent Effects of Liver Disease and Chronic Alcoholism on Thyroid Function and Size: The Possibility of a Toxic Effect of Alcohol on the Thyroid Gland. *Metabolism* 37:229–233.

Henahan, R. 1988. Grounds for Heavy Coffee Drinkers to Use Filters. *Medical Tribune* (December 29):11.

Hubert, H. B., et al. 1983. Obesity as an Independent Risk Factor for Cardiovascular Disease: A 26-Year Follow-up of Participants in the Framingham Heart Study. *Circulation* 67(5):968–977.

Hunding, A.; Jordahl, R.; and Pauley, P. E. 1981. Running Anemia and Iron Deficiency. *Acta Medica Scandinavica* 209:315–318.

Jajich, C. L.; Ostfeld, A. M.; and Freeman, H., Jr. 1984. Smoking and Coronary Heart Disease. Mortality in the Elderly. *Journal of the American Medical Association* 252:2831–2834.

Kerr, R. A. 1988. Indoor Radon: The Deadliest Pollutant. *Science* 240:606–608.

Klein, L. W. 1987. Cigarette Smoking and Coronary Artery Disease: Recent Findings and Implications for Patient Management. *Cardiovascular Reviews & Reports* 8(February):74–78.

Klerman, G. L., and Weissman, M. M. 1989. Increasing Rates of Depression. *Journal of the American Medical Association* 261:2229–2235.

LaCroiz, A. Z., et al. 1986. Coffee Consumption and the Incidence of Coronary Heart Disease. *New England Journal of Medicine* 315:977–982.

Lall, K. B.; Barar, M.; and Pande, S. K. 1980. Probable Tobacco Addiction in a Three-Year-Old Child. *Clinical Pediatrics* 19:56–58.

Leonard, T. K., et al. 1986. Nutrient Intakes: Cancer Causation and Prevention. *Progress in Food and Nutrition Science* 10:237–277.

Lieber, C. S. 1983. Hepatic, Metabolic, and Nutritional Complications of Alcoholism. *Resident and Staff Physician* 29(August):79–96.

———. The Influence of Alcohol on Nutritional Status. *Nutritional Review* 46(July):241:254.

254 BIBLIOGRAPHY

MacDonald, T. L., and Martin, R. B. 1988. Aluminum in Biological Systems. *Trends in Biological Sciences* 13(January):15–19.

Mackay, J. 1988. The Tobacco Epidemic Spreads. *World Health* (October):9–12.

Manson, J. E., et al. 1987. Body Weight and Longevity. *Journal of the American Medical Association* 257:353–358.

Marshall, E. 1989. Clean Air? Don't Hold Your Breath. *Science* 244:517–520.

Matteo, S. 1988. The Risk of Multiple Addictions/Guidelines for Assessing a Woman's Alcohol and Drug Use. *Western Journal of Medicine* 149:741–745.

Mattson, M. E., et al. 1989. Passive Smoking on Commercial Airline Flights. *Journal of the American Medical Association* 261:867–872.

Mattson, M. E.; Pollack, E. S.; and Cullen, J. W. 1987. What Are the Odds That Smoking Will Kill You? *American Journal of Public Health* 77:425–431.

McGuire, R. 1988. Running Immunity Ragged. *Medical Tribune* (November 24):5.

Merz, B. 1987. New Framingham Data Indicate That Smoking Is Also a Risk Factor for Stroke. *Journal of the American Medical Association* 257:2132–2134.

Michaels, M.; Willwerth, J.; et al. 1989. How America Has Run out of Time. *Time* (April 24):58.

Mickley, D. W. 1988. Eating Disorders. *Hospital Practice* (November 30):58–79.

Milhorn, H. T., Jr. 1989. Nicotine Dependence. *American Family Physician* 39:214–224.

Nero, A. V., Jr. 1988. Controlling Indoor Air Pollution. *Scientific American* 258 (May):42–48.

Olsen-Noll, C. G., and Bosworth, M. F. 1989. Alcohol Abuse in the Elderly. *American Family Physician* 39:173–179.

Peck, P. 1989. Pollution: Medicine's Next AIDS. *Physician's Management* 29(5):40–47.

Phillips, P. 1988. Concomitant Nicotine and Alcohol Addiction Require Special Care. *Medical World News* (June 13):30–31.

Puddey, I. B.; Beilin, L. J.; and Vandongen, R. 1987. Regular Alcohol Use Raises Blood Pressure in Treated Hypertensive Subjects. *The Lancet* I: 647–651.

Raloff, J. 1989. Lead Effects Show in Child's Balance. *Science News* 135:54.

———. 1989. Blood-Lead Climbs as Old Bones Decline. *Science News* 135:181.

Rapoport, J. L. 1988. The Neurobiology of Obsessive-Compulsive Disorder. *Journal of the American Medical Association* 260:2888–2890.

Ricer, R. E. 1987. Smokeless Tobacco Use. *Postgraduate Medicine* 81(4):89–94.

Rosenberg, L., et al. 1988. Coffee Drinking and Nonfatal Myocardial Infarction in Men Under 55 Years of Age. *American Journal of Epidemiology* 128:570–578.

Rosenberg, L., et al. 1985. Myocardial Infarction and Cigarette Smoking in Women Younger Than 50 Years of Age. *Journal of the American Medical Association* 253:2965–2974.

Rowbotham, M. C. 1988. Neurologic Aspects of Cocaine Abuse. *Western Journal of Medicine* 149:442–448.

Ruoff, G. E. 1986. Cigarettes and Peptic Ulcers. *Drug Therapy* (November):51–62.

Samet, J. M., and Nero, A. V., Jr. 1989. Indoor Radon and Lung Cancer. *New England Journal of Medicine* 320:591–593.

Sherlock, S. 1988. Liver Disease in Women/Alcohol, Autoimmunity, and Gallstones. *Western Journal of Medicine* 149:683–686.

Shocken, D. D.; Holloway, J. D.; and Powers, P. S. 1989. Weight Loss and the Heart. *Archives of Internal Medicine* 149:877–881.

Siegel, A. J.; Hennekens, C. H.; and Soloman, H. S. 1979. Exercise-Related Hematuria: Findings in a Group of Marathon Runners. *Journal of the American Medical Association* 241:391.

Silbergeld, E. K. 1987. Lead Poisoning Imperils Millions of Americans. *Environmental Defense Fund Letter* (March).

Slattery, M. L., et al. Cigarette Smoking and Exposure to Passive Smoke Are Risk Factors for Cervical Cancer. *Journal of the American Medical Association* 261:1593–1633.

Stampfer, M. J., et al. 1988. A Prospective Study of Moderate Alcohol Consumption and the Risk of Coronary Disease and Stroke in Women. *New England Journal of Medicine* 319:267–273.

Tell, G., et al. 1989. Cigarette Smoking Cessation and Extracranial Carotid Atherosclerosis. *Journal of the American Medical Association* 261:1178–1180.

Torres, M., and Brecher, D. B. 1987. Smokeless Tobacco: A New Health Hazard. *Medical Times* (February):73–80.

Underwood, B. A. 1986. The Diet-Cancer Conundrum. *Public Health Review* 14:191–212.

Unger, K. B. 1988. Chemical Dependency in Women/Meeting the Challenges of Accurate Diagnosis and Effective Treatment. *Western Journal of Medicine* 149:746–750.

Urbano-Marquez, A., et al. 1989. The Effects of Alcoholism on Skeletal and Cardiac Muscle. *New England Journal of Medicine* 320:409–415.

U.S. Department of Health and Human Services. 1986. *The Health Consequences of Involuntary Smoking: A Report of the Surgeon General.* DHHS(CDC):87–8398.

U.S. Department of Health and Human Services. 1988. *The Health Consequences of Smoking: Nicotine Addiction: A Report of the Surgeon General.* DHHS(CDC):88–8406.

Van Itallie, T. B. 1985. Health Implications of Overweight and Obesity: an American Perspective. *Annals of Internal Medicine* (December).

———. 1979. Obesity: Adverse Effects on Health and Longevity. *American Journal of Clinical Nutrition* 32:2723–2733.

Vander Zwaag, R., et al. 1988. The Effect of Cigarette Smoking on the Pattern of Coronary Atherosclerosis: A Case-Control Study. *Chest* 94:290–295.

Wehrmacher, W. H. 1988. Effect of Alcohol on the Heart: Good or Bad? *Internal Medicine* 9(April):118–120.

Wehrmacher, W. H., and Doot, M. 1988. Alcoholism in the Elderly. *Internal Medicine* 9 (October 15):134–140.

Winniford, M., et al. 1987. Cigarette Smoking-Induced Coronary Vasoconstriction in Atherosclerotic Coronary Artery Disease and Prevention by Calcium Antagonists and Nitroglycerin. *American Journal of Cardiology* 59:203–207.

Woods, J. H.; Katz, J. L.; and Winger, G. 1988. Use and Abuse of Benzodiazepines. *Journal of the American Medical Association* 260:3476–3479.

PART II

Chapter 1: Vitamins and Minerals

Alexander, M.; Newmark, H.; and Miller, R. G. 1985. Oral Beta Carotene Can Increase the Number of OKT4+ Cells in Human Blood. *Immunology Letters* 9:221–224.

Anderson, J.J.B., and Switzer, B. R. 1987. Effects of Alcohol on Nutritional Status: Part I—Minerals. *Internal Medicine* 8(August):69–94.

Anderson, R. A. 1986. Chromium Metabolism and Its Role in Disease Processes in Man. *Clinical Physiology and Biochemistry* 4:31–41.

Anderson, R.; Theron, A. J.; and Ras, G. J. 1987. Regulation by the Antioxidants Ascorbate, Cysteine, and Dapsone of the Increased Extracellular and Intracellular Generation of Reactive Oxidants by Activated Phagocytes from Cigarette Smokers. *American Review of Respiratory Diseases* 135:1027–1032.

Anderson, R., et al. 1988. Ascorbic Acid Neutralizes Reactive Oxidants Released by Hyperactive Phagocytes from Cigarette Smokers. *Lung* 166:149–159.

Anderson, S. H.; Vickery, C. A.; and Nicol, A. D. 1986. Adult Thiamine Requirements and the Continuing Need to Fortify Processed Cereals. *The Lancet* II: 85–89.

Anonymous. 1986. Can B_6 Add to Asthma Therapy? *Medical World News* (August 11):63.

Anonymous. 1987. Copper Deficiency and Hypercholesterolemia. *Nutrition Reviews* 45(April):116–117.

Anonymous. 1988. Hypomagnesemia Found in 25% of Eating Disorders. (report) *Internal Medicine News* 21(July 1–14):47.

Anonymous. 1987. Micronutrient Interactions in the Prevention of Cancer. *Nutrition Reviews* 45(May):139–141.

Anonymous. 1987. Vitamin B_{12} Confirmed as Effective Sulfite Allergy Blocker. *Allergy Observer* 4(March–April):1.

Anonymous. 1985. Zinc Deficiency Impairs Ethanol Metabolism. *Nutrition Reviews* 43(May):158–159.

Arsenio, L., et al. 1986. Effectiveness of Long-Term Treatment with Pantethine in Patients with Dyslipidemia. *Clinical Therapeutics* 8:537–541.

Beard, J., and Myfanwy, B. 1988. Iron Deficiency and Thermoregulation. *Nutrition Today* 23(September/October):41–45.

Beck, W. S. 1988. Cobalamin and the Nervous System. *New England Journal of Medicine* 318:1752–1754.

Becker, D. V., et al. 1984. The Use of Iodine as a Thyroidal Blocking Agent in the Event of a Reactor Accident. *Journal of the American Medical Association* 252:659–661.

Belko, A. Z., et al. 1983. Effects of Exercise on Riboflavin Requirements of Young Women. *American Journal of Clinical Nutrition* 37:509–517.

Bendich, A. 1988. Antioxidant Vitamins and Immune Responses, in Chandra, R. K., ed. *Nutrition and Immunology*. New York: Alan R. Liss, Inc., 125–147.

———. 1988. The Safety of B-Carotene. *Nutrition and Cancer* 11:207–214.

Bertolini, S., et al. 1986. Lipoprotein Changes Induced by Pantethine in Hyperlipoproteinemic Patients: Adults and Children. *International Journal of Clinical Pharmacology, Therapy and Toxicology* 24:630–637.

Biale, Y., and Lewenthal, H. 1984. Effect of Folic Acid Supplementation on Congenital Malformations Due to Anticonvulsive Drugs. *European Journal of Obstetrics, Gynecology and Reproductive Biology* 18:211–216.

Bjorneboe, G. A., et al. 1988. Diminished Serum Concentration of Vitamin E in Alcoholics. *Annals of Nutrition and Metabolism* 32:56–61.

Bon, G. B., et al. 1986. In Vitro Effect of Pantethine on Platelet Aggregation. *Current Therapeutic Research* 40:464.

Brady, R. A., and Westerfeld, W. W. 1947. The Effect of B-Complex Vitamins on the Voluntary Consumption of Alcohol by Rats. *Quarterly Journal of Studies on Alcohol* 7:499–505.

Bright-See, E. 1983. Vitamin C and Cancer Prevention. *Seminars in Oncology* X(September):294–298.

Brown, W. T., et al. 1986. High Dose Folic Acid Treatment of Fragile (X) Males. *American Journal of Medical Genetics* 23:263–271.

Buckley, J. E. 1984. Hypomagnesemia after Cisplatin Combination Chemotherapy. *Archives of Internal Medicine* 144:2347–2348.

Burton, G. W., and Ingold, K. U. 1984. Beta Carotene: An Unusual Type of Lipid Antioxidant. *Science* 224:569–573.

Calabrese, E., et al. 1985. Influence of Dietary Vitamin E on Susceptibility to Ozone Exposure. *Bulletin of Environmental Contamination and Toxicology* 34:417–422.

Campbell, C. H. 1984. The Severe Lacticacidosis of Thiamine Deficiency: Acute Pernicious or Fulminating Beriberi. *The Lancet* II: 446–449.

Carrara, P., et al. 1984. Pantethine Reduces Plasma Cholesterol and the Severity of Arterial Lesions in Experimental Hypercholesterolemic Rabbits. *Atherosclerosis* 53:255–264.

Centerwall, B. S., and Criqui, M. H. 1978. Prevention of the Wernicke-Korsakoff Syndrome. *New England Journal of Medicine* 299:285–289.

Cighetti, G., et al. 1987. Pantethine Inhibits Cholesterol and Fatty Acid Syntheses and Stimulates Carbon Dioxide Formation in Isolated Rat Hepatocytes. *Journal of Lipid Research* 28:152–161.

Collipp, P. J., et al. 1975. Pyridoxine Treatment of Childhood Bronchial Asthma. *Annals of Allergy* 35:93–97.

Conner, P. L., et al. 1986. Fifteen-Year Mortality in Coronary Drug Project Patients: Long-Term Benefit with Niacin. *Journal of the American College of Cardiology* 8:1245–1255.

Connor, H. J., et al. 1985. Effect of Increased Intake of Vitamin C on the Mutagenic Activity of Gastric Juice and Intragastric Concentrations of Ascorbic Acid. *Carcinogenesis* 6:1675–1676.

Correa, P. 1985. Dietary Determinants of Gastric Cancer in South Louisiana Inhabitants. *Journal of the National Cancer Institute* 75:645–653.

Corwin, M.; Gordon, R. K.; and Shloss, J. 1981. Studies of the Mode of Action of Vitamin E in Stimulating T-Cell Mitogenesis. *Scandinavian Journal of Immunology* 14:565–571.

Cross, C. E., et al. 1987. Oxygen Radicals and Human Disease. (conference) *Annals of Internal Medicine* 107:526–545.

258 BIBLIOGRAPHY

Crowle, A. J.; Ross, E. J.; and May, M. H. 1987. Inhibition by 1,25(OH)$_2$-Vitamin D3 of the Multiplication of Virulent Tubercle Bacilli in Cultured Human Macrophages. *Infection and Immunity* 55:2945–2950.

Davies, K.J.A., et al. 1982. Free Radicals and Tissue Damage Produced by Exercise. *Biochemical and Biophysical Research Communications* 107:1198–1205.

DiSorbo, D. M., and Nathanson, L. 1983. High-Dose Pyridoxal Supplemented Culture Medium Inhibits the Growth of a Human Malignant Melanoma Cell Line. *Nutrition and Cancer* 5(1):10–15.

Dubey, A., and Solomon, R. 1989. Magnesium, Myocardial Ischaemia and Arrhythmias/The Role of Magnesium in Myocardial Infarction. *Drugs* 37:1–7.

Dworkin, B. M., et al. 1986. Selenium Deficiency in the Acquired Immunodeficiency Syndrome. *Journal of Parenteral and Enteral Nutrition* 10:405–407.

Eckardt, M. J.; Parker, E. S.; and Vanderveen, E. 1981. Health Hazards Associated with Alcohol Consumption. *Journal of the American Medical Association* 246:648–666.

Embry, C. K., and Lippmann, S. 1987. Use of Magnesium Sulfate in Alcohol Withdrawal. *American Family Physician* 35:167–170.

Emilia, A., et al. 1986. Vitamin E Enhances the Chemotherapeutic Effects of Adriamycin on Human Prostatic Carcinoma Cells *in Vitro*. *The Journal of Urology* 136:529–531.

Flombaum, C. D. 1984. Hypomagnesemia Associated with Cisplatin/Combination Chemotherapy. (editorial) *Archives of Internal Medicine* 144:2336–2337.

Forster, R. E., ed. 1986. Oxidants and Antioxidants in the Lung. *Annual Review of Physiology* 48:655–731.

Fraker, P. J., et al. 1986. Interrelationships Between Zinc and Immune Function. *Federation Proceedings* 45:1479.

Franz, K. B. 1985. Physiologic Changes During a Marathon, with Special Reference to Magnesium. *Journal of the American College of Nutrition* 4:187–194.

Freeland-Graves, J. H. 1988. Manganese: An Essential Nutrient for Humans. *Nutrition Today* (November/December):13–19.

Frei, B.; Stocker, R.; and Ames, B. 1988. Antioxidant Defense and Lipid Peroxidation in Human Blood Plasma. *Proceedings of the National Academy of Sciences* 85:9748–9752.

Froster-Iskenius, U., et al. 1986. Folic Acid Treatment in Males and Females with Fragile -(X)- Syndrome. *American Journal of Medical Genetics* 23:273–289.

Gaddi, A. 1984. Controlled Evaluation of Pantethine, a Natural Hypolipidemic Compound, in Patients with Different Forms of Hyperlipoproteinemia. *Atherosclerosis* 50:73–83.

Garland, C. F., and Garland, F. C. 1980. Do Sunlight and Vitamin D Reduce the Likelihood of Colon Cancer? *International Journal of Epidemiology* 9:227–231.

Garland, C., et al. 1985. Dietary Vitamin D and Calcium and Risk of Colorectal Cancer: A 19-Year Prospective Study in Men. *The Lancet* I: 307–309.

Gensini, G. F., et al. 1985. Changes in Fatty Acid Composition of the Single Platelet Phospholipids Induced by Pantethine Treatment. *International Journal of Clinical Pharmacology Research* 5:309–318.

Gerschman, R., et al. 1954. Oxygen Poisoning and X-Irradiation: A Mechanism in Common. *Science* 112(May):623–626.

Gladston, M., et al. 1987. Antioxidant Activity of Serum Ceruloplasmin and Transferrin/Available Iron-Binding Capacity in Smokers and Nonsmokers. *American Review of Respiratory Disease* 135:783–787.

Granger, D. N.; Hernandez, L. A.; and Grisham, M. B. 1986. Reactive Oxygen Metabolites: Mediators of Cell Injury in the Digestive System. *Viewpoints on Digestive Diseases* 18(September):13–16.

Gridley, D. S., et al. 1988. In Vivo and in Vitro Stimulation of Cell-Mediated Immunity by Vitamin B$_6$. *Nutrition Research* 8:201–207.

Gustavson, K., et al. 1985. Effect of Folic Acid Treatment in the Fragile X Syndrome. *Clinical Genetics* 27:463–467.

Hagerman, R. J., et al. 1986. Oral Folic Acid Versus Placebo in the Treatment of Males with the Fragile X Syndrome. *American Journal of Medical Genetics* 23:241–262.

Harman, D. 1988. Free Radicals in Aging. *Molecular and Cellular Biochemistry* 84:155–161.

———. 1983. Free Radical Theory of Aging: Consequences of Mitochondrial Aging. *Age* 6(July):86–94.

Heimburger, D. C., et al. 1988. Improvement in Bronchial Squamous Metaplasia in Smokers Treated with Folate and Vitamin B$_{12}$. *Journal of the American Medical Association* 259:1525–1530.

Hendler, S. S. 1986. *Complete Guide to Anti-Aging Nutrients.* New York: Fireside.

Hennekens, C. H. 1986. Micronutrients and Cancer Prevention. *New England Journal of Medicine* 315:1288–1289.

Hillman, R. S., and Steinberg, S. E. 1982. The Effects of Alcohol on Folate Metabolism. *Annual Review of Medicine* 33:345–354.

Hoffman, B., et al. 1987. Effect of Pantethine on Platelet Functions in Vitro. *Current Therapeutic Research* 41:791–801.

Holbrook, T. L.; Barrett-Connor, E.; and Wingard, D. L. 1988. Dietary Calcium and Risk of Hip Fracture: 14-Year Prospective Population Study. *The Lancet* II: 1046–1049.

Hunding, A.; Jordahl, R.; and Pauley, P. E. 1981. Runners' Anemia and Iron Deficiency. *Acta Medica Scandinavica* 209:315–318.

Ip, C., and White, G. 1987. Mammary Cancer Chemoprevention by Inorganic and Organic Selenium: Single Agent Treatment or in Combination with Vitamin E and Their Effects on *In Vitro* Immune Functions. *Carcinogenesis* 8:1763–1766.

Jacobsen, D. W.; Simon, R. A.; and Singh, M. 1984. Sulfite Oxidase Deficiency and Cobalamin Protection in Sulfite Sensitive Asthmatics (SSA). (abstract) *Journal of Allergy and Clinical Immunology* (supplement) 73:135.

Karkkainen, P., et al. 1988. Alcohol Intake Correlated with Serum Trace Elements. *Alcohol & Alcoholism* 23:279–282.

Katz, M. A. 1986. The Expanding Role of Oxygen Free Radicals in Clinical Medicine. *Western Journal of Medicine* 144:441–446.

Kiremidjian-Schumacher, L., and Stotzky, G. 1987. Selenium and Immune Responses. *Environmental Research* 42:277–303.

Knapp, R. H., et al. 1985. Contrasting Effects of Unmodified and Time Release Forms of Niacin on Lipoproteins in Hyperlipidemic Subjects: Clue to Mechanism of Action of Niacin. *Metabolism* 34:442.

260   BIBLIOGRAPHY

Kok, F. J., et al. 1989. Decreased Selenium Levels in Acute Myocardial Infarction. *Journal of the American Medical Association* 261:1161–1164.

———. 1987. Selenium Status and Chronic Disease Mortality: Dutch Epidemiological Findings. *International Journal of Epidemiology* 16:329–331.

Korpela, H., et al. 1985. Decreased Serum Selenium in Alcoholics as Related to Liver Structure and Function. *American Journal of Clinical Nutrition* 42(July):147–151.

Krivit, W., et al. 1983. Prevention of Cyclophosphamide (CYT) Induced Hemorrhagic Cystitis (HC) by Use of Ascorbic Acid (AA) to Reduce Urinary pH. (abstract) *American Society of Clinical Oncology* 2:27.

Kune, G. A., et al. 1989. Serum Levels of Beta Carotene, Vitamin A, and Zinc in Male Lung Cancer Cases and Controls. *Nutrition and Cancer* 12:169–176.

Kuvibidila, S. 1987. Iron Deficiency, Cell-Mediated Immunity and Resistance Against Infections: Present Knowledge and Controversies. *Nutrition Research* 7:989–1003.

Lampe, J. W.; Slavin, J. L.; and Apple, F. S. 1986. Poor Iron Status of Women Runners Training for a Marathon. *International Journal of Sports Medicine* 7:111–114.

Laurence, K. M. Prevention of Neural Tube Defects by Improvement in Maternal Diet and Periconceptional Folic Acid Supplementation. In Marcois, M., ed. 1985. *Prevention of Physical and Mental Congenital Defects (Part B)* New York: Alan R. Liss.

Laurence, K. M., et al. 1981. Double-Blind Randomized Controlled Trial of Folate Treatment Before Conception to Prevent Recurrence of Neural Tube Defects. *British Medical Journal* 282:1509–1511.

Leo, M. A., and Lieber, C. S. 1982. Hepatic Vitamin A Depletion in Alcoholic Liver Injury. *New England Journal of Medicine* 307:597–601.

Levenson, S. M., et al. 1984. Supplemental Vitamin A Prevents the Acute Radiation-Induced Defect in Wound Healing. *Annals of Surgery* 200:494–512.

Lieber, C. S. 1988. Biochemical and Molecular Basis of Alcohol-Induced Injury to Liver and Other Tissues. *New England Journal of Medicine* 319:1639–1650.

———. 1988. The Influence of Alcohol on Nutritional Status. *Nutritional Reviews* 46(July):241–254.

Lindenbaum, J., et al. 1988. Neuropsychiatric Disorders Caused by Cobalamin Deficiency in the Absence of Anemia or Macrocytosis. *New England Journal of Medicine* 318:1720–1727.

Liu, L.; Borowski, G.; and Rose, L. I. 1983. Hypomagnesemia in a Tennis Player. *The Physician and SportsMedicine* 11(May):79–80.

Luria, M. H. 1988. Effect of Low-Dose Niacin on High Density Lipoprotein Cholesterol and Total Cholesterol/High Density Lipoprotein Cholesterol Ratio. *Archives of Internal Medicine* 148:2493–2495.

McCarron, D. A. 1989. Calcium: Confirming an Inverse Relationship. *Hospital Practice* (February 15):229–244.

McClain, C. J., and Su, L. 1983. Zinc Deficiency in the Alcoholic: A Review. *Alcoholism* 7:5–10.

Machlin, L. J., and Bendich, A. 1987. Free Radical Tissue Damage: Protective Role of Antioxidant Nutrients. *Federation of the American Societies of Experimental Biology Journal* 1:441–445.

Marx, J. L. 1987. Oxygen Free Radicals Linked to Many Diseases. *Research News* (January 30):529–531.

Mazzola, V. 1986. Asthma Symptoms Eased by Vitamin B_6. *Agricultural Research* (October):4–5.

Menkes, M. S., et al. 1986. Serum Beta-Carotene, Vitamins A and E, Selenium, and the Risk of Lung Cancer. *New England Journal of Medicine* 315:1250–1254.

Meydani, S. N., et al. 1986. Vitamin E Supplementation Suppresses Prostaglandin E_2 Synthesis and Enhances the Immune Response of Aged Mice. *Mechanism of Ageing and Development* 34:191–201.

Mohsenin, V.; Dubois, A. B.; and Douglas, J. S. 1983. Effect of Ascorbic Acid on Response to Methacholine/Challenge in Asthmatic Subjects. *American Review of Respiratory Diseases* 127:143–147.

Molloy, D. W. 1987. Hypomagnesemia and Respiratory-Muscle Weakness in the Elderly. *Geriatric Medicine Today* 6(February):53–61.

Moore, J. A.; Noiva, R.; and Wells, I. C. 1984. Selenium Concentrations in Plasma of Patients with Arteriographically Defined Coronary Atherosclerosis. *Clinical Chemistry* 30:1171–1173.

Munoz, N., et al. 1987. Effect of Riboflavin, Retinol, and Zinc on Micronuclei of Buccal Mucosa and of Esophagus: A Randomized Double-Blind Intervention Study in China. *Journal of the National Cancer Institute* 79:687–691.

Nielsen, F. H. 1988. Dietary Magnesium, Manganese and Boron Affect the Response of Rats to High Dietary Aluminum. *Magnesium* 7:133–147.

Oski, F. A. 1980. Vitamin E—A Radical Defense. (editorial) *New England Journal of Medicine* 303:454–455.

Pacht, E. R., et al. 1986. Deficiency of Vitamin E in the Alveolar Fluid of Cigarette Smokers. *American Society for Clinical Investigation* 77:789–796.

Palgi, A. 1984. Vitamin A and Lung Cancer: A Perspective. *Nutrition and Cancer* 6:105–120.

Perkins, J. 1988. A Radical View of Chemistry. *New Scientist* (August 11):41.

Peto, R.; Doll, R.; Buckley, J. D.; and Sporn, M. B. 1981. Can Dietary Beta Carotene Materially Reduce Human Cancer Rates? *Nature* 290:201–208.

Prisco, D. 1984. Effect of Pantethine Treatment on Platelet Aggregation and Thromboxane A_2 Production. *Current Therapeutic Research* 35:700–706.

Raloff, J. 1988. New Misgivings About Low Magnesium. (report) *Science News* 133:356.

Rasmussen, H. S., et al. 1989. Influence of Magnesium Substitution Therapy on Blood Lipid Composition in Patients with Ischemic Heart Disease. *Archives of Internal Medicine* 149:1050–1053.

Reiser, S., et al. 1987. Effect of Copper Intake on Blood Cholesterol and Its Lipoprotein Distribution in Men. *Nutrition Reports International* 36:641–649.

Richter, C.; Park, J. W.; and Ames, B. N. 1988. Normal Oxidative Damage to Mitochondrial and Nuclear DNA Is Extensive. *Proceedings of the National Academy of Sciences* 85:6465–6467.

Roe, D. 1976. *Drug-Induced Nutritional Deficiencies.* Westport, Conn.: AVI Publishing Co.

Rolla, G. 1987. Reduction of Histamine-Induced Bronchoconstriction by Magnesium in Asthmatic Subjects. *Allergy* 42:186–188.

Romney, S. L., et al. 1985. Plasma Vitamin C and Uterine Cervical Dysplasia. *American Journal of Obstetrics and Gynecology* 151:976–980.

Salonen, J. T. 1984. Association Between Serum Selenium and the Risk of Cancer. *American Journal of Epidemiology* 120:342–349.

Salonen, J. T., et al. 1985. Risk of Cancer in Relation to Serum Concentrations of Selenium and Vitamins A and E: Matched Case-Control Analysis of Prospective Data. *British Medical Journal* 290:417–420.

Saltiel, E., and McGuire, W. 1983. Doxorubicin (Adriamycin) Cardiomyopathy. *Western Journal of Medicine* 139:332–341.

Seelig, M. 1986. Magnesium, Exercise, and Stress. *Medical Tribune* (July 23): 42.

Seifter, E., et al. 1984. Morbidity and Mortality Reduction by Supplemental Vitamin A or Beta Carotene in Mice Given Total Body Gamma Radiation. *Journal of the National Cancer Institute* 73:1167–1177.

Sethi, V. S., et al. 1983. Vitamin C Lowers Vincristine Toxicity in Rhesus Monkeys. (abstract) *American Association of Cancer Research*: 286.

Shariff, R., et al. 1988. Vitamin E Supplementation in Smokers. *American Journal of Clinical Nutrition*. (abstract) 47:758.

Sherlock, S. 1984. Nutrition and the Alcoholic. *The Lancet* I: 436–439.

Simonoff, M., et al. 1984. Low Plasma Chromium in Patients with Coronary Artery and Heart Disease. *Biological Tract Element Research* 6:431.

Simon-Schnasa, I., and Pabst, H. 1988. Influence of Vitamin E on Physical Performance. *International Journal for Vitamin and Nutrition Research* 58:49–54.

Sklan, D. 1987. Vitamin A in Human Nutrition. *Progress in Food and Nutrition Science* 11:39–55.

Smith, J. A.; Dardin, P. A.; and Brown, W. T. 1951. The Treatment of Alcoholism by Nutritional Supplement. *Quarterly Journal of Studies on Alcohol* 12:381.

Sokol, R. J. 1989. Vitamin E and Neurologic Function in Man. *Free Radical Biology & Medicine* 6:189–207.

Som, S.; Chatterjee, M.; and Banerjee, M. R. 1984. Beta Carotene Inhibition of 7, 12-dimethylbenz[a]anthracene Induced Transformation of Murine Mammary Cells. *In Vitro Carcinogenesis* 5:937–940.

Southorn, P. A., and Powis, G. 1988. Free Radicals in Medicine. I. Chemical Nature and Biologic Reactions. *Mayo Clinic Proceedings* 63:381–389.

———.1988. Free Radicals in Medicine. II. Involvement in Human Disease. *Mayo Clinic Proceedings* 63:390–403.

Spanhake, E. W., and Menkes, H. A. 1983. Vitamin C—New Tricks for an Old Dog. (editorial) *American Review of Respiratory Disease* 127:139–140.

Stead, R. J., et al. 1985. Selenium Deficiency and Possible Increased Risk of Carcinoma in Adults with Cystic Fibrosis. *The Lancet* II: 862–863.

Stendig-Lindberg, G., et al. 1987. Changes in Serum Magnesium Concentration After Strenuous Exercise. *Journal of the American College of Nutrition* 6(1):35–40.

Stich, H. F., et al. 1988. Vitamin A Therapy for Oral Cancer. Reported in *Science News* 133:381.

Stryker, W. S. 1988. The Relation of Diet, Cigarette Smoking, and Alcohol Consumption to Plasma Beta Carotene and Alpha-Tocopherol Levels. *American Journal of Epidemiology* 127:283–296.

Sundaram, G. S., et al. 1981. d-Tocopherol and Serum Lipoproteins. *Lipids* 16:223–227.

Switzer, B. R., and Anderson, J.J.B. 1987. Effects of Alcohol on Nutritional Status: Part II—Vitamins. *Internal Medicine* 8(September):62–71.

Tanaka, J. 1979. Vitamin E and Immune Response. *Immunology* 38:727–734.

Tannenbaum, S. R. 1989. N-Nitroso Compounds: A Perspective on Human Exposure. *The Lancet* I: 629–632.

Tannenbaum, S. R., and Mergens, W. 1980. Reaction of Nitrite with Vitamins C and E. *Annals of The New York Academy of Sciences* 355(December 1):267–277.

Travis, J. 1987. Oxidants and Antioxidants in the Lung. (editorial) *American Review of Respiratory Disease* 135:773.

Trickler, D., and Shkler, G. 1987. Prevention by Vitamin E of Experimental Oral Carcinogenesis. *Journal of the National Cancer Institute* 78:165–169.

Trulson, M. F.; Fleming, R.; and Stare, F. J. 1954. Vitamin Medication in Alcoholism. *Journal of the American Medical Association* 155:114–119.

Watanabe, A., et al. 1985. Lowering of Blood Acetaldehyde but Not Ethanol/Concentrations by Pantethine Following Alcohol Ingestion: Different Effects in Flushing and Nonflushing Subjects. *Alcoholism: Clinical and Experimental Research* 9(3):272–276.

Watson, R. R., and Moriguchi, S. 1985. Cancer Prevention by Retinoids: Role of Immunological Modification. *Nutrition Research* 5:663–675.

Weinstein, M. C. 1978. Prevention That Pays for Itself. (editorial) *New England Journal of Medicine* 299:307–308.

Willett, W. C., et al. 1983. Prediagnostic Serum Selenium and Risk of Cancer. *The Lancet* II: 130–134.

Williams, A.J.K., and Barry, R. E. 1987. Free Radical Generation by Neutrophils: A Potential Mechanism of Cellular Injury in Acute Alcoholic Hepatitis. *Gut* 28:1157–1161.

Williams, R. J. 1947. The Etiology of Alcoholism: A Working Hypothesis Involving the Interplay of Hereditary and Environmental Factors. *Quarterly Journal of Studies on Alcohol* 7:567.

————. 1981. *Prevention of Alcoholism Through Nutrition*. New York: Bantam Books.

Williams, R. J.; Beerstecher, E.; and Berry, L. J. 1950. The Concept of Genetotrophic Disease. *The Lancet* I: 287–289.

Windham, C. T.; Wyse, B. W.; and Hansen, R. G. 1983. Alcohol Consumption and Nutrient Density of Diets in the Nationwide Food Consumption Survey. *Journal of the American Dietetic Association* 82:364–373.

Yates, J.R.W., et al. 1987. Is Disordered Folate Metabolism the Basis for the Genetic Predisposition to Neural Tube Defects? *Clinical Genetics* 31:279–287.

Yunis, J. J., and Soreng, A. L. 1984. Constitutive Fragile Sites and Cancer. *Science* 226:119–120.

Chapter 2: Amino Acids

Anonymous. 1985. Branched-Chain Amino Acids Reverse Hepatic Encephalopathy. *Internal Medicine News* 18(18):5.

264 BIBLIOGRAPHY

Anonymous. 1984. L-Tryptophan Interval Therapy Is Effective in Chronic Insomnia. *Internal Medicine News* 17(18):11.

Anonymous. 1987. Tryptophan Aids Adjustment to Jet Lag, Shift Work. *Internal Medicine News* 20(4):53.

Baker, A. L. 1979. Amino Acids in Liver Disease: A Cause of Hepatic Encephalopathy? (editorial) *Journal of the American Medical Association* 242:355–356.

Bloom, F. E. 1988. Neurotransmitters: Past, Present and Future Direction. *Federation of American Societies for Experimental Biology Journal* 2:32–41.

Blum, K., et al. 1987. Enkephalinase Inhibition: Regulation of Ethanol Intake in Genetically Predisposed Mice. *Alcohol* 4:449–456.

Budd, K. 1983. Use of D-Phenylalanine, an Enkephalinase Inhibitor, in the Treatment of Intractable Pain. *Advances in Pain Research and Therapy* 5:305.

Chang, R.S.S., and Pomeranz, B. 1980. A Combined Treatment with d-Amino Acids and Electroacupuncture Produces a Greater Analgesia than Either Treatment Alone; Naloxone Reverses These Effects. *Pain* 8:231–236.

Cooper, J. R.; Bloom, F. E.; and Roth, R. H. 1986. *The Biochemical Basis of Neuropharmacology*, Fifth Edition. New York and Oxford: Oxford University Press.

DiChiara, G., and Imperato, A. 1988. Drugs Abused by Humans Preferentially Increased Synaptic Dopamine Concentrations in the Mesolimbic System of Freely Moving Rats. *Proceedings of the National Academy of Sciences* 85:5274–5278.

Ehrenpreis, S. 1982. D-Phenylalanine and Other Enkephalinase Inhibitors as Pharmacological Agents: Implications for Some Important Therapeutic Application. *Substance and Alcohol Actions/Misuse* 3:231–239.

Fincle, L. P. 1961. The Effect of L-Glutamine on Psychiatric Hospitalized Alcoholic Patients. *Bedford Research*. Bedford, Massachusetts Veteran's Administration Hospital 7(January 2):2.

———. 1964. Experiments in Treating Alcoholics with Glutamic Acid and Glutamine. Paper presented at symposium, Biochemical and Nutritional Aspects of Alcoholism. Symposium sponsored by the Christopher D. Smithers Foundation and the Clayton Foundation Biochemical Institute, University of Texas, Austin. New York: 26–37, October 1.

Flot, Carry, and Rosier. 1964. Some Clinical Results in the Treatment of Alcoholism with L-Glutamic Acid Monoamide. *Le Journal de Médecine de Lyon* 45:1067.

Gelenberg, A. J., et al. 1980. Tyrosine for the Treatment of Depression. *American Journal of Psychiatry* 137(5):622–623.

Gold, M. S.; Washton, A.; and Dackis, C. A. 1985. Cocaine Abuse Neurochemistry, Phenomenology, and Treatment. NIDA Research Monograph. 16:130–150.

Goleman, D. 1988. Food and Brain: Psychiatrists Explore Use of Nutrients in Treating Disorders. *New York Times* (March 1):15.

Hartmann, E. 1977. L-Tryptophan: A Rational Hypnotic with Clinical Potential. *American Journal of Psychiatry* 134:366.

Hartmann, E., and Spinweber, C. L. 1979. Sleep Induced by L-Tryptophan. Effect of Dosages Within the Normal Dietary Intake. *Journal of Nervous and Mental Disease* 167:497.

Hyodo, M.; Kitada, T.; and Hosoka, E. 1983. Study on the Enhanced Analgesic Effect Induced by Phenylalanine During Acupuncture Analgesia in Humans. *Advances in Pain Research and Therapy* 5:577.

Jackson, D. V., et al. 1988. Amelioration of Vincristine Neurotoxicity by Glutamic Acid. *American Journal of Medicine* 84:1016–1022.

King, R. B. 1980. Pain and Tryptophan. *Journal of Neurosurgery* 53:44.

Koop, G. F., and Bloom, F. E. 1988. Cellular and Molecular Mechanisms of Drug Dependence. *Science* 242:715–723.

Kravitz, H. M.; Sabelli, H. C.; and Fawcett, J. 1984. Dietary Supplements of Phenylalanine and Other Amino Acid Precursors of Brain Neuroamines in the Treatment of Depressive Disorders. *Journal of the American Osteopathic Association* 84:119.

Lieber, C. S. 1988. The Influence of Alcohol on Nutritional Status. *Nutrition Reviews* 46(7):241–254.

Lyness, W. H. 1983. Effect of L-Tryptophan Pretreatment on d-Amphetamine Self-Administration. *Substance and Alcohol Actions/Misuse* 4:305–312.

Ravel, J. M., et al. 1955. Reversal of Alcohol Toxicity by Glutamine. *Journal of Biological Chemistry* 214:497.

Reinstein, D. K.; Lehnert, H.; and Wurtman, R. J. 1985. Dietary Tyrosine Suppresses the Rise in Plasma Corticosterone Following Acute Stress in Rats. *Life Sciences* 37:2157–2163.

Rogers, L. L., and Pelton, R. B. 1957. Glutamine in the Treatment of Alcoholism. *Quarterly Journal of Studies on Alcohol* 18:581.

Rogers, L. L.; Pelton, R. B.; and Williams, R. J. 1956. Amino Acid Supplementation and Voluntary Alcohol Consumption by Rats. *Journal of Biological Chemistry* 220:321–323.

————.1955. Voluntary Alcohol Consumption by Rats Following Administration of Glutamine. *Journal of Biological Chemistry* 214:503–506.

Rosecrans, J. S. 1983. The Treatment of Cocaine Abuse with Imipramine, L-tyrosine and L-tryptophan. Reported before the Seventh World Congress of Psychiatry, Vienna, Austria.

Seltzer, S.; Marcus, R.; and Stoch, R. 1981. Perspectives in the Control of Chronic Pain by Nutritional Manipulation. *Pain* 11:141–148.

Seltzer, S., et al. 1982. The Effects of Dietary Tryptophan on Chronic Maxillofacial Pain and Experimental Pain Tolerance. *Journal of Psychiatric Research* 17:181.

Sener, A. I., et al. 1986. Comparison of the Suppressive Effects of L-Aspartic Acid and Chlorpromazine + Diazepam Treatments on Opiate Abstinence Syndrome in Men. *Arzneimittel-Forschung* 36:1684–1686.

Shive, W. 1964. Glutamine as a Metabolic Agent Protecting Against Alcohol Poisoning. Paper presented at symposium, Biochemical and Nutritional Aspects of Alcoholism. Symposium sponsored by the Christopher D. Smithers Foundation and the Clayton Foundation Biochemical Institute, University of Texas, Austin. New York: 17–25, October 2.

Shpeen, S. E.; Morse, D. R.; and Furst, M. L. 1984. The Effect of Tryptophan on Postoperative Endodontic Pain. *Oral Surgery, Oral Medicine and Oral Pathology* 58:446.

Tennant, F., and Berman, M. L. 1988. Stepwise Detoxification from Cocaine. *Postgraduate Medicine* 84(2):225–235.

Walsh, N. E., et al. 1986. Analgesic Effectiveness of D-phenylalanine in Chronic Pain Patients. *Archives of Physical Medicine and Rehabilitation* 67:436.

Wang, Q., et al. 1989. Effects of Taurine on Bleomycin-Induced Lung Fibrosis in Hamsters. *Proceedings of the Society for Experimental Biology and Medicine* 190:330–338.

Watanabe, A., et al. 1985. Effect of Taurine on Blood Acetaldehyde Elevation Following Alcohol Ingestion. *Research Communications in Substances of Abuse* 6(4):247–250.

Williams, R. J. 1981. *The Prevention of Alcoholism Through Nutrition*. New York: Bantam Books.

Williams, R. J., and Davis, D. R. 1986. Differential Nutrition—A New Orientation from which to Approach the Problems of Human Nutrition. *Perspectives in Biology and Medicine*. 29(2):199–202.

Wurtman, R. J. 1987. Nutrients Affecting Brain Composition and Behavior. *Integrative Psychiatry* 5:226–257.

Wyatt, R. J., et al. 1970. Effects of L-tryptophan (a natural sedative) on Human Sleep. *The Lancet* II: 842.

Chapter 3: Lipids

Alling, C. 1983. Alcohol Effects on Cell Membrane. *Substance and Alcohol Actions/Misuse* 4:67–72.

Atoba, M. A.; Ayoola, E. A.; and Ogunseyinde, O. 1985. Effect of Essential Phospholipid Choline on the Course of Acute Hepatitis-B Infection. *Tropical Gastroenterology* 6(2):96–99.

Cohen, B. M.; Lipinski, J. F.; and Altesman, R. I. 1982. Lecithin in the Treatment of Mania: Double-Blind, Placebo-Controlled Trials. *American Journal of Psychiatry* 139:1162–1164.

Gelenberg, A. J.; Doller-Wojcik, J. C.; and Growdon, J. H. 1979. Choline and Lecithin in the Treatment of Tardive Dyskinesia: Preliminary Results from a Pilot Study. *American Journal of Psychiatry* 136(June):6.

Goldstein, D. B. 1985. Drunk and Disorderly: How Cell Membranes Are Affected by Alcohol. *Nutrition Today* (March/April):4–9.

Gorlin, R. 1988. The Biological Actions and Potential Clinical Significance of Dietary ω-3 Fatty Acids. *Archives of Internal Medicine* 148:2043–2048.

Growdon, J. H. 1987. Use of Phosphatidylcholine in Brain Diseases: An Overview. In Hanin, I., and Ansell, G. B., eds. *Lecithin: Technological, Biological and Therapeutic Aspects*. New York: Plenum Press, 121–136.

Growdon, J. H.; Wheeler, M. A.; and Graham, H. N. 1984. Plasma Choline Responses to Lecithin-Enriched Soup. *Psychopharmacology* 20:603–606.

Hanin, I., and Ansell, G. B., eds. 1987. *Lecithin: Technological, Biological and Therapeutic Aspects*. New York: Plenum Press.

Hegner, D., and Platt, D. 1975. Effect of Essential Phospholipids on the Properties of ATPases of Isolated Rat Liver Plasma Membranes of Young and Old Animals. *Mechanisms of Ageing and Development* 4:191–200.

Heron, D. S.; Shinitzky, M.; and Samuel, D. 1982. Alleviation of Drug Withdrawal Symptoms by Treatment with a Potent Mixture of Natural Lipids. *European Journal of Pharmacology* 83:253–261.

Hitzemann, R.; Hirschowitz, J.; and Garver, D. 1984. Membrane Abnormalities in the Psychoses and Affective Disorders. *Journal of Psychiatric Research* 18(3):319–326.

Jackson, I. V., et al. 1979. Treatment of Tardive Dyskinesia with Lecithin. *American Journal of Psychiatry* 136(November):11.

Jenkins, P. J., et al. 1982. Use of Polyunsaturated Phosphatidyl Choline in HBsAg Negative Chronic Active Hepatitis: Results of Prospective Double-Blind Controlled Trial. *Liver* 2:77–81.

Kamido, H.; Matsuzawa, Y.; and Tarui, S. 1988. Lipid Composition of Platelets from Patients with Atherosclerosis: Effect of Purified Eicosapentaenoic Acid Ethyl Ester Administration. *Lipids* 23(10)917–923.

Kosina, F., et al. 1981. Essential Cholinephospholipids in the Treatment of Virus Hepatitis (translated from Czech) *Casopis Lekaru Ceskych* 120(August 13):957–960.

La Droitte, P., et al. 1984. Sensitivity of Individual Erythrocyte Membrane Phospholipids to Changes in Fatty Acid Composition in Chronic Alcoholic Patients. *Alcoholism: Clinical and Experimental Research* 9(2):135–137.

Leaf, A., and Weber, P. C. 1988. Cardiovascular Effects of n-3 Fatty Acids. *New England Journal of Medicine* 318(9):539–557.

Levine, P. H., et al. 1989. Dietary Supplementation with Omega-3 Fatty Acids Prolongs Platelet Survival in Hyperlipidemic Patients with Atherosclerosis. *Archives of Internal Medicine* 149:1113–1116.

Little, A., et al. 1985. A Double-Blind, Placebo Controlled Trial of High-Dose Lecithin in Alzheimer's Disease. *Journal of Neurology, Neurosurgery and Psychiatry* 48:736–742.

Lyte, M., and Shinitzky, M. 1985. A Special Lipid Mixture for Membrane Fluidization. *Biochimica et Biophysica Acta* 812:133–138.

Ma, W. C. 1931. A Cytopathological Study of Acute and Chronic Morphinism in the Albino Rat. *Chinese Journal of Physiology* 5:251–278.

Rabinowich, H., et al. 1987. Augmentation of Mitogen Responsiveness in the Aged by a Special Lipid Diet AL 721. *Mechanisms of Ageing and Development* 40:131–138.

Raloff, J. 1988. No-Fault Fat: More Praise for Fish Oil. *Science News* 134:228.

Sarin, P. S., et al. 1985. Effects of a Novel Compound (AL 721) on HTLV-III Infectivity *In Vitro*. *New England Journal of Medicine* 313:1289–1290.

Vbraski, S. R., et al. 1988. Influence of High-Protein Diets on Brain Phospholipid, Ganglioside and Monogalactosyl Glycolipid Content Previously Altered by Long-Term Low-Protein and Ethanol Administration. *Journal of Studies on Alcohol* 49(4):369–374.

Visco, G. 1985. Polyunsaturated Phosphatidylcholine in Association with Vitamin B Complex in the Treatment of Acute Viral Hepatitis B. (translated from Italian) *Clinica Terapeutica* 114:183–188.

Von Schacky, C. 1987. Prophylaxis of Atherosclerosis with Marine Omega-3 Fatty Acids. *Annals of Internal Medicine* 107:890–899.

Wood, J. L., and Allison, R. G. 1982. Effects of Consumption of Choline and Lecithin on Neurological and Cardiovascular Systems. *Federation Proceedings* 41(14):3015–3021.

Wurtman, R. J.; Hefti, F.; and Melamed, E. 1981. Precursor Control of Neurotransmitter Synthesis. *Pharmacological Reviews* 32(4):315–335.

Chapter 4: Seaweed

Besterman, E. M. M., and Evans, J. 1957. Antilipaemic Agent Without Anticoagulant Action. *British Medical Journal* (February 9):310–312.

Ehresmann, D. W.; Deig, E. F.; and Hatch, M. T. 1979. Anti-Viral Properties of Algal Polysaccharides and Related Compounds. In Hoppe, H. A.; Levring, T.; and Tanaka, Y., eds. *Marine Algae in Pharmaceutical Science*. Berlin and New York: Walter de Gruyter, 293–302.

Gonzalez, M. E.; Alarcon, B.; and Carrasco, L. 1987. Polysaccharides as Antiviral Agents: Antiviral Activity of Carrageenan. *Antimicrobial Agents and Chemotherapy* 31(9):1388–1393.

Hoppe, H. A.; Levring, T.; and Tanaka, Y., eds. 1979. *Marine Algae in Pharmaceutical Science*. Berlin and New York: Walter de Gruyter.

Nakashima, H., et al. 1987. Antiretroviral Activity in a Marine Red Alga: Reverse Transcriptase Inhibition by an Aqueous Extract of *Schizymenia Pacifica*. *Journal of Cancer Research and Clinical Oncology* 113:413–416.

———.1987. Purification and Characterization of an Avian Myeloblastosis and Human Immunodeficiency Virus Reverse Transcriptase Inhibitor, Sulfated Polysaccharides Extracted from Sea Algae. *Antimicrobial Agents and Chemotherapy* 31(10):1524–1528.

Neushul, M. 1988. Method for the Treatment of AIDS Virus and Other Retroviruses. United States Patent: 4,783,446 (November 8).

Stein, J. R., and Border, C. A. 1984. Causative and Beneficial Algae in Human Disease Conditions: A Review. *Phycologia* 23(4):485–501.

Tanaka, Y., and Stara, J. F. 1979. Algal Polysaccharides: Their Potential Use to Prevent Chronic Metal Poisoning. In Hoppe, H. A.; Levring, T.; and Tanaka, Y., eds. *Marine Algae in Pharmaceutical Science*. Berlin and New York: Walter de Gruyter, 525–543.

Yamamoto, I, and Maruyama, H. 1985. Effect of Dietary Seaweed Preparations on 1, 2-Dimethylhydrazine-Induced Intestinal Carcinogenesis in Rats. *Cancer Letters* 26:241–251.

Chapter 5: Herbs

Abe, H., et al. 1987. Effects of Glycyrrhizin and Glycyrrhetinic Acid on Growth and Melanogenesis in Cultured B16 Melanoma Cells. *European Journal of Cancer & Clinical Oncology* 23(10):1549–1555.

Anand, C. L. 1971. Effect of Avena Sativa on Cigarette Smoking. *Nature* 233(October):496.

Baba, M., and Shigeta, S. 1987. Antiviral Activity of Glycyrrhizin Against Varicella-Zoster Virus *In Vitro*. *Antiviral Research* 7:99–107.

Bullock, C. 1984. Two Chinese Herbs Show Blooming Anticancer Potential. *Medical Tribune* (March 28):5.

Connor, J., et al. 1975. The Pharmacology of Avena Sativa. *Journal of Pharmacy and Pharmacology* 27:92–98.

Floersheim, G. L., et al. 1978. Effects of Penicillin and Silymarin on Liver Enzymes and Blood Clotting Factors in Dogs Given a Boiled Preparation of Amanita Phalloides. *Toxicology and Applied Pharmacology* 46:455–462.

Han, B. H., et al. 1985. Chemical and Biochemical Studies on Antioxidant Components of Ginseng. *Advances in Chinese Medicinal Materials Research.* Singapore: World Scientific Publishing Company, 485–498.

Ito, M., et al. 1987. Inhibitory Effect of Glycyrrhizin on the *In Vitro* Infectivity and Cytopathic Activity of the Human Immunodeficiency Virus (HIV [HTLV-III/LAV]) *Antiviral Research* 7:127–137.

———.1988. Mechanism of Inhibitory Effect of Glycyrrhizin on Replication of Human Immunodeficiency Virus (HIV). *Antiviral Research* 10:289–298.

Kiso, Y., et al. 1984. Mechanism of Antihepatotoxic Activity of Glycyrrhizin I. Effect on Free Radical Generation and Lipid Peroxidation. *Planta Medica* 50:298.

Lee, F. C., et al. 1987. Effects of Panax Ginseng on Blood Alcohol Clearance in Man. *Clinical and Experimental Pharmacology & Physiology* 14:543–546.

Macek, C. 1984. East Meets West to Balance Immunologic Yin and Yang. *Journal of the American Medical Association* 251:433–439.

———. 1984. Herbs and Heat in Chinese Armamentarium. *Journal of the American Medical Association* 251 (4):439–441.

Nakashima, H., et al. 1987. A New Anti-Human Immunodeficiency Virus Substance, Glycyrrhizin Sulfate: Endowment of Glycyrrhizin with Reverse Transcriptase-Inhibitory Activity by Chemical Modification. *Japanese Journal of Cancer Research* 78(August):767–771.

Nebelkopk, E. 1988. Herbs and Substance Abuse Treatment: A 10-Year Perspective. *Journal of Psychoactive Drugs* 20:349–354.

Pompei, R., et al. 1979. Glycyrrhizic Acid Inhibits Virus Growth and Inactivates Virus Particles. *Nature* 281(October):689–690.

Smith, M. 1979. Acupuncture and Natural Healing in Drug Detoxification. *American Journal of Acupuncture* 7:97–107.

Sun, Y., et al. 1983. Immune Restoration and/or Augmentation of Local Graft Versus Host Reaction by Traditional Chinese Medicinal Herbs. *Cancer* 52(1)70–73.

Takeda, A.; Yonezawa, M.; and Katoh, N. 1981. Restoration of Radiation Injury by Ginseng. I. Responses of X-Irradiated Mice to Ginseng Extract. *Journal of Radiation Research* 22:323–335.

———. 1981. Restoration of Radiation Injury by Ginseng. II. Some Properties of the Radioprotective Substances. *Journal of Radiation Research* 22:336–343.

Valenzuela, A.; Guerra, R.; and Garrido, A. 1987. A Silybin Dihemisuccinate Protects Rat Erythrocytes Against Phenylhydrazine-Induced Lipid Peroxidation and Hemolysis. *Planta Medica* 53(5):402–405.

Valenzuela, A.; Guerra, R.; and Videla, L. A. 1986. Antioxidant Properties of the Flavonoids Silybin and (+)-cyanidanol-3: Comparison with Butylated Hydroxyanisole and Butylated Hydroxytoluene. *Planta Medica* 52(6):438–440.

Valenzuela, A.; Lagos, C.; and Schmidt, K. 1985. Silymarin Protection Against Hepatic Lipid Peroxidation Induced by Acute Ethanol Intoxication in the Rat. *Biochemical Pharmacology* 34(12):2209–2212.

Vengerovski, A. I., et al. 1987. Liver Protective Action of Silybinene in Experimental CCl₄ Poisoning. *Farmakologiya I Toksikologiya* 50(5):67–69.

Vogel, G. 1981. A Peculiarity Among the Flavonoids. Silymarin, a Compound Active on the Liver. *Munich Proceedings of the International Bioflavonoid Symposium:* 461–480.

Vogel, G., et al. 1975. Studies on the Pharmacodynamics Including Site and Mode of Action of Silymarin. The Antihepatotoxic Principle from Silybum Mar. (L) Gaertn. *Arzneimittel-Forschung Drug Research* 25(1):82–89;(2):179–188.

Wagner, H. 1986. Antihepatotoxic Flavonoids. *Progress in Clinical and Biology Research* 213:319–331.

Wagner, H., et al. 1968. The Chemistry of Silymarin (silybim), the Active Principle of the Fruits of Silybum Marianum (L) Gaertn. (Carduus Marianus) (L). *Arzneimittel-Forschung Drug Research* 18:688–696.

Weiss, R. F. 1988. Valeriana Officinalis (Valerian). *Herbal Medicine.* England: Beaconsfield Publishers Ltd., 281–285.

Zuin, M., et al. 1987. Effects of a Preparation Containing a Standardized Ginseng Extract Combined with Trace Elements and Multivitamins Against Hepatotoxin-Induced Chronic Liver Disease in the Elderly. *The Journal of International Medical Research* 15:276–281.

Chapter 6: Pharmaceuticals

Anonymous. 1985. Easing Cocaine Withdrawal. *Medical World News* (November 11):128.

Anonymous. 1987. Serotonin Uptake Inhibitor Cuts Yearnings for Excess Booze, Food. *Medical World News* (March 23):58–59.

Banys, P. 1988. The Clinical Use of Disulfiram (Antabuse): A Review. *Journal of Psychoactive Drugs* 20:243–262.

Barnes, D. M. 1988. Breaking the Cycle of Addiction. *Science* 241:1029–1030.

Benfield, P.; Heel, R. C.; and Lewis, S. P. 1986. Fluoxetine: A Review of Its Pharmacodynamic and Pharmacokinetic Properties, and Therapeutic Efficacy in Depressive Illness. *Drugs* 32:481–508.

Benowitz, N. L. 1988. Pharmacologic Aspects of Cigarette Smoking and Nicotine Addiction. *New England Journal of Medicine* 319:1318–1330.

Bray, G. A., and Gray, D. S. 1988. Obesity Part II—Treatment. *Western Journal of Medicine* 149:555–571.

Carmody, T. P., et al. 1988. Nicotine Polacrilex: Clinic-Based Strategies with Chronically Ill Smokers. *Journal of Psychoactive Drugs* 20:269–274.

Cummings, S. R., et al. 1988. Internists and Nicotine Gum. *Journal of the American Medical Association* 260:1565–1569.

de la Fluente, J.-R., et al. 1989. A Controlled Study of Lithium Carbonate in the Treatment of Alcoholism. *Mayo Clinic Proceedings* 64:177–180.

Dencker, S. J., et al. 1978. Piracetam and Chlormethiazole in Acute Alcohol Withdrawal: A Controlled Clinical Trial. *Journal of International Medical Research* 6:395–400.

Dole, V. P. 1988. Implications of Methadone Maintenance for Theories of Narcotic Addiction. *Journal of the American Medical Association* 260:3025–3029.

Edwards, N. B., et al. 1988. Doxepin in the Treatment of Nicotine Withdrawal. *Psychosomatics* 29:203–206.

Emerit, J.; Loeper, J.; and Chomette, G. 1981. Superoxide Dismutase in the Treatment of Post-Radiotherapeutic Necrosis and of Crohn's Disease. *Clinical Respiratory Physiology* 17:287–288.

Fortmann, S. P., et al. 1988. Minimal Contact Treatment for Smoking Cessation. *Journal of the American Medical Association* 260:1575–1580.

Gawin, F. H., and Ellinwood, E. H., Jr. 1988. Cocaine and Other Stimulants: Action, Abuse and Treatment. *New England Journal of Medicine* 318(18):1173–1182.

Gelenberg, A. J. 1978. Amantadine in the Treatment of Benztropine-Refractory Extrapyramidal Disorders Induced by Antipsychotic Drugs. *Current Therapeutic Research* 23:375–380.

Glassman, A. H., et al. 1988. Heavy Smokers, Smoking Cessation, and Clonidine. *Journal of the American Medical Association* 259:2863–2866.

Gossop, M. 1988. Clonidine and the Treatment of the Opiate Withdrawal Syndrome. *Drug and Alcohol Dependence* 21:253–259.

Gupta, A. K., and Jha, B. K. 1988. Clonidine in Heroin Withdrawal Syndrome: A Controlled Study in India. *British Journal of Addiction* 83:1079–1084.

Hajek, P.; Belcher, M.; and Feyerabend, C. 1988. Preference for 2 MG Versus 4 MG Nicotine Chewing Gum. *British Journal of Addiction* 83:1089–1093.

Hajek, P.; Jackson, P.; and Belcher, M. 1988. Long-Term Use of Nicotine Chewing Gum. *Journal of the American Medical Association* 260:1593–1596.

Hayden, J., and Comstock, E. 1975. Use of Activated Charcoal in Acute Poisoning. *Clinical Toxicology* 8:515–533.

Herridge, P., and Gold, M. S. 1988. Pharmacological Adjuncts in the Treatment of Opioid and Cocaine Addicts. *Journal of Psychoactive Drugs* 20:233–242.

Horowitz, R. I.; Gottlieb, L. D.; and Kraus, M. L. 1989. The Efficacy of Atenolol in the Outpatient Management of the Alcohol Withdrawal Syndrome. *Archives of Internal Medicine* 149:1089–1093.

Hughes, J. R. 1988. Clonidine, Depression, and Smoking Cessation. (editorial) *Journal of the American Medical Association* 259:2901–2902.

Hughes, J. R., and Miller, S. A. 1984. Nicotine Gum to Help Stop Smoking. *Journal of the American Medical Association* 252:2855–2838.

Hughes, J. R., et al. 1989. Nicotine vs. Placebo Gum in General Medical Practice. *Journal of the American Medical Association* 261:1300–1305.

Jackson, G. G.; Muldoon, R. L.; and Ackers, L. W. 1963. Serological Evidence for Prevention of Influenzal Infection in Volunteers by an Antiinfluenza Drug, Amantadine Hydrochloride. *Antimicrobial Agents and Chemotherapeutics* 3:703.

Jain, N. K.; Patel, V. P.; and Pitchumoni, C. S. 1986. Activated Charcoal, Simethicone, and Intestinal Gas: A Double-Blind Study. *Annals of Internal Medicine* 105:61–62.

———. 1986. Efficacy of Activated Charcoal in Reducing Intestinal Gas: A Double-Blind Clinical Trial. *American Journal of Gastroenterology* 81:532–535.

Jarvik, M. E., and Schneider, N. G. 1984. Degree of Addiction and Effectiveness of

272   BIBLIOGRAPHY

Nicotine Gum Therapy for Smoking. *American Journal of Psychiatry* 141:790–791.

Jarvis, M. J., et al. 1982. Randomised Controlled Trial of Nicotine Chewing-Gum. *British Medical Journal* 285:537–540.

Jonas, J. M., and Gold, M. S. 1986. Naltrexone Reverses Bulimic Symptoms. *The Lancet* I: 807.

Katona, B.; Siegel, E.; and Cluxton, R. 1987. The New Black Magic: Activated Charcoal and New Therapeutic Users. *Journal of Emergency Medicine* 5:9–18.

Kuusisto, P., et al. 1986. Effect of Activated Charcoal on Hypercholesterolaemia. *The Lancet* II: 366–367.

McNabb, M. E.; Ebert, R. V.; and McCusker, K. 1982. Plasma Nicotine Levels Produced by Chewing Nicotine Gum. *Journal of the American Medical Association* 248:865–868.

Manschreck, T. C. 1988. Cocaine Abuse Medical and Psychopathologic Effects. *Drug Therapy:* 26–44.

Michelson, A. M. 1987. Medical Aspects of Superoxide Dismutase. *Life Chemistry Reports* 6(1).

Murphy, J. M., et al. 1988. Effects of Fluoxetine on the Intragastric Self-Administration of Ethanol in the Alcohol Preferring P Line of Rats. *Alcohol* 5:283–286.

Naranjo, C. A.; Sellers, E. M.; and Lawrin, M. O. 1986. Modulation of Ethanol Intake by Serotonin Uptake Inhibitors. *Journal of Clinical Psychiatry* 47:(4)16–22 (suppl).

Ockene, J. K., et al. 1988. Sure-Fire Smoking Cessation. *Patient Care* (December 15):83–116.

Ornish, S. A.; Zisook, S.; and McAdams, L. A. 1988. Effects of Transdermal Clonidine Treatment on Withdrawal Symptoms Associated with Smoking Cessation. *Archives of Internal Medicine* 148:2027–2031.

Preliminary Observations on Naltrexone for Treatment of Alzheimer's Type Dementia. 1987. *Journal of the American Geriatrics Society* 35:369–370.

Prochazka, A. V., and Boyko, E. J. 1988. How Physicians Can Help Their Patients Quit Smoking. A Practical Guide. *Western Journal of Medicine* 149(2):188–194.

Reisberg, B., et al. 1983. Effects of Naloxone in Senile Dementia: A Double-Blind Trial. *New England Journal of Medicine* 308:721–722.

Sannerud, C. A., and Griffiths, R. R. 1988. Amantadine: Evaluation of Reinforcing Properties and Effect on Cocaine Self-Injection in Baboons. *Drug and Alcohol Dependence* 21:195–202.

Sees, K. L., and Clark, H. W. 1988. Use of Clonidine in Nicotine Withdrawal. *Journal of Psychoactive Drugs* 20:263–268.

Skondia, V., and Kabes, J. 1985. Piracetam in Alcoholic Psychoses: A Double-Blind, Crossover, Placebo Controlled Study. *Journal of International Medical Research* 13:185–187.

Sugrue, M. F. 1987. Neuropharmacology of Drugs Affecting Food Intake. *Pharmacology and Therapeutics* 32:145–182.

Tennant, F., and Berman, M. L. 1988. Stepwise Detoxification from Cocaine. *Postgraduate Medicine* 84:225–235.

Tennant, F. S., Jr., and Sagherian, A. A. 1987. Double-Blind Comparison of Amantadine and Bromocriptine for Ambulatory Withdrawal from Cocaine Dependency. *Archives of Internal Medicine* 147:109–112.

Tonnesen, P., et al. 1988. Effect of Nicotine Chewing Gum in Combination with Group Counseling on the Cessation of Smoking. *New England Journal of Medicine* 318:15–18.

Weiss, R. D. 1988. Relapse to Cocaine Abuse after Initiating Desipramine Treatment. *Journal of the American Medical Association* 260:2545–2546.

Werther, N. M., and Dayal, H. H. 1988. How to Help Patients Stop Smoking. *Postgraduate Medicine* 83(1):277–284.

Wurtman, J., et al. 1987. Fenfluramine Suppresses Snack Intake Among Carbohydrate Cravers but Not Among Noncarbohydrate Cravers. *International Journal of Eating Disorders* 6(6):687–699.

Chapter 7: Food, Water, and Air

Abraham, Z. D., and Mehta, T. 1988. Three-Week Psyllium-Husk Supplementation: Effect on Plasma Cholesterol Concentrations, Fecal Steroid Excretion, and Carbohydrate Absorption in Men. *American Journal of Clinical Nutrition* 47:67–74.

Anderson, G. J., and Connor, W. E. 1989. On the Demonstration of ω-3 Essential-Fatty-Acid Deficiency in Humans. (editorial) *American Journal of Clinical Nutrition* 49:585–587.

Anderson, J. W., et al. 1988. Cholesterol-Lowering Effects of Psyllium Hydrophilic Mucilloid for Hypercholesterolemic Men. *Archives of Internal Medicine* 148:292–296.

———. 1984. Hypocholesterolemic Effects of Oat-Bran or Bean Intake for Hypercholesterolemic Men. *American Journal of Clinical Nutrition* 40:1146–1155.

Anonymous. 1984. Thirst and Osmoregulation in the Elderly. (editorial) *The Lancet* II: 1017–1018.

Aoki, T., et al. 1984. Antibodies to HTLV I and III in Sera from Two Japanese Patients, One with Possible Pre-AIDS. *The Lancet* II: 936–937.

Bang, H. O., and Dyerberg, J. 1972. Plasma Lipids and Lipoproteins in Greenlandic West-Coast Eskimos. *Acta Medica Scandinavica* 192:85–94.

Bang, H. O.; Dyerberg, J.; and Nielsen, A. B. 1971. Plasma Lipid and Lipoprotein Pattern in Greenlandic West-Coast Eskimos. *The Lancet* I: 1143–1146.

Berlin, E.; Matusik, E. J.; and Young, C., Jr. 1980. Effect of Dietary Fat on the Fluidity of Platelet Membrane. *Lipids* 15(8):604–608.

Block, E. 1985. The Chemistry of Garlic and Onions. *Scientific American* (March):114–128.

Carper, J. 1988. *The Food Pharmacy.* New York: Bantam Books.

Chandra, R. K. 1988. There Is More to Fish Than Fish Oils. *Nutrition Research* 8:1–2.

Connor, S. L., and Connor, W. E. 1989. *The New American Diet.* New York: Fireside.

Cooper, R. A. 1977. Abnormalities of Cell-Membrane Fluidity in the Pathogenesis of Disease. *New England Journal of Medicine* 297(7):371–377.

Cranston, D.; McWhinnie, D.; and Collin, J. 1988. Dietary Fibre and Gastrointestinal Disease. *British Journal of Surgery* 75:508–512.

Danielsson, A., et al. 1979. Effect of Long-Term Treatment with Hydrophilic Colloid on Serum Lipids. *Acta Hepato-Gastroenterologica* 26:148–153.

DeGroot, A. P.; Luyken, R.; and Pikaar, N. A. 1963. Cholesterol-Lowering Effect of Rolled Oats. *The Lancet* II: 303–304.

Dehmer, G. J., et al. 1988. Reduction in the Rate of Early Restenosis after Coronary Angioplasty by a Diet Supplemented with n-3 Fatty Acids. *New England Journal of Medicine* 319(12):733–740.

Dougherty, R. M., et al. 1987. Lipid and Phospholipid Fatty Acid Composition of Plasma, Red Blood Cells, and Platelets and How They Are Affected by Dietary Lipids: A Study of Normal Subjects from Italy, Finland, and the USA. *American Journal of Clinical Nutrition* 45:443–455.

Driss, F., et al. 1984. Inhibition of Platelet Aggregation and Thromboxane Synthesis After Intake of Small Amount of Eicosapentaenoic Acid. *Thrombosis Research* 36:389–396.

Eastwood, M. A., and Passmore, R. 1983. Dietary Fibre. *The Lancet* II: 202–205.

Florholmen, J., et al. 1982. The Effect of Metamucil on Postprandial Blood Glucose and Plasma Inhibitory Peptide in Insulin-Dependent Diabetics. *Acta Medica Scandinavica* 212:237–239.

Fox, P. L., and DiCorleto, P. E. 1988. Fish Oils Inhibit Endothelial Cell Production of Platelet-Derived Growth Factor-Like Protein. *Science* 241:453–456.

Garvin, J. E., et al. 1965. Lowering of Human Serum Cholesterol by an Oral Hydrophilic Colloid. *Proceedings of the Society for Experimental Biology and Medicine* 120:744–746.

Gold, K. V., and Davidson, D. M. 1988. Oat Bran as a Cholesterol-Reducing Dietary Adjunct in a Young, Healthy Population. *Western Journal of Medicine* 148:299–302.

Goodnight, S. H., Jr.; Harris, W. S.; and Connor, W. E. 1981. The Effects of Dietary ω-3 Fatty Acids on Platelet Composition and Function in Man. A Prospective, Controlled Study. *Blood* 58:880–885.

Graham, D. Y., et al. 1988. Spicy Food and the Stomach. Evaluation by Videoendoscopy. *Journal of the American Medical Association* 260(23):3473–3475.

Harris, L. J. 1979. *The Book of Garlic*. Berkeley, Calif.: Aris Books/Harris Publishing Company.

Harris, W. S. 1988. Effects of a Low Saturated Fat, Low Cholesterol Fish Oil Supplement in Hypertriglyceridemic Patients. A Placebo-Controlled Trial. *Annals of Internal Medicine* 109:465–470.

Heaton, K. W. 1983. Dietary Fibre in Perspective. *Clinical Nutrition* 37C:151–170.

Hendler, S. S. 1986. *Complete Guide to Anti-Aging Nutrients*. New York: Fireside.

———. 1989. *Oxygen Breakthrough*. New York: William Morrow.

Judd, P. A., and Truswell, A. S. 1981. The Effect of Rolled Oats on Blood Lipids and Fecal Steroid Excretion in Man. *American Journal of Clinical Nutrition* 34:2061–2067.

Kamada, T., et al. 1986. Dietary Sardine Oil Increases Erythrocyte Membrane Fluidity in Diabetic Patients. *Diabetes* 35:604–611.

Kendler, B. S. 1987. Garlic (Allium sativum) and Onion (Allium cepa): A Review of Their Relationship to Cardiovascular Disease. *Preventive Medicine* 16:670–685.

Kirby, R. W. 1981. Oat-Bran Intake Selectively Lowers Serum Low-Density Lipoprotein Cholesterol Concentrations of Hypercholesterolemic Men. *American Journal of Clinical Nutrition* 34:824–829.

Klaassen, C. D.; Amdur, M. O.; and Doull, J., eds. 1986. *Casarett and Doull's Toxicology*, Third Edition. New York, Toronto, London: Macmillan, 825–853.

Knapp, H. R., and Fitzgerald, G. A. 1989. The Antihypertensive Effects of Fish Oil. A Controlled Study of Polyunsaturated Fatty Acid Supplements in Essential Hypertension. *New England Journal of Medicine* 320(16):1037–1043.

Knox, C. 1988. The Air You Breathe May Hurt Your Ears. *Science News* (November 19):327.

Kremer, J. M., et al. 1987. Fish-Oil Fatty-Acid Supplementation in Active Rheumatoid Arthritis. *Annals of Internal Medicine* 106(4):497–506.

Kromhout, D.; Bosschieter, E. B.; and Coulander, D. de L. 1985. The Inverse Relation Between Fish Consumption and 20-Year Mortality from Coronary Heart Disease. *New England Journal of Medicine* 312:1205–1209.

Krotkiewski, M. 1984. Effect of Guar Gum on Body-Weight, Hunger Ratings and Metabolism in Obese Subjects. *British Journal of Nutrition* 52:97–105.

Kumar, N., et al. 1984. Do Chillies Influence Healing of Duodenal Ulcer? *British Medical Journal* 288:1803–1804.

Leaf, A. 1984. Dehydration in the Elderly. (editorial) *New England Journal of Medicine* 311(12):791–792.

Lorenz, R., et al. 1983. Platelet Function, Thromboxane Formation and Blood Pressure Control During Supplementation of the Western Diet with Cod Liver Oil. *Circulation* 67(3):504–509.

Lourau, M., and Lartique, O. 1950. Influence du régime alimentaire sur les effets biologiques produits par une irradiation unique de tout le corps (Rayons X). *Experientia* 6:25.

Mori, T. A., et al. 1987. New Findings in the Fatty-Acid Composition of Individual Platelet Phospholipids in Man after Dietary Fish Oil Supplementation. *Lipids* 22(10):744–750.

Niukian, K.; Schwartz, J.; and Shklar, G. 1987. *In Vitro* Inhibitory Effect of Onion Extract on Hamster Buccal Pouch Carcinogenesis. *Nutrition and Cancer* 10(3):137–143.

Nuovo, J. 1989. Use of Dietary Fiber to Lower Cholesterol. *American Family Physician* 39(4):137–140.

Osilesi, O., et al. 1985. Use of Xanthan Gum in Dietary Management of Diabetes Mellitus. *American Journal of Clinical Nutrition* 42:597–603.

Phillips, P. A., et al. 1984. Reduced Thirst After Water Deprivation in Healthy Elderly Men. *New England Journal of Medicine* 311:753–759.

Rivnay, B., et al. 1980. Correlations Between Membrane Viscosity, Serum Cholesterol, Lymphocyte Activation and Aging in Man. *Mechanisms of Ageing and Development* 12:119–126.

Sanders, T.A.B. 1987. Fish and Coronary Artery Disease. (editorial) *British Heart Journal* 57:214–219.

Sartor, G.; Carlstrom, S.; and Schersten, B. 1981. Dietary Supplementation of Fibre (Lunelax) as a Mean to Reduce Postprandial Glucose in Diabetics. *Acta Medica Scandinavica* (suppl) 656:51–53.

Saynor, R.; Verel, D.; and Gillot, T. 1984. The Long-Term Effect of Dietary Supplementation with Fish Lipid Concentrate on Serum Lipids, Bleeding Time, Platelets and Angina. *Atherosclerosis* 50:3–10.

Schneeman, B. O. 1987. Dietary Fiber and Gastrointestinal Function. *Nutritional Reviews* 45(5):129–132.

Shiga, T., and Maeda, N. 1980. Influence of Membrane Fluidity on Erythrocyte Functions. *Biorheology* 17:485–499.

Shiga, T., et al. 1979. Rheological and Kinetic Dysfunctions of the Cholesterol-Loaded, Human Erythrocytes. *Biorheology* 16:363–369.

Shurtleff, W., and Aoyagi, A. 1975. *The Book of Tofu.* New York: Ballantine Books.

————. 1976. *The Book of Miso.* New York: Ballantine Books.

Slavin, J. L., and Levine, A. S. 1986. Dietary Fiber and Gastrointestinal Disease. Part I: What Is Fiber and How Much Should You Take? *Practical Gastroenterology* X(3):56–59.

————. 1986. Dietary Fiber and Gastrointestinal Disease. Part II. How to Use Fiber to Treat Disease. *Practical Gastroenterology* X(4):19–24.

Spector, H., and Calloway, D. H. 1959. Reduction of X-Radiation Mortality by Cabbage and Broccoli. *Proceedings of the Society for Experimental Biology and Medicine.* 100:405–407.

Srivastava, K. C. 1986. Onion Exerts Antiaggregatory Effects by Altering Arachidonic Acid Metabolism in Platelets. *Prostaglandins, Leukotrienes and Medicine* 24:43–50.

Superko, H. R. 1985. Decreasing Blood Cholesterol Levels with a Dietary Additive: An Additional Approach to Diet and Drugs. *Cardiovascular Reviews* 6(11):1253–1265.

Thomas, R.D., ed. 1986. *Drinking Water and Health—Volume 6.* Washington, D.C.: National Academy Press.

Van Horn, L. V., et al. 1986. Serum Lipid Response to Oat Product Intake with a Fat-Modified Diet. *Journal of the American Dietetic Association* 86:759–764.

Visudhiphan, S., et al. 1982. The Relationship Between High Fibrinolytic Activity and Daily Capsicum Ingestion in Thais. *American Journal of Clinical Nutrition* 35:1452–1458.

Wagner, H.; Wierer, M.; and Fessler, B. 1987. Effects of Garlic Constituents on Arachidonate Metabolism. *Planta Medica* 53:305–306.

Wattenberg, L. W. 1977. Inhibition of Carcinogenic Effects of Polycyclic Hydrocarbons by Benzyl Isothiocyanate and Related Compounds. *Journal of the National Cancer Institute* 58:395–398.

————. 1981. Inhibition of Carcinogen-Induced Neoplasia by Sodium Cyanate, tert-Butyl Isocyanate, and Benzyl Isothiocyanate Administered Subsequent to Carcinogen Exposure. *Cancer Research* 41(August):2991–2994.

Wattenberg, L. W., and Loub, W. D. 1978. Inhibition of Polycyclic Aromatic Hydrocarbon-Induced Neoplasia by Naturally Occurring Indoles. *Cancer Research* 38:1410–1413.

Weber, N., et al. 1988. Antiviral Activity of Allium Sativum (Garlic). (abstract) 88th Annual Meeting of American Society for Microbiology.

Weiner, B. H., et al. 1986. Inhibition of Atherosclerosis by Cod-Liver Oil in a Hyperlipidemic Swine Model. *New England Journal of Medicine* 315(14)841–846.

Yang, P., and Banwell, J. G. 1986. Dietary Fiber. Its Role in the Pathogenesis and Treatment of Constipation. *Practical Gastroenterology* X(6):28–32.

Chapter 8: Light

Dilsaver, S. C., and Coffman, J. A. 1988. Seasonal Depression. *American Family Physician* 38(4):173–176.

Kiev, A. 1986. Seasonal Affective Disorders. *Medical Tribune* (October 8):24.

Kripke, D. F.; Risch, S. C.; and Janowsky, D. S. 1983. Bright White Light Alleviates Depression. *Psychiatry Research* 10:105–112.

———. 1983. Lighting Up Depression. *Psychopharmacology Bulletin* 19:526–530.

Lewy, A. J., et al. 1987. Antidepressant and Circadian Phase-Shifting Effects of Light. *Science* 235:352–353.

———. 1982. Bright Artificial Light Treatment of a Manic-Depressive Patient with a Seasonal Mood Cycle. *American Journal of Psychiatry* 139:1496–1498.

Rosenthal, N. E., et al. 1985. Antidepressant Effects of Light in Seasonal Affective Disorder. *American Journal of Psychiatry* 142:163.

———. 1984. Seasonal Affective Disorder. A Description of the Syndrome and Preliminary Findings with Light Therapy. *Archives of General Psychiatry*. 41:72–80.

Tapp, W. N., and Natelson, B. H. 1986. Life Extension in Heart Disease: An Animal Model. *The Lancet* I: 238–240.

Terman, M. 1988. On the Question of Mechanism in Photo Therapy for Seasonal Affective Disorder. Consideration of Clinical Efficacy and Epidemiology. *Journal of Biological Rhythms* 3(2):155–172.

Vogel, S. 1988. "Lightening Up" Alcohol Withdrawal. *Medical Tribune* (July 28):2.

Wurtman, R. J., and Wurtman, J. J. 1989. Carbohydrates and Depression. *Scientific American* 260(1):68–75.

Chapter 9: Exercise, Relaxation, and Stress Management

Adams, M. L., et al. 1987. Increased Plasma β-endorphin Immunoreactivity in Scuba Divers After Submersion. *Medicine and Science in Sports and Exercise* 19(2):87–90.

Anonymous. 1987. Long-Distance Runners Experiencing Gastrointestinal Bleeding. *Internal Medicine World Report* 2(3):11.

Bortz, W. M., II. 1982. Disuse and Aging. *Journal of the American Medical Association* 248(10):1203–1208.

Briner, W. W., Jr. 1988. Shinsplints. *American Family Physician* 37(2):155–160.

Brummund, W., and Fink, J. N. 1985. Recognition and Management of Exercise-Induced Anaphylaxis. *Internal Medicine* 6:97–106.

Christenson, S. 1988. Stressless Strolls. (report) *American Health* (September):44.

Constant, J. 1987. The Relationship Between Stress and Atherosclerotic Coronary Disease. *Internal Medicine* 8(8):137–144.

DeBenedette, V. 1988. Getting Fit for Life: Can Exercise Reduce Stress? *The Physician and SportsMedicine* 16(6):185–200.

———. 1988. Keeping Pace with the Many Forms of Walking. *The Physician and SportsMedicine* 16(8):145–150.

deCoverley, Veale D.M.W. 1987. Exercise Dependence. *British Journal of Addiction* 82:735–740.

Eichner, E. R. 1986. The Anemias of Athletes. *The Physician and SportsMedicine* 14(9):122–130.

———. 1987. Exercise and the Heart: Benefits and Risks. *Internal Medicine* 8(13):119–128.

———. 1989. Gastrointestinal Bleeding in Athletes. *The Physician and SportsMedicine* 17(5):128–140.

Farrell, P. A. 1984. Exercise as a Stimulus to the Endogenous Opiate System. In *Opioid Peptides in the Periphery,* Fraol; Isidori; and Mazzetti, eds. New York: Elsevier Science Publishers, 179–186.

Fisher, R. L., et al. 1986. Gastrointestinal Bleeding in Competitive Runners. (abstract) *Journal of the American Medical Association* 31:1226–1228.

Friedell, A. 1948. Automatic Attentive Breathing in Angina Pectoris. *Minnesota Medicine* 31:875–881.

Hendler, S. S. 1989. *Oxygen Breakthrough.* New York: William Morrow.

Higdon, H. 1988. 12 Minutes Does It. *American Health* 41–47.

———. 1988. Heart and Sole. *American Health* (March):38.

Hunding, A.; Jordahl, R.; and Pauley, P. E. 1981. Runners' Anemia and Iron Deficiency. *Acta Medica Scandinavica* 209:315–318.

Klein, R., et al. 1986. Nasal Airflow Asymmetries and Human Performance. *Biological Psychology* 23:127–137.

Kono, I., et al. 1988. Weight Reduction in Athletes May Adversely Affect the Phagocytic Function of Monocytes. *The Physician and SportsMedicine* 16(7): 56–65.

Koplan, J. P., et al. 1982. An Epidemiologic Study of the Benefits and Risks of Running. *Journal of the American Medical Association* 248(23):3118–3121.

McGuire, R. 1988. Exercise Restraint? *American Health* (September):40.

———. 1988. Running Immunity Ragged. *Medical Tribune* (November 24):5.

Martinsen, E. W.; Mendus, A.; and Sandvik, L. 1985. Effects of Aerobic Exercise on Depression: A Controlled Study. *British Medical Journal* 291:109.

Mellion, M. B. 1985. Exercise Therapy for Anxiety and Depression. 1. Does the Evidence Justify Its Recommendation? (editorial) *Postgraduate Medicine* 77(3):59–66.

———. 1985. Exercise Therapy for Anxiety and Depression. 2. What Are the Specific Considerations for Clinical Application? (editorial) *Postgraduate Medicine* 77(3):91–95.

Monahan, T. 1987. Is "Activity" as Good as Exercise? *The Physician and Sports-Medicine* 15(10):181–186.

Nagarathna, R., and Nagendra, H. R. 1985. Yoga for Bronchial Asthma: A Controlled Study. *British Medical Journal* 291:1077–1079.

Nash, H. L. 1989. Reemphasizing the Role of Exercise in Preventing Heart Disease. *The Physician and SportsMedicine* 17(3):219–225.

Olson, B. R. 1989. Exercise-Induced Amenorrhea. *American Family Physician* 39(2):213–221.

Ornish, D., et al. 1983. Effects of Stress Management Training and Dietary Changes in Treating Ischemic Heart Disease. *Journal of the American Medical Association* 247:54–59.

Raymond, C. 1989. Distrust, Rage May Be "Toxic Core" That Puts "Type A" Person at Risk. *Journal of the American Medical Association* 261(6):813.

Rippe, J., et al. 1989. The Cardiovascular Benefits of Walking. *Practical Cardiology* 15(1):66–72.

Rosanski, A., et al. 1988. Mental Stress and the Induction of Silent Myocardial Ischemia in Patients with Coronary Artery Disease. *New England Journal of Medicine* 218(16):1005–1012.

Schneider, E. L. 1987. Exercise and Longevity: Fact Versus Fiction. *Hospital Medicine* (April):109–118.

Shannahoff-Khalsa, D. 1986. Breathing for the Brain. *American Health* 16–18.

———. 1984. Rhythms and Reality: The Dynamics of the Mind. *Psychology Today* 72–73.

Sheehan, G. 1986. Walking: The Best Exercise of All. *The Physician and Sports-Medicine* 14(10):41.

Shoenfeld, Y., et al. 1980. Walking: a Method for Rapid Improvement of Physical Fitness. *Journal of the American Medical Association* 243(20):2062–2063.

Simon, H. B. 1987. Exercise and Infection. *The Physician and SportsMedicine* 15(10):135–142.

Stanley, I.; Wolf, M. D.; and Lampl, K. L. 1988. Pulmonary Rehabilitation: The Use of Aerobic Dance as a Therapeutic Exercise for Asthmatic Patients. *Annals of Allergy* 61:357–360.

Szabadi, E. 1988. Physical Exercise and Mental Health. *British Medical Journal* 296:659–660.

Thompson, P.D., and Mitchell, J. H. 1984. Exercise and Sudden Cardiac Death. (editorial) *New England Journal of Medicine* 311(14):914–915.

Werntz, D.; Bickford, R. G.; and Shannahoff-Khalsa, D. S. 1987. Selective Hemispheric Stimulation by Unilateral Forced Nostril Breathing. *Human Neurobiology* 6:165–171.

Wishnitzer, R., et al. 1986. Decreased Cellularity and Hemosiderin of the Bone Marrow in Healthy and Overtrained Competitive Distance Runners. *The Physician and SportsMedicine* 14(7):86–100.

PART III

Chapter 1: Alcohol

Anderson, J.J.B., and Switzer, B. R. 1987. Effects of Alcohol on Nutritional Status: Part I—Minerals. *Internal Medicine* 8(8):69–91.

Anonymous. 1985. The Leaky Gut of Alcoholism. *Nutrition Reviews* 43(3):72–74.

Ballenger, J., et al. 1979. Alcohol and Central Serotonic Metabolism in Man. *Archives of General Psychiatry* 36:224–227.

Beasley, J. D. 1987. *Wrong Diagnosis, Wrong Treatment.* Durant, Dallas, New York: Creative Infomatics.

Bergman, M. M., and Gleckman, R . A. 1988. Infectious Complications in Alcohol Abusers. *Hospital Practice* (September 15):145–156.

Bjarnason, I., et al. 1984. The Leaky Gut of Alcoholism: Possible Route of Entry for Toxic Compounds. *The Lancet* I: 79–82.

280 BIBLIOGRAPHY

Blum, K., et al. 1978. Putative Role of Isoquinoline Alkaloids in Alcoholism: A Link to Opiates. *Alcoholism* 2:113–120.

Bower, B. 1988. Alcoholism's Elusive Genes. *Science News* 134:74–76.

———. 1988. Intoxicating Habits. *Science News* 134:88–89.

Collin-Williams, C. 1988. Oral Use of Cromolyn in Food Allergy. In *Food Allergy: A Practical Approach to Diagnosis and Management.* Chiaramonte, L. T.; Schneider, A. T.; and Lifshitz, F. eds. New York: Marcel Dekker, 377–391.

DiChiara, G., and Imperato, A. 1988. Drugs Abused by Humans Preferentially Increase Synaptic Dopamine Concentrations in the Mesolimbic System of Freely Moving Rats. *Proceedings of the National Academy of Science* 85:5274–5278.

Eckardt, M. J., et al. 1981. Health Hazards Associated with Alcohol Consumption. *Journal of the American Medical Association.* 246:648–666.

Forest, J. L., et al. 1987. Alcoholism Rx: How You Can Help. *Patient Care* (January 15):85–97.

Genazzani, A. R., et al. 1982. Central Deficiency of Beta-Endorphin in Alcoholics. *Journal of Clinical Endocrinology and Metabolism* 55:485–488.

Hayashida, M., et al. 1989. Comparative Effectiveness and Costs of Inpatient and Outpatient Detoxification of Patients with Mild-to-Moderate Alcohol Withdrawal Syndrome. *New England Journal of Medicine* 320(6):358–365.

Kirn, T. F. 1989. Research Increasingly Focuses on Possible Genetic Factors in Complex Problem of Alcohol Abuse. *Journal of the American Medical Association* 261:2170–2172.

Klerman, G. L. 1989. Treatment of Alcoholism. (editorial) *New England Journal of Medicine* 320(6):394–395.

Kocoshis, S., and Gryboski, J. 1979. Use of Cromolyn in Combined Gastrointestinal Allergy. *Journal of the American Medical Association* 242:1169–1173.

Koob, G. F., and Bloom, F. E. 1988. Cellular and Molecular Mechanisms of Drug Dependence. *Science* 42:715–723.

Leo, M. A., and Lieber, C. S. 1982. Hepatic Vitamin A Depletion in Alcoholic Liver Injury in Man. *New England Journal of Medicine* 37:597–601.

Lieber, C. S. 1988. Biochemical and Molecular Basis of Alcohol-Induced Injury to Liver and Other Tissues. *New England Journal of Medicine* 319(25):1639–1650.

———. 1983. Hepatic, Metabolic, and Nutritional Complications of Alcoholism. *Resident & Staff Physician* 79–96.

———. 1988. The Influence of Alcohol on Nutrition Status. *Nutrition Reviews* 46(7):241–254.

Lindsay-Miller, A. C., and Chambers, A. 1987. Group Comparative Trial of Cromolyn Sodium and Terfenadine in the Treatment of Seasonal Allergic Rhinitis. *Annals of Allergy* 58:28–32.

MacGregor, R. R. 1986. Alcohol and Immune Defense. *Journal of the American Medical Association* 256:1474–1479.

Milhorn, H. T. 1988. The Diagnosis of Alcoholism. *American Family Physician* 37(6):175–183.

Moore, R. D., et al. 1989. Prevalence, Detection, and Treatment of Alcoholism in Hospitalized Patients. *Journal of the American Medical Association* 261:403–407.

Myers, R. D. 1989. Emerging Biochemical Theories of Alcoholism. *Medical Times* 117(2):113–116.

Sherlock, S. 1984. Nutrition and the Alcoholic. *The Lancet* I: 436–439.

Switzer, B. R., and Anderson, J.J.B. 1987. Effects of Alcohol on Nutritional Status: Part II—Vitamins. *Internal Medicine* 8(9):62–71.

Trachtenberg, M. C., and Blum, K. 1987. Alcohol and Opioid Peptides: Neuropharmacological Rationale for Physical Craving of Alcohol. *American Journal of Drug and Alcohol Abuse* 13(3):365–372.

Trubo, R. 1989. Drying Out Is Just a Start: Alcoholism. *Medical World News* (February 13):56–65.

Williams, R. J. 1947. The Etiology of Alcoholism: A Working Hypothesis Involving the Interplay of Hereditary and Environmental Factors. *Quarterly Journal of Studies on Alcohol* 7:567–587.

Chapter 2: Nicotine/Smoking

Benowitz, N. L. 1988. Pharmacologic Aspects of Cigarette Smoking and Nicotine Addiction. *New England Journal of Medicine* 319:1318–1330.

Botvin, G. J. 1986. The Psychology of Cigarette Smoking. *Primary Care & Cancer* 22–31.

Brown, R.; Pinkerton, R.; and Tuttle, M. 1987. Respiratory Infections in Smokers. *American Family Physician* 36(5):133–140.

Burton, R. C. 1983. Smoking, Immunity, and Cancer. *The Medical Journal of Australia* (October 29):411–412.

Cohen, S. J., et al. 1989. Encouraging Primary-Care Physicians to Help Smokers Quit. A Randomized, Controlled Trial. *Annals of Internal Medicine* 110:648–656.

Cummings, S. R., et al. 1989. Training Physicians in Counseling about Smoking Cessation. *Annals of Internal Medicine* 110:640–647.

DiChiara, G., and Imperato, A. 1988. Drugs Abused by Humans Preferentially Increase Synaptic Dopamine Concentrations in the Mesolimbic System of Freely Moving Rats. *Proceedings of the National Academy of Science* 85:5274–5278.

Ferguson, T. 1987. *The No-Nag, No-Guilt, Do-It-Your-Own-Way Guide to Quitting Smoking.* New York: Ballantine Books.

Fisher, E. B., and Rost, K. 1986. Smoking Cessation: A Practical Guide for the Physician. *Clinics in Chest Medicine* 7(4):551–565.

Fletcher, D. J. 1985. Kicking the Nicotine Habit. *Postgraduate Medicine* 77(3):123–129.

Hall, G. H., and Morrison, C. F. 1973. New Evidence for a Relationship Between Tobacco Smoking, Nicotine Dependence and Stress. *Nature* 243:199–201.

Hughes, J. R., et al. 1989. Nicotine vs. Placebo Gum in General Medical Practice. *Journal of the American Medical Association* 261:1300–1305.

Hurt, R. D., et al. 1988. Long-Term Follow-up of Persons Attending a Community-Based Smoking-Cessation Program. *Mayo Clinic Proceedings* 63:681–690.

Kottke, T. E., et al. 1989. A Randomized Trial to Increase Smoking Intervention by Physicians. *Journal of the American Medical Association* 261:2101–2106.

Kozlowski, L. T., et al. 1989. Comparing Tobacco Cigarette Dependence with Other

Drug Dependencies. *Journal of the American Medical Association* 261:898–901.

Mattson, M. E.; Pollack, E. S.; and Cullen, J. W. 1987. What Are the Odds That Smoking Will Kill You? *American Journal of Public Health* 77(4):425–431.

Milhorn, H. T. 1989. Nicotine Dependence. *American Family Physician* 39(3):214–224.

Novotny, T. E. 1988. Cessation of Smoking and the Social Milieu. (editorial) *Mayo Clinic Proceedings* 63:729–731.

Ockene, J. K.; Sachs, D.P.L.; and Solberg, L. I. 1988. Sure-Fire Smoking Cessation. *Patient Care* (December 15):83–115.

Orleans, C. T. 1985. Understanding and Promoting Smoking Cessation: Overview and Guidelines for Physician Intervention. *Annual Review of Medicine* 36: 51–61.

Perkins, K. A., et al. 1989. The Effect of Nicotine on Energy Expenditure During Light Physical Activity. *New England Journal of Medicine* 320:898–903.

Prochazka, A. V., and Boyko, E. J. 1988. How Physicians Can Help Their Patients Quit Smoking—A Practical Guide. *Western Journal of Medicine* 149:188–194.

Rigotti, N. A. 1989. Cigarette Smoking and Body Weight. (editorial) *New England Journal of Medicine.* 320:931–933.

Sopori, M. L., et al. 1989. Cigarette Smoke Causes Inhibition of the Immune Response to Intratracheally Administered Antigens. *Toxicology and Applied Pharmacology* 97:489–499.

Chapter 3: Caffeine

Clementz, G. L., and Dailey, J. W. 1988. Psychotropic Effects of Caffeine. *American Family Physician* 37(5):168–172.

Curatolo, P. W., and Robertson, D. 1983. The Health Consequences of Caffeine. *Annals of Internal Medicine* 98:641–653.

Henahan, R. 1988. Grounds for Heavy Coffee Drinkers to Use Filters. *Medical Tribune* (December 29):11.

Johnson, E. S., et al. 1955. Efficacy of Feverfew as Prophylactic Treatment of Migraine. *British Medical Journal* 291:569–573.

LaCroix, A. Z., et al. 1986. Coffee Consumption and the Incidence of Coronary Heart Disease. *New England Journal of Medicine* 315:977–982.

Murphy, J. J.; Heptinstall, S.; and Mitchell, J.R.A. 1988. Randomised Double-Blind Placebo-Controlled Trial of Feverfew in Migraine Prevention. *The Lancet* II: 189–192.

Chapter 4: Cocaine and Amphetamines

Anonymous. 1985. Easing Cocaine Withdrawal. *Medical World News* (November 11):128.

Ashley, R. 1975. *Cocaine: Its History, Uses and Effects.* New York: Warner Books.

Barnes, D. M. 1988. The Biological Tangle of Drug Addiction. *Science* 241(July):415–417.

———. 1988. Breaking the Cycle of Addiction. *Science* 241(August):1029–1030.

Dackis, C. A., and Gold, M. S. 1985. New Concepts in Cocaine Addiction. The Dopamine Depletion Hypothesis. *Neuroscience and Biobehavioral Research* 9:469–477.

Daigle, R. D., et al. 1988. A Primer on Neurotransmitters and Cocaine. *Journal of Psychoactive Drugs* 20:283.

DiChiara, G., and Imperato, A. 1988. Drugs Abused by Humans Preferentially Increase Synaptic Dopamine Concentrations in the Mesolimbic System of Freely Moving Rats. *Proceedings of the National Academy of Science* 85(July):5274–5278.

Gawin, F., and Kleber, H. 1986. Pharmacological Treatments of Cocaine Abuse. *Psychiatric Clinics of North America* 9:573–583.

Gawin, F. H., and Ellinwood, E. H. 1988. Cocaine and Other Stimulants. *New England Journal of Medicine* 318:1173–1182.

Giannini, J. A., and Gold, M. S. 1988. Cocaine Abuse: Demons Within. *Emergency Decisions* (October):34–37.

Koob, G. F., and Bloom, F. E. 1988. Cellular and Molecular Mechanism of Drug Dependence. *Science* 242(November):715–723.

Manschreck, T. C. 1988. Cocaine Abuse—Medical and Psychopathologic Effects. *Drug Therapy* (August):26–44.

Miller, N. S.; Gold, M. S.; and Millman, R. L. 1989. Cocaine. *American Family Physician* 39(2):115–120.

Smith, D. K., et al. 1979. *Amphetamine Use, Misuse and Abuse.* Boston: G. K. Hall.

Vereby, K., and Gold, M. S. 1984. The Psychopharmacology of Cocaine. *Annals of Psychiatry* 14:714–723.

Chapter 5: Opioids

DiChiara, G., and Imperato, A. 1988. Drugs Abused by Humans Preferentially Increase Synaptic Dopamine Concentrations in the Mesolimbic System of Freely Moving Rats. *Proceedings of the National Academy of Science* 85(July):5274–5278.

Kleber, H. D. 1981. Detoxification from Narcotics. In Lowinson, J. H., and Ruz, P., eds. *Substance Abuse: Clinical Problems and Perspectives.* Baltimore: Williams and Wilkin.

Koob, G. F., and Bloom, F. E. 1988. Cellular and Molecular Mechanisms of Drug Dependence. *Science* 242:715–723.

Levinthal, C. F. 1988. *Opiates and the Brain.* New York: Anchor Press.

Moore, D. F. 1989. The Abuse of Opiates and CNS Depressants. *Medical Times* (January):99–103.

Synder, S. H., and Childers, S. R. 1979. Opiate Receptors and Opioid Peptides. *Annual Review of Neuroscience* 2:35–64.

Yahya, M. D., and Watson, R. R. 1987. Immunomodulation by Morphine and Marijuana. *Life Sciences* 41:2503–2510.

Chapter 6: Benzodiazepines/Barbiturates

Garner, S. J., et al. 1989. Buspirone, an Anxiolytic Drug That Stimulates Respiration. *American Review of Respiratory Diseases* 139:946–950.

Murphy, S. M.; Owen, R. T., and Tyrer, P. J. 1984. Withdrawal Symptoms After Six Weeks Treatment with Diazepam. *The Lancet* II: 1389.

Novak, R. F., and Swift, T. J. 1972. Barbiturate Interaction with Phosphatidylcholine. *Proceedings of the National Academy of Science* 69(3):640–642.

Roy-Byrne, P. P., and Hommer, D. 1988. Benzodiazepine Withdrawal: Overview and Implications for the Treatment of Anxiety. *American Journal of Medicine* 84:1041–1052.

Winokur, A., et al. 1984. Withdrawal Reaction from Long-Term Low-Dosage Administration of Diazepam. *Archives of General Psychiatry* 37:101.

Woods, J. H.; Katz, J. L.; and Winger, G. 1988. Use and Abuse of Benzodiazepines. *Journal of the American Medical Association* 260:3476–3480.

Chapter 7: Cholesterol/Fats/Stagnant Blood/Excess Weight

Caballero, B. 1987. Brain Serotonin and Carbohydrate Craving in Obesity. *International Journal of Obesity* II, Supplement 3, 179–183.

Connor, S. L., and Connor, W. E. 1989. *The New American Diet*. New York: Fireside.

Flatt, J. P. 1987. Effect of Carbohydrate and Fat Intake on Postprandial Substrate Oxidation and Storage. *Topics in Clinical Nutrition* 2(2):15–27.

McCarty, M. F. 1986. The Unique Merits of a Low-Fat Diet for Weight Control. *Medical Hypotheses* 20:183–197.

Chapter 8: Chemotherapy/Radiotherapy Detoxification

Aisner, J., et al. 1988. Studies of High-Dose Magestrol Acetate: Potential Applications in Cachexia. *Seminars in Oncology* 68–75 (Supplement 1).

Borek, C. 1985. The Induction and Control of Radiogenic Transformation *In Vitro*: Cellular and Molecular Mechanism. *Pharmacology and Therapeutics* 27:99–142.

Buckley, J. E., et al. 1984. Hypomagnesemia After Cisplatin Combination Chemotherapy. *Archives of Internal Medicine* 144:2347–2348.

Ceruti, P. A. 1985. Prooxidant States and Tumor Promotion. *Science* 227:375–381.

Jackson, D. V., et al. 1988. Amelioration of Vincristine Neurotoxicity by Glutamic Acid. *American Journal of Medicine* 84:1016–1022.

Krivit, W., et al. 1983. Prevention of Cyclophosphamide (CYT) Induced Hemorrhagic Cystitis (HC) by Use of Ascorbic Acid (AA) to Reduce Urinary PH. (abstract C-105) *American Society of Clinical Oncology* 2:27.

Marklund, S. L., et al. 1982. Copper- and Zinc-Containing Superoxide Dismutase, Manganese-Containing Superoxide Dismutase, Catalase, and Glutathione Peroxidase in Normal and Neoplastic Human Cell Lines and Normal Human Tissues. *Cancer Research* 42(May):1955–1962.

Racker, E. 1972. Bioenergetics and the Problem of Tumor Growth. *American Scientist* 60:56–63.

Ripoll, E.A.P.; Ram, B. N.; and Webber, M. M. 1986. Vitamin E Enhances the Chemotherapeutic Effects of Adriamycin on Human Prostatic Carcinoma Cells *In Vitro*. *The Journal of Urology* 136:529–531.

Saltiel, E., and McGuire, W. 1983. Doxorubicin (Adriamycin) Cardiomyopathy. *Western Journal of Medicine* 139:332–341.

Sethi, V. 1983. Vitamin C Lowers Vincristine Toxicity in Rhesus Monkeys. (abstract 1129) *Proceedings of the American Association of Cancer Research* 286.

Smith, A. E., and Kenyon, D. H. 1973. A Unifying Concept of Carcinogenesis and Its Therapeutic Implications. *Oncology* 27:459–479.

Sun, Y., et al. 1983. Immune Restoration and/or Augmentation of Local Graft Versus Host Reaction by Traditional Chinese Medicinal Herbs. *Cancer* 52(1):70–73.

Takeda, A.; Yonezawa, M.; and Katoh, N. 1981. Restoration of Radiation Injury by Ginseng. I. Responses of X-Irradiated Mice to Ginseng Extract. *Journal of Radiation Research* 22:323–335.

————. 1986. Restoration of Radiation Injury by Ginseng. II. Some Properties of the Radioprotective Substances. *Journal of Radiation Research* 22:336–343.

Tchekmedyian, N. S., et al. 1987. High-Dose Magestrol Acetate. A Possible Treatment for Cachexia. *Journal of the American Medical Association* 257:1195–1198.

Totter, J. R. 1980. Spontaneous Cancer and Its Possible Relationship to Oxygen Metabolism. *Proceedings of the National Academy of Science* 77(4):1763–1767.

Warbrug, O. 1956. On the Origin of Cancer Cells. *Science* 123(3191):309–314.

Chapter 9: Environmental Toxins/Allergens/Other Noxious Substances

Borek, C. 1985. The Induction and Control of Radiogenic Transformation *In Vitro:* Cellular and Molecular Mechanisms. *Pharmacology and Therapeutics* 27:99–142.

Demichiel, M. E., and Nelson, L. 1988. Allergic Rhinitis. *American Family Physician* 37(4):251–263.

Kirkpatrick, J. N. 1987. Occult Carbon Monoxide Poisoning. *Western Journal of Medicine* 146(1):52–56.

Lieberman, P. 1988. Rhinitis—Allergic and Nonallergic. *Hospital Practice* (June 15):117–145.

Lifshitz, F. 1988. "Food Intolerance." In Chiaramonte, L. T.; Schneider, A. T. and Lifshitz, F., eds. *Food Allergy—A Practical Approach to Diagnosis and Management:* 3–21. New York and Basel: Marcel Dekker.

Macdonald, T. L., and Martin, B. R. 1988. Aluminum Ion in Biological Systems. *Trends in Biochemical Sciences:* 13–19.

Mazow, J. B. 1989. Formulating the Best Treatment Plan. *Consultant* (April 1): 143–155.

Russell, M. 1988. Ozone Pollution: The Hard Choices. *Science* 241:1275–1276.

Schechter, S. R., and Monte, T. 1988. *Fighting Radiation with Foods, Herbs, & Vitamins.* Brookline, Massachusetts: East West Health Books.

Index